S0-ANR-953

Religious Bodies Politic

Buddhism and Modernity

A SERIES EDITED BY DONALD S. LOPEZ JR.

RECENT BOOKS IN THE SERIES:

From Stone to Flesh: A Short History of the Buddha
DONALD S. LOPEZ JR. (2013)

The Museum on the Roof of the World: Art, Politics, and the Representation of Tibet
CLARE E. HARRIS (2012)

Bonds of the Dead: Temples, Burial, and the Transformation of Contemporary Japanese Buddhism
MARK MICHAEL ROWE (2011)

Locations of Buddhism: Colonialism and Modernity in Sri Lanka
ANNE M. BLACKBURN (2010)

In the Forest of Faded Wisdom: 104 Poems by Gendun Chopel, a Bilingual Edition
EDITED AND TRANSLATED BY DONALD S. LOPEZ JR. (2009)

Religious Bodies Politic

Rituals of Sovereignty in Buryat Buddhism

ANYA BERNSTEIN

The University of Chicago Press   Chicago and London

PUBLICATION OF THIS BOOK HAS BEEN AIDED
BY A GRANT FROM THE BEVINGTON FUND.

ANYA BERNSTEIN is assistant professor of anthropology and
social studies at Harvard University.

The University of Chicago Press, Chicago 60637
The University of Chicago Press, Ltd., London
© 2013 by The University of Chicago
All rights reserved. Published 2013.
Printed in the United States of America

22 21 20 19 18 17 16 15 14 13   1 2 3 4 5

ISBN-13: 978-0-226-07255-5 (cloth)
ISBN-13: 978-0-226-07272-2 (paper)
ISBN-13: 978-0-226-07269-2 (e-book)
DOI: 10.7208/chicago/9780226072692.001.0001

Library of Congress Cataloging-in-Publication Data

Bernstein, Anya.
    Religious bodies politic : rituals of sovereignty in Buryat buddhism /
Anya Bernstein.
        pages cm — (Buddhism and modernity)
    Includes bibliographical references.
    ISBN 978-0-226-07255-5 (cloth : alkaline paper) —
ISBN 978-0-226-07272-2 (paperback : alkaline paper) —
ISBN 978-0-226-07269-2 (e-book)   1. Buddhism—Russia
(Federation)—Buriatiia—21st century.   2. Monastic and religious
life (Buddhism)—Russia (Federation)—Buriatiia.   3. Buddhist
monasticism and religious orders—Russia (Federation)—Buriatiia.
4. Buriatiia (Russia)—Religious life and customs—21st century.
5. Buriats—Religion.   6. Eurasian school—Religious aspects—
Buddhism.   I. Title.   II. Series: Buddhism and modernity.
    BQ709.R85B87834 2013
    294.3'9209575—dc22

                                                2013013420

♾ This paper meets the requirements of ANSI/NISO Z39.48–1992
(Permanence of Paper).

To my parents, Lev and Elena Bernstein

Contents

Acknowledgments

First and foremost, I thank the Buryat and Tibetan Buddhist monks, nuns, lamas, and laypeople in Russia and India who gave so generously of their time toward this project. I offer my deepest gratitude to the monks of the Drepung Gomang Monastic College in India and the Ivolginsk Monastery in Buryatia; monks, nuns, and lay pilgrims in Dharamsala; and multiple ethnographic consultants in Buryatia who shared their thoughts on many personal subjects with me.

This book would have never been possible without the expert supervision of Bruce Grant, professor of anthropology at New York University, who guided this project from the first day of its inception, through fieldwork, and, most critically, during the writing stage. His bold and sophisticated twists on this material, insightful and inspiring feedback, and general positive outlook on life made both the writing of this text and the study on which it was based an intellectual experience for which I have been grateful.

Years of conversation with Fred Myers and Faye Ginsburg on mediation, materiality, and the circulation of culture shaped many themes of this book. Faye Ginsburg was a major source of support and encouragement for my formation as a visual anthropologist, particularly during the shooting, production, and distribution of my feature-length film, *In Pursuit of the Siberian Shaman*. In Buryatia, long and productive discussions with Nikolai Tsyrempilov and Tatiana Skrynnikova were central to my understanding of many of the issues addressed here. Katherine Verdery, Gray Tuttle, Tejaswini Ganti, and Johan Elverskog offered invaluable and detailed comments on earlier versions of this text. Lucas Bessire and Nica Davidov read and critiqued individual chapters and articles. I am also thankful to Marjorie Mandelstam Balzer, who has been very supportive of this project since its early stages.

This project's beginnings came in a master's program in visual anthropology at the University of Manchester, which enabled me to travel to India and to Buryatia in 2001, producing a film, *Join Me in Shambhala*, about a Tibetan lama with "Buryat roots." I extend my gratitude to Yeshe Lodrö Rinpoche and his disciple Tenzin for allowing me to follow them during their busy summer ritual schedule and record many personal encounters. Paul Henley at the Granada Center for Visual Anthropology was a wonderful mentor. Postdoctoral colleagues at the University of Michigan Society of Fellows also contributed to this project through excellent conversations, discussions, and advice.

I presented early versions of several chapters of this book at the annual meetings of the American Anthropological Association, the American Academy of Religion, the International Association of Tibetan Studies, Soyuz, and the Central Eurasian Studies Society, and at workshops, conferences, or lectures at Harvard University, Scripps College, George Mason University, Duke University, the Max Planck Institute for Social Anthropology, the Institute for International and Regional Studies at Princeton University, the Center for Russian, Eurasian, and East European Studies at the University of Michigan, the Anthropology and History Workshop at the University of Michigan, the Michigan Society of Fellows, the American Museum of Natural History, the Fulbright Foundation, the Tibetan Buddhist Resource Center/Rubin Foundation Scholars Seminar, St. Petersburg State University, the Center for Social Anthropology at the Russian State University for the Humanities, and the Buryat Scientific Center of the Siberian Branch of the Russian Academy of Sciences. I am grateful to panel organizers, discussants, and audiences at these events, who offered many helpful thoughts and suggestions.

The research for and writing of this book were sponsored by a postdoctoral fellowship from the Michigan Society of Fellows, the Social Science Research Council Postdoctoral Fellowship for Transregional Research: Inter-Asian Contexts and Connections, a Mellon/American Council for Learned Societies Dissertation Completion Fellowship, a Fulbright IIE Fellowship for Field Research, a Wenner-Gren Dissertation Fieldwork Grant, the Social Science Research Council Eurasia Program, a Foreign Language and Area Studies Fellowship of the US Department of Education, and summer fellowships from New York University. I thank I. F. Popova and I. V. Kul'ganek of St. Petersburg's Institute of Oriental Manuscripts for their assistance with archival work.

An earlier version of chapter 1 appeared as "Pilgrims, Fieldworkers, and Secret Agents: Buryat Buddhologists and the History of a Eurasian Imaginary," *Inner Asia* 11, no. 1 (2009): 23–45 (2009). Chapter 3 appeared as "The Post-Soviet Treasure Hunt: Time, Space, and Necropolitics in Siberian Buddhism," *Comparative Studies in Society and History* 53, no. 3 (2011): 623–653. Some material from chapter 2 and the introduction appeared as "More Alive Than All the Living: Sovereign Bodies and Cosmic Politics in Buddhist Siberia." *Cultural Anthropology* 27, no. 2 (2012): 261–285. I thank the publishers for kindly allowing me to reprint these materials.

I thank my parents, Lev and Elena Bernstein, for their unwavering support through all the stages of life that accompanied this research. Wladimir Quénu, Ksenia Pimenova, Nica Davidov, David Kaye, and Katia Belousova were among the best friends one could hope for. Derek Martin appeared in my life as the writing of this work began, and I suspect it would not have been finished without his love and encouragement. Auriel Valentin, who came into the world not long before this book, remains a preverbal but generous font of support. He is looking forward to reading it one day.

A Note on Transliteration

For terms in Russian and Buryat, the Library of Congress Cyrillic transliteration system is used, prefaced by "Rus." and "Bur.," respectively. The only exceptions are Russian and Buryat proper and geographic names with well-established English spellings. For example, Stcherbatsky is used instead of Shcherbatskii and Buryatia instead of Buriatiia. For the Buryat highest ecclesiastical title, I have used the transliterated Russian version, Pandito Khambo Lama.

For Tibetan, Turrell Wylie's system is used (based on his paper "A Standard System of Tibetan Transcription," *Harvard Journal of Asiatic Studies* 22 [1959]: 261–267). Tibetan transcriptions are prefaced by "Tib." Conventional English spellings are used for the well-known lamas, such as the Dalai Lama and the Panchen Lama.

All Sanskrit terms are prefaced by "Skt."

Chronology of Events

Some dates are only approximate.

ca. 1625–1661	Russians settle in the Cisbaikal
ca. 1638–1689	Russians settle in the Transbaikal
1635	First Jebdzundamba Khutugtu is born in Khalkha Mongolia
1644	Qing dynasty is established in China
ca. mid-1600s	First Buddhist yurt-temples are established in Buryatia
1689	The Treaty of Nerchinsk; Buryat-Mongol communities in the Lake Baikal area are fixed as Russian subjects
1712	150 Tibetan and Mongolian lamas arrive in Buryatia
1727	The Treaty of Khyakhta finalizes Sino-Russian frontiers; all of Buryatia becomes part of the Russian empire
1727–1732	Damba-Darzha Zaiaev travels to Tibet
1728	Count Sava Raguzinskii issues the instruction to the border patrols prohibiting foreign lamas from traveling to Buryat regions
1741	Empress Elizabeth recognizes Buddhism in Buryatia as independent from Mongolian and Tibetan Buddhism
1764	The institution of Pandito Khambo Lamas is established
1822	Speranskii's statute establishes Buryat steppe dumas (local self-government)
1846	The number of monasteries reaches thirty-four, and the number of lamas—4,509
1846	Soodoi Lama is born

1853	The Statute on Lamaist Clergy in Eastern Siberia is issued
1854	Agvan Dorzhiev is born
ca. 1890s	Increased Russification policies; local self-government is gradually being abolished; start of the Buryat nationalist movement
1899–1902	Gombozhab Tsybikov travels to Tibet
1905–1907	Bazar Baradiin travels to Tibet
1911	Fall of the Qing empire; Outer Mongolia declares independence
1913	Buddhist temple opens in St. Petersburg
1917	Start of the Buryat Buddhist reform movement
1917	February Revolution in Russia; the tsar is deposed; Provisional Government is formed
1917	Buryat National Committee (*Burnatskom*) is formed
1917	October Revolution in Russia; Bolsheviks take power
1922	Central Spiritual Board of Buddhists is formed
1923	Buryat-Mongol Autonomous Soviet Socialist Republic is formed
1924	Mongolian People's Republic (MPR) is formed
1924	Eighth Jebdzundamba dies, MPR declares him to be the last Jebdzundamba
1927	Lama Itigelov passes away
1927	Buryat pilgrims Agvan Nyima, Thubten Nyima, and Galsan Legden arrive in Tibet
late 1920s–late 1930s	Buryat Buddhism is repressed, monasteries cease to function, lamas are purged
1937	The republic is divided into three parts
1937	Bazar Baradiin is shot
1938	Agvan Dorzhiev dies in prison
1943	Yeshe Lodrö Rinpoche is born in Litang, Kham (China)
1946	Ivolginsk Monastery is built; Aginsk Monastery is reopened
1950	China invades Tibet
1959	The Dalai Lama flees to India; Chinese repressions of Buddhism in Tibet
ca. 1955–1959	Galsan Legden serves as abbot of Drepung Gomang in Tibet
1958	The suffix "Mongol" is dropped from the republic's name
1968	Bakula Rinpoche visits Buryatia
1976	End of the Cultural Revolution in China
1976	Galsan Legden's reincarnation is born in Nepal
1977–1980	Avgan Nyima serves as abbot of Drepung Gomang in India
1987	Perestroika starts in the USSR
1989	Religious revival starts in Buryatia
1989	Several Buryat lamas visit India for short-term study and pilgrimages

1990	Buryatia declares sovereignty; the republic is renamed Buryat Soviet Socialist Republic
1991	Collapse of the Soviet Union
1991	The republic is renamed Republic of Buryatia
1991	250 Years of Buddhism in Russia celebrated
1991	Ninth Jebdzundamba is recognized in India
1993	Yeshe Lodrö Rinpoche arrives in Buryatia
1995	The first group of Buryat monks leaves to study at the Drepung Gomang Monastery in India
1995	Aiusheev is elected as the Twenty-Fourth Khambo Lama
1997	A preamble to the 1997 Russian Federal Law on Freedom of Conscience and Religious Associations acknowledges a special role of Russia's four "traditional religions"
1997	Schism in the Sangha
2000	Vladimir Putin is inaugurated president, formulates National Security Policy
2002	Buryatia drops some of the sovereignty clauses from its constitution
2002	Itigelov is exhumed
2004	Yeshe Lodrö Rinpoche opens his temple in Ulan-Ude
2005	Yanzhima is revealed as a self-arisen image
2006	Ust'-Orda Buryat Autonomous District is abolished
2008	Dmitrii Medvedev is elected president
2008	Aga Buryat Autonomous District is abolished
2008	Itigelov's Palace is open
2009	Dmitrii Medvedev declared the emanation of the White Tārā
2009	Buryatia drops the last sovereignty clause

In August 2009, President Dmitrii Medvedev of Russia was declared an incarnation of the Buddhist goddess White Tārā. The Pandito Khambo Lama, the leader of Buryat Buddhists, made the declaration during the president's official visit to the Buddhist Ivolginsk Monastery in Siberia (fig. 1). The news set off a storm among the Russian commentators: from the left, decrying such unseemly alliances between church and state, and from the right, over the choice of the church in question, proclaiming that a "Russian Orthodox president" cannot also be a Buddhist goddess. In Buryatia, however, where there is a long tradition of binding Russian emperors to the most popular female deity in the Tibetan Buddhist pantheon, the announcement was received as a logical extension of local practice. While some considered such a "nomination" an obsequious and politically opportunist gesture or, conversely, an ultimate recognition of Russian sovereignty over Buryats, other local leaders viewed this as a reverse "incorporation"—not of Buryatia into Russia, but of Russia into the larger Buddhist cosmos through laying claim to the president's body.

The summer of 2009 turned out to be eventful for Buryatia, a relatively trouble-free Siberian multinational region. Though officially a semiautonomous republic within the greater Russian Federation, Buryatia made headlines when the Russian Constitutional Court required it to remove all references to "sovereignty" from its constitution.[1]

---

1. The process of removing references to sovereignty in republics started in the first years of this century, when the Constitutional Court stated that "the

FIGURE 1. President Medvedev with lamas, Ivolginsk Monastery, 2009. Photo courtesy of RIA Novosti.

Eighteen years after Boris Yeltsin's famous invitation to Russian regions to "take as much sovereignty as you can handle," this order signaled a significant reversal of the freedoms of the perestroika era. Relations between the Russian center and its diverse populations are once again being redefined as the central government reconsiders just how "multinational" it wants to be in an age of authoritarian revival. This complex relationship between religion and politics is the focus of this book.

The establishment in 1727 of the border between the Russian empire and Qing China is considered a canonical beginning of the formation of Buryats as a separate community out of several large northern Mon-

---

multinational people of Russia is to be considered the only carrier of sovereignty and the only source of power in the Russian Federation." The sovereignty of the Russian Federation, it was argued, cannot allow for the existence of two levels of sovereign powers within one state. During that period, some republics, including Buryatia, followed this order and removed references to sovereignty from their constitutions (the republics that did not remove them include Tatarstan, Bashkorkostan, Sakha, and Tyva). However, many did not remove the clause about the people of the republic as a "source of power." In June 2009, the Russian Supreme Court raised this issue again, stating that the people of the republic cannot be the source of power, since the only source of power is the multinational people of Russia (Rus. *mnogonatsional'nyi narod Rossii*). This time, Buryatia, Tatarstan, Bashkorkostan, Kabardino-Balkaria, Komi, and Chechnya were ordered to remove the clauses from their constitutions as soon as possible (Anonymous 2009).

gol clans that became Russian subjects.[2] According to Buryat chronicles, Buddhism in this region was quite insignificant until the arrival in 1712 of 150 Tibetan and Mongolian lamas, who established themselves among the Selenga and Khori clans.[3] At this time, Buryats had no stationary monasteries, but mobile yurt-temples were reported in the Transbaikal as early as the mid-1600s. By 1846, there were 4,509 lamas, thirty-four monasteries, and 144 freestanding temples (Poppe 1940: 49–55). Around the same time, Russian imperial politics had started to undergo a major shift, with the official ideology now expressed in Count Sergei Uvarov's formula of "Orthodoxy, Autocracy, and Nationality." The unprecedented growth of Buddhism in the Transbaikal, which until then had been overlooked by the government in order to keep this sensitive border region stable, now presented a problem for the spread of Christianity. The government was urgently inventing new ways to solve "the Buddhist question."

From the very beginning, similarly limiting "free worship" was a regular strategy to restrain Buryat Buddhists from contact with their foreign coreligionists. The 1728 instruction to the border patrols issued by Count Sava Raguzinskii, a diplomat who played the key role in the establishment of the Sino-Russian border, stated that "foreign lamas, as subjects of other states, are not to be admitted into the company of tribute-paying natives, and are to make use only of those lamas who stayed here after the separation, so that the property of Russian subjects does not go to the foreigners" (Galdanova, Gerasimova, and Dashiev 1983: 16–17). Over the past 250 years, Buryats, a Mongolian people who currently number some five hundred fifty thousand across Eurasia (fig. 2), have been subject to the various policies of the Russian imperial, later Soviet, and now postsocialist Russian federal government. For all the changes, the central government's reluctance to see its Buddhist subjects cross borders has remained the same. This policy continues today. In 2000, Vladimir Putin's National Security Policy identified foreign religious organizations as an explicit threat to stability. At the Ivolginsk Monastery in the summer of 2009, his successor, Dmitrii Medvedev, stated that no help "from abroad" was needed to permit Russia's Buddhist peoples to rebuild monasteries destroyed dur-

2. The Treaty of Nerchinsk in 1689 had already fixed much of the Sino-Russian frontier; the 1727 treaty finalized the southern frontier.

3. In the Buryat and Mongolian context, the word "lama" is often used interchangeably with "monk." Most contemporary Buryat lamas are not monks in the strict sense of the word, since they are not celibate (see chap. 4).

FIGURE 2. Buryatia within Russia. Map by Jeffrey E. Levy.

ing Soviet times. Despite such efforts, Buryats have long taken a great interest in life beyond their immediate territory (fig. 3). From imperial times to the present, numerous Buryats have undertaken pilgrimages to Mongolia and Tibet; in the late 1980s, these journeys were extended to Tibetan exile monasteries in India.[4]

This book tracks the changing profiles of this very cosmopolitan Siberian Buddhist community over the past hundred years. I became interested in how early Buryat monks, some of whom once traveled to Mongolia and Tibet to receive religious education, adapted to the Soviet internationalist project after 1917 and, seven decades later, with the fall of the Soviet Union, deftly moved again to reestablish ties with the Tibetan exile community dispersed across northern and southern India. What became of these men, and what might their experiences tell

4. The starting points for overland pilgrimages varied. The route marked in figure 3 corresponds to the route followed by the monks discussed in chapter 2, starting at the Atsagat Monastery, about thirty miles away from what is today Ulan-Ude.

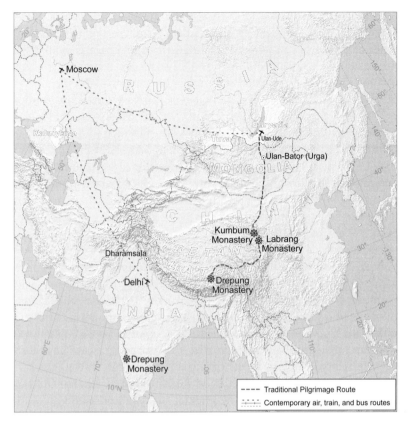

FIGURE 3. Eurasia with historic pilgrimage routes and contemporary air, bus, and train travel. Map by Jeffrey E. Levy.

us about shifting cultural politics across these vast territories? I make the case that the extraordinary flow of revolutionary events crystallized in the life stories of specific monks, whose incarnations and reincarnations adroitly captured the parallel refashionings of secular space experienced by many Buryats. Thus, these "religious bodies politic" became fascinating illustrations, not only of past and present Buddhist transnational processes across northern and southern Asia, where I did field and archival research for this book, but for the crucially changing "Eurasian" geopolitical imaginaries that so many Buryats contemplate today.

Most broadly, I argue that under conditions of rapid social transformation such as those that accompanied the Russian Revolution, the Cold War, and the dissolution of the Soviet Union, certain persons, and especially their bodies, became key sites through which Buryats have negotiated their relationship with the Russian state and the larger Eurasian world.[5] During my field research, I encountered many such kinds of emblematic bodies—the dead bodies of famous monks, the temporary bodies of reincarnated lamas, the celibate bodies of Buddhist monastics, the dismembered bodies of lay disciples offered as imaginary gifts to the spirits, and, finally, the Russian leader's body, which has historically been a key site for uniting competing universes of meaning and for creating flexible political alliances. I suggest that for Buryats to have maintained their long-standing mobility—across the spatial borders of nation-states and the temporal horizons between life and death, as well as across multiple sites of belonging—they have collectively developed and continue to employ a characteristically Buddhist "body politics." This body politics is an assertion of cultural sovereignty that allows Buryats to preserve a careful balance between a greater Eurasian Buddhist cosmos and their loyalties to Russia. Through such transnational flows of bodies and minds, Buryat Buddhists are challenging the dominant biopolitical regimes of limited mobility imposed by nation-states on their indigenous populations. In so doing, they have also been developing hybrid forms of subjectivity, gender categories, and exchange relations that often fall outside the conventional anthropological categories for discussing religious practice under and after socialism. In what follows I tell the story of the intricate intersections of religion and politics in the post-Soviet period. I ask: What does religion look like after socialism? What can the emerging forms of religious practice tell us about broader postsocialist transformations, including economic practices, moral and political imaginaries, and ideas of space and time? Through ethnographic analysis of everyday religion, I begin to untangle the often-surprising ways in which Buddhism lies at the heart of the ongoing restructuring of Buryat social worlds in the wake of the collapse of state socialism and the rise of global market capitalism.

5. My approach here is consonant with Katherine Verdery's work on the political life of dead bodies (1999). My material, however, is not limited to dead bodies, focusing on a broad range of Buddhist bodies. In this, I also draw on Caroline Humphrey's recent work, in which she argues that tumultuous events, such as revolutions, uprisings, and religious revivals, create crystallized personalities. While Humphrey was not interested in bodies expressly, my approach here is very much in agreement with her observations from the people of the Urad district in Inner Mongolia, China that one can track key events through certain charismatic personalities (Humphrey 2008).

Rituals of Sovereignty

The years 1741 and 1764 are iconic in the history of Buryat Buddhism. The first marks the recognition of Buryat Buddhism by the empress Elizabeth as one of the legitimate religions of the Russian empire.[6] The second marks the establishment of the institution of Pandito Khambo Lamas, the supreme ecclesiastical Buryat leaders. Many in Buryatia today consider these two events a guarantee of a de facto "autocephality" (Rus. *avtokefal'nost'*) of the Buryat "Buddhist church" vis-à-vis the authority of the Tibetan Dalai Lamas and Mongolian Jebdzundambas. Unlike these reincarnated hierarchs endowed with charismatic, magical authority, the Pandito Khambo Lama was created as an elected post by the tsarist administration, which was understandably wary of the possible uncontrollable factors that an institution of reincarnation could present.[7] This move, as many researchers have pointed out, was highly strategic: by granting an autocephalous status to a non-Christian religion in the sensitive borderlands while cutting its ties with Mongolia and Tibet, Empress Catherine the Great seemingly ensured the successful incorporation of Buryats into the empire (Galdanova, Gerasimova, and Dashiev 1983: 18–26; Ukhtomskii 1904: 11; Gerasimova 1957: 22–24). For this legitimating gesture, the empress is said to have been proclaimed by Buryats the first Russian emanation of the goddess White Tārā.[8] From the Buryat point of view, however, as has been argued re-

6. I thank the historian Nikolai Tsyrempilov for pointing out to me that this popularly famous decree supposedly signed by the empress has never been discovered in the archives, so there are doubts whether it ever existed. He also noted that she seized power only in late November 1741 as a result of a palace revolution. With no previous experience, Empress Elizabeth found herself the head of a great empire, and it is not clear then how she could have familiarized herself with the situation in the Transbaikal in less than a month (Tsyrempilov, personal communication, 2008).

7. While many today believe that it was Empress Catherine the Great who conferred the title of "Bandido Khambo Lama" upon the first leader of Buryat Buddhists, Damba-Darzha Zaiaev (this is also an official point of view of the Buddhist Traditional Sangha), most researchers emphasize the fact that Zaiaev must have first conferred this title upon himself, and then had it approved by the local administration in 1764 (Galdanova, Gerasimova, and Dashiev 1983: 24; Poppe 1940: 49). Yet others state that while he might have invented the title himself, most important, he secured its ultimate approval by the empress during his 1767 visit to Moscow (Ukhtomskii 1904: 11; Pozdneev ca. 1888).

8. The origins of this identification are unclear. It is well documented that various Central and Inner Asian (both Turkic- and Mongolian-speaking) peoples referred to Russian emperors as "White Tsars" (for detailed analysis of this phenomenon, see Trepavlov 2007). Buryat folklore researcher M. I. Tulokhonov quotes an early eighteenth-century Buryat song about Peter I, where he was named the White Tārā. The song was written after Peter I graciously received the Buryat delegation in Moscow in 1703 (Tulokhonov 1973: 100). The nineteenth-century Russian

cently by a prominent native scholar, Nikolai Tsyrempilov, the title given to the empress is rather an example of the use of the Buddhist "skillful means" doctrine (Skt. *upāya*)—a key Mahāyāna doctrine that facilitated the propagation of Buddhism—to advance the dharma to the "West" (European Russia). Thus, Buryat Buddhists present a competing view of "incorporation." From their perspective, it was Russia that had been drawn into the "Pax Buddhica" by claiming the empress's body (Tsyrempilov 2009). In this book, I also adopt this view, suggesting that practices such as proclaiming the Russian president to be an emanation of a Buddhist goddess, far from being an obsequious gesture, is only one recent instance of a long-running ritual traffic in bodies in ways that can both conform to and diplomatically challenge Russian logics of sovereignty.

As the example of President Medvedev's body already begins to tell us, bodies, understood here in the most broad sense as "contingent formations of space, time, and materiality" (Lock and Farquhar 2007), often figure prominently in performances of sovereignty across cultures. Most famously, sovereignty has been linked to bodies of leaders, who were believed to have two bodies: a body natural and a body politic (Kantorowicz 1957). While the context of medieval kingship might no longer be relevant, Kantorowicz's notion of the "two bodies of the king" remains foundational as a point of translation in thinking of how bodies of present-day leaders often become sites for assertions of sovereignty. Shifting attention from the bodies of leaders to ordinary bodies, more recent studies have focused on them as sites of performance of sovereign power, sites that become most visible in extreme conditions, such as war and other "states of exception" (Agamben 1998 [1995]; Foucault 1980). These insights have been fruitfully explored by scholars, who have argued that besides being an object of sovereign violence, the body can also be its ultimate site of resistance, as exemplified by the figure of a civil disobedience campaigner, a hunger striker, or, in the most extreme case, a suicide bomber (Hansen and Stepputat 2004; Feldman 1991; Mbembe 2003). This book contributes to these accounts of "sovereign bodies"—a broad notion that includes a range of historical actors, "from states, nations, communities, self-appointed big-

scholar G. N. Potanin noted that Mongols also identified Russian empresses as reincarnations of one of Chinggis Khan's daughters, who herself was viewed as a reincarnation of the White Tārā (Potanin 1883: 869). In 1893, in his report to the tsar Aleksandr III, Petr Badmaev mentions that Mongol Buddhists "consider the white tsar to be a reincarnation of their goddess Dara Ekhe (Bur. White Tārā). She is reincarnated into the white tsar in order to soften the character of the northern countries' inhabitants" (Badmaev 2001: 65–66).

men and leaders, to mobile individuals and political outfits" (Hansen and Stepputat 2005: 5)—by considering the processes through which specific, highly mobile Buddhist bodies become key sites for broader claims of religiopolitical sovereignty.

As early postperestroika hopes for Buryat territorial sovereignty were slowly eroding, indigenous politics reorganized itself around claims usefully defined elsewhere in terms of "cultural sovereignty"—a broad notion signifying strategies to maintain and develop cultural alterity, as well as assert autonomy from external control (Coffey and Tsosie 2001). Such expressions of sovereignty are usually disaggregated from territorial nationalism and are primarily nonjuridical and strategic, often executed on equal footing but in *interdependence* with other sovereignties (Cattelino 2008; Winegar 2006). Cultural sovereignty discourse has become especially vital for Buryats since the collapse of the USSR, as, against the earlier hopes of indigenous elites, their long-standing marginality seems to have been increased in post-Soviet Russia. Having long been discursively defined by others as belonging to the various peripheries, such as those of empires and states—Mongolian, Chinese, Russian, Soviet, and now the Russian Federation—most recently Buryats have unexpectedly found themselves pushed into yet another cultural fringe, this time that of the cosmopolitan world of Asian Buddhism. Almost as removed from Moscow as from Lhasa, Buryats are a minority not only within larger Russia (despite being the largest ethnic group in Siberia) but also within the nominally autonomous republic, which bears their name but where they now constitute only 29.5% of the population.[9] Despite their eagerness to reestablish ties with their Asian coreligionists, in a transnational context, they are often cast as the northernmost fringe of the "forest" Mongols, who received Tibetan Buddhism much later than most of their Asian counterparts, subsequently undergoing mass Russification and Sovietization—a final blow to an already "incomplete" religious transmission. In particular, many in the Tibetan exile community consider Buryats' current attempts to revive their Buddhist traditions to be of dubious authenticity and in need of Tibetan "missionaries" to help them with this task. In this context, a major arena where assertions of cultural sovereignty take place today is the contemporary practice of Buryat Buddhism, which many local leaders consider the most important cultural currency. Thus, what is at stake in such regionally particular religious domains is not only

---

9. 2010 Russian census data (available at http://www.perepis-2010.ru/).

Buryats' relationship with the Russian federal government and the phenomenon of the so-called regional sovereignty mentioned above, but also the issue of cultural recognition within the larger Mongol-Tibetan world.

Besides a complex and uneasy engagement with Tibetan Buddhists across Asia (and now the world), Buryats' relationship with the Russian state is also fraught with contradictions. If the Russian imperial government tried to solve the "Buddhist question" by regulating the number of approved lamas and restricting Buryats' physical mobility, the Soviet Union's solution to this issue strikes one as even more pointedly *biopolitical*.

The Body Soviet and the Body Buddhist

The Soviet Union, although not usually invoked in discussions of biopolitics, certainly exemplifies how governments produce subjects and manage human populations through regulating health, hygiene, diet, and sexuality (my use of the notion of biopolitics here is consistent with Foucault 2003: 239–264). The Soviet body was highly regulated, as the socialist state attempted to greatly diminish private space through various surveillance institutions that put bodies permanently on display (Buck-Morss 2000: 199). Much literature has been devoted to the production of the New Soviet Person, especially in the domains of health, physical culture, and gender. The Soviet body was conceptualized as a machine: strong, masculine, productive, autonomous, and subject exclusively to reason (Starks 2008; Attwood 1990; Livers 2004).

While the workings of biopolitics in these domains have been well studied, the religious domain has been relatively neglected. Unlike secularization in the West, Soviet secularization attempted to expel religion not only from the public space, but also from the body. Scholars generally agree that this secularization produced mixed results, with convincing evidence that religious life actively continued in the private sphere (Dragadze 1993; Steinberg and Wanner 2008; Rogers 2009). What matters here is that there was a serious and sustained attempt to create what I call "closed" bodies, whose sovereignty would be based on physical and moral strength, autonomy, and their impenetrability to religious influences. Religion was viewed as an "opium" for the body that was not to be ingested orally or intravenously; it was conceptualized as a disease that might eventually destroy the body. In particular, religion was related to the classical biopolitical concern with health and hygiene, as Orthodox icons became sites of infections through saliva, and Central Asian Muslim veils were claimed to cause birth defects (Starks 2008: 32). Lamas were accused of spreading unsanitary conditions, due to their adherence to the Buddhist doctrine of nonviolence, which supposedly did not allow them to kill lice. According to one atheist cultural worker, lamas also prevented believers from using soap to wash their hands and clothes, due to the "savage superstition" that happiness was washed away with the dirt (Erbanov 1959: 27). While hygiene can be viewed as surface purification, the body also had to be purged from the inside: of supernatural abilities, spirits, and deities that might inhabit it. Shamans were thrown off helicopters to see if they could "really" fly (Vitebsky 1995: 136). Incarnate lamas were convinced to renounce their status as false (Norbaev 1927).[10] Monks, in particular, presented a biopolitical hindrance, since they refused to participate in sexual reproduction and socialist labor.

This biopolitics also affected mobility, as fears of contamination of bodies by alien ideologies became an additional justification for the iron curtain. In order to be allowed to travel abroad, one had to pass the test of ideological solidity. The permeable bodies of religious adepts, which might emanate divinities or allow deities to penetrate them, had to be first purified and then closed or, in the case of resistant "infections," destroyed. In this context, some aspects of Soviet secularization can be viewed as a kind of hygienic treatment to expel extraneous agents, religious subjectivities and dispositions, as well as a subsequent symbolic "closing" of the body in at attempt to constrain and circumscribe it in strictly materialist and unitary terms. Here, the Soviet purification was only partially successful: it was specifically the bodies that resisted such practices that would become important sites for postsocialist assertions of cultural sovereignty. The bodies of the Buryat Buddhists that I discuss in this study stand in stark contrast to the Soviet secularized body: mobile, permeable, enduring, they have become productive arenas for the creative refashioning of what it means to be sovereign.[11]

---

10. Some Buryat monks supported this "purification"—albeit for different reasons—calling for the return to the rules of the Vinaya (monastic code of early Indian Buddhism, which did not include the institution of reincarnation). Danzan Norbaev, an incarnate lama otherwise known as Ganzhurva-gegen, wrote a letter to the editor of the newspaper *Buryat-Mongol Pravda*, renouncing his status as an incarnate (Norbaev 1927).

11. See Bernstein 2012 for specific elaborations on the links between bodily and cultural sovereignty.

The physical body, in the pan-Buddhist view that many diverse Buddhist cultures appear to share, is not an "independent entity set against others, 'me' contrasted with and in opposition to 'you,' but is just the coming together in a patterned heap of a collection of material elements," where the patterning is defined by karmic processes over time (Williams 1997: 207). This notion of the body is intricately connected to the Buddhist doctrine of "no-self," which holds that what we perceive as an unchanging and permanent "self" is a constantly changing collection of elements that constitute a psychophysical complex, which is conventionally understood as a "self." In the Buddhist view, this self is an illusion, falsely imagined to exist somewhere among the various constituents of mind and body. By this logic, the ownership of one's own body is theoretically impossible, since there is no entity, such as a permanent "self" or "I," that could claim ownership of it. Sovereignty, in the Buddhist sense, is achieved not through claiming the boundaries of one's body, but through using one's body as a vehicle to reach enlightenment. Although in Buddhism, the body is often viewed as repulsive and disgusting, something to which people erroneously cling and which should be overcome through special training, such as meditations on the foulness of the body, the human body is also valued as the best vehicle for traversing the path to enlightenment (Collins 1997; Williams 1997). Mastering death, in particular, offers an especially striking way to sovereignty in a Buddhist context.

Death, one of the four main forms of human suffering in Buddhist thought (along with birth, old age, and sickness), "exemplifies the very problem that the Buddhist soteriological project is to overcome." The idea of stopping the cycle of rebirths and attaining *nirvāṇa* signifies the defeat not only of desire and attachment but also of death, demonstrated by the Buddha, who "attained to the deathless" (Cuevas and Stone 2007: 1). Other methods of controlling death include certain techniques of the body, such as the ability of some extraordinary individuals to control their future rebirths (incarnate lamas), to stop the decomposition of their bodies after death ("incorruptible" bodies of certain saints and yogins), or to separate consciousness from the body in order to dismember one's own corpse and offer it as food to the spirits (practitioners of what is known as a *chöd* ritual).

Yet, strikingly, overcoming mortality is one goal that early socialist and classical Buddhist projects might have had in common. Early socialists were equally concerned with overcoming death, albeit through rather different methods. Influenced by apocalyptic and utopian turn-of-the-century philosophers, such as N. F. Fedorov, early Bolsheviks attempted to liberate mankind from death with the "miracle-working powers of technology" (Tumarkin 1997: 181). For all their atheist ambitions, these Russian revolutionary visionaries advocated a means to eliminate death and achieve physical immortality through a unique blending of cutting-edge science and deeply religious ideas, which eventually came to influence millions of people who lived in the USSR.[12]

Negotiations of Death

In 1924, the Immortalization Commission, a group of Soviet scientists, revolutionized what might today still be considered the traditional perspective on a leader's two bodies. Not only was Lenin's *body politic* declared immortal through the ubiquitous slogan "Lenin lives, Lenin lived, Lenin will live!" but his *body natural* was also made eternal though experimental techniques of embalming. Influenced by contemporary futuristic theories that technology would soon enable the resurrection of the dead, scientists considered it their moral duty to preserve great historical figures.[13] Thus, after Lenin, Stalin's embalmed body entered the same mausoleum in 1953 while great leaders of other socialist countries were sent to Russia for mummification (Bulgarian communist leader Georgi Dimitrov in 1949, Mongolian leader Choibalsan in 1952, Vietnam's Ho Chi Minh in 1969, Angola's Agostino Neto in 1979, Guyana's Lindon Forbes Burnham in 1985) (Tumarkin 1997: 184–189; Buck-Morss 2000: 78–79).[14]

12. The ideas of N. F. Fedorov (1828–1903), who believed that technology would help mankind achieve immortality, profoundly influenced the Bolshevik intelligentsia, most notably L. B. Krasin (1870–1926), the scientist who supervised the preservation of Lenin's body; the Marxist scientist A. A. Bogdanov (1873–1928), who believed that blood transfusions would lead to eternal life (eventually dying from these experiments); and polymath A. V. Lunacharsky (1875–1933), who was to become the first Soviet "people's commissar of enlightenment" (responsible for culture and education) and one of the leading architects of the Lenin cult (Tumarkin 1997: 19–22). British Sovietologist Peter Wiles once wrote that this particular "Russian passion for immortality" had its origins not in communism, but in prerevolutionary folk culture and religion, which, however, "fits ideally into communism." Besides the cult of dead bodies, he also cites the prominent place of gerontology in the Soviet health system and reports of Caucasian mountain tribesmen who live to 150—a prominent feature of the Russian imaginary even today—as indicative of the Russian/Soviet obsession with eternal life (Wiles 1965: 125–143).

13. Besides cutting-edge science, as Tumarkin convincingly argues, another major influence upon the emergent cult of Lenin in early Soviet Russia was the Russian Orthodox tradition of venerating saints' relics (1997: 4–6).

14. Mao Zedong was mummified by the Chinese in 1976. Stalin was removed from the mausoleum in 1961, as a consequence of the de-Stalinization campaign. In 1995, after the fall of the Soviet Union, Korea's dead leader Kim Il Sung was embalmed by the same Moscow laboratory (Buck-Morss 2000: 78–79).

While socialism was characterized by the drive to immortalize "great bodies," one of the most important processes in the postsocialist period was exhumations and reburials. In the midnineties, calls to remove Lenin from the mausoleum and give him a "proper human burial" created controversy on the Russian political scene, one which is still not resolved today. Similarly, other countries in the postsocialist bloc, both in Eastern Europe and across the world—in Latin America, Asia, and Africa—have been swept by what Katherine Verdery called a "parade of dead bodies." Statues were being toppled, famous corpses and bones moved around—some removed from their former places and others brought from abroad to be reburied at home with great fanfare (Gal 1991; Todorova 2009; Verdery 1999). Why is all this activity around dead bodies happening in the postsocialist period, and how does it differ from similar examples in other times and places? Verdery attempts to answer these questions by investigating how certain bodies—revolutionary leaders, heroes, religious figures, and sometimes even anonymous dead, such as those buried in mass graves—have taken on a political life of their own since the collapse of communism. She argues that rather than being simple metaphors of the death of the communist system, we should view these ritual dead-body manipulations as crucial to the central transformations of postsocialism: reconfiguring not only the notions of authority, the sacred, and the moral order but also time and space itself, as the past is being revisited and the present reoriented (1999: 33–53). These highly influential studies, however, do not question the present-day ambiguity and biopolitical negotiations of death, which create liminal beings, who hover between life and death, being neither persons nor cadavers. While these issues have been richly explored by medical anthropologists (e.g., Kaufman and Morgan 2005; Sharp 2007), the religious dimensions have received less attention.

More Alive Than All the Living

Consider one such case of a key religious body and its political ramifications. In September 2002, lamas of the Ivolginsk Monastery accompanied by forensic experts performed an exhumation of the body of Dashi-Dordzho Itigelov, the last Khambo Lama elected during the existence of the Russian empire, who died in 1927. The body of the lama, found seated in the lotus position, allegedly had not deteriorated, and soon rumors spread that the lama was alive and had returned to Buryatia, as he had promised. According to the stories told by senior monks, before his death, Itigelov asked to have his body exhumed thirty years later. He was first exhumed in 1955 (a little short of thirty years) by his relatives and lamas in secret, out of fear of being discovered by the Soviet authorities. The body was intact, so they reburied him right away. In 2002 he was exhumed again. Since then, the lama's body has been encased in a glass display at the Ivolginsk Monastery and shown to the public and pilgrims seven times per year on major Buddhist holidays.

Seven years later, debates regarding the state of his body continue. Many, including the traditional Buddhist leadership and some members of the Russian and Buryat academic community, maintain that Itigelov is simply alive, in ways yet unknown to modern science.[15] Reports of Itigelov's growing nails, hair, and allegedly warm body temperature consistently make headlines in the local and national press. Those who are more careful claim that he is "neither dead, nor alive," being in a special state of consciousness known as deep Buddhist mediation. Yet others claim that he did die, reaching the state of nirvāṇa and stopping the cycle of rebirth, but he deliberately left his incorruptible body behind, knowing in advance that only a magical feat such as his would inspire strong faith during these difficult postsocialist times. To many believers, Itigelov's body, said to have magical powers to grant any sincere wish and instantaneously correct one's karma, is a beacon of hope. To the leading Buryat Buddhist organization, the Buddhist Traditional Sangha of Russia, Itigelov is a guarantee of its autocephality, since he is a fully local leader who never traveled to Tibet and yet achieved such remarkable realizations. And to me, Itigelov is only one example of many such sovereign Buddhist bodies, which, in one way or another, exercised control over their own mortality, thus challenging the logics of larger sovereignties, whether of the Russian imperial, Soviet, or postsocialist states or those of Tibetan or Mongolian religious orbits.

The incorruptible body has a long history in Buddhism, most famously in the Lotus Sutra. Such famous figures as Tsongkhapa were said to have incorruptible bodies. Mummification of great lamas, such as the Dalai Lamas, has also been an important practice, and it has

---

15. See Quijada 2012 for an analysis of the view of Itigelov as a "scientifically proven miracle" and its significance for the postsocialist renegotiation of Soviet discourses on science and religion.

continued in Tibetan exile communities with the mummification of the Dalai Lama's senior tutor Ling Rinpoche. In Itigelov's case, it has to be emphasized that although rumors that salt has been used to preserve his body currently circulate, the official point of view of the Buddhist Sangha is that his body is miraculously *self-preserved* and not deliberately mummified or embalmed.

Yet the notion of the preservation of the body of a leader as a display of sovereignty, exemplified by famous socialist corpses, such as Lenin, Stalin, and Mao, is not lost on Itigelov's commentators. Shortly after Lenin's death in 1924 and before the decision to embalm him was made, Soviet poet Vladimir Mayakovsky inadvertently created what would become a ubiquitous slogan posted in every classroom in the Soviet Union:

Lenin i teper' zhivee vsekh zhivykh
(Lenin is even now more alive than all the living)

The same poem further specified the metonymic connections between Lenin and Soviet sovereignty vested in the Communist Party by what has become another famous slogan: "When we say 'Lenin' / We mean 'Party' / When We Say 'Party,' / We mean 'Lenin.'"[16] Similarly to how the "undead" Lenin has been metonymized into the sovereignty of the party, Itigelov has come to embody the autocephality of Buryat Buddhism. Comparisons of Itigelov with Lenin are indeed ubiquitous in both Buryat and broader Russian media, from condemnations by those opposing the display of Itigelov, who argue that he should be buried in a stupa (reliquary),[17] to humorous quips by journalists, paraphrasing the slogan above: "More Alive Than All the Living: Not Lenin but Lama Itigelov" (the title of an article in *Izvestiia*, a high-circulation Russian daily newspaper; Klin 2006). Rumors, sometimes quite wild, relating socialist dead bodies to Itigelov continue to circulate: a tabloid recently claimed that Itigelov gave advice regarding Lenin's embalmment in 1924 (Anonymous 2006; the Sangha lamas denied this claim). Another journalist called Itigelov the "Buryat Lenin," while others argue that the lama's body is superior to that of Lenin, since Itigelov does not need any special preservation or embalmment.[18] Yet many

---

16. V. Mayakovskii, "V. I. Lenin" (1924).

17. Similarly, the Russian Orthodox Church maintains that Lenin should be removed from the mausoleum and given a "proper human burial."

18. Quijada reports a similar sentiment expressed by one of her Buryat informants, who claimed that while "Lenin is artificial," Itigelov is the "real thing." Whereas Itigelov is a "scientifi-

popular news stories covering socialist dead body politics put Itigelov firmly alongside Lenin and Mao (Anonymous 2005, 2007). As life and death today are increasingly approached through their biopolitical negotiation, Itigelov joins the growing numbers of "liminal beings who hover in an ambiguous zone between life and death," similarly to "not-dead-but-not-fully-alive" biomedical subjects, whose personhood is negotiated through intersubjective knowledge (Kaufman and Morgan 2005: 300). If sovereignty has to do with "making" live or "letting" die (Foucault 2003), Buryat Buddhists' ability to make decisions about life, death, and the different values of different (quasi) lives demonstrates how long-standing pan-Buddhist practices could be deployed as assertions of countersovereignty in the domain of cultural and even cosmic politics.

While Itigelov is undoubtedly the most famous Buddhist body in Russia, he is not the only Buryat lama who is believed to have managed to overcome his own mortality.[19] Stories of Buryat lamas defying death abound in contemporary Buryat folklore, often structured by the memories of violence inscribed in their bodies during the Soviet period, when lamas were sent to work in labor camps and forced to marry. Monastic disciplines of self-denial, which produce ascetic bodies, as Foucault notes, are unlike other societal disciplines aimed at creating famously "docile bodies." Ascetic discipline, although it involves obedience to others, has as its main function to increase mastery of each individual over his own body rather than increase its productive utility (Foucault 1979 [1975]: 137). Those bodies which did not comply with the new requirements of obligatory labor and reproductive sexuality indicated a biopolitical threat to the socialist state. The bodies, displaying noncompliance, were to be destroyed, purged without a trial. Or were they?

"When I aimed my gun at the lama and was about to pull the trigger, the lama just disappeared," said the Soviet guard at a labor camp, who was ordered by his superiors to shoot a lama in 1937. "After a few seconds, he appeared again, but he was

---

cally proven miracle," Lenin is "merely a miracle of science." Itigelov's "authenticity retroactively exposes Lenin to have been the copy, the Soviet faith in science, which tried to usurp the place of religious faith, a mere duplicate of the real, scientifically proven miracle" (Quijada 2012: 148).

19. Interestingly, the Russian Orthodox Church also reports miraculously incorruptible bodies, such as the body of the saint Aleksandr Svirskii, who is sometimes mentioned in the press in connection with Itigelov (Klin 2006). Svirskii's remains, however, are clearly treated as sacred *relics*; claims that he is alive are not being made. While Buryat Buddhism might have been, in some ways, influenced by Russia's dominant religion, it is the distinct pan-Buddhist conceptions of life, death, and the body that enable phenomena like Itigelov.

about thirty steps from the place where he was before. I quickly aimed and shot again. The lama again disappeared! After some time I saw him floating in the air, over the pine tree tops, I shot at him again. My hands were shaking, I was overcome by panic and fear. All of a sudden the lama appeared again, close to me, stretching his hands toward me and saying something. I vaguely remember that I reloaded my gun and shot again. The lama fell on the ground; his chest was covered with blood. All of a sudden a white lotus flower of giant dimensions appeared in the air. Its aroma was so strong that I started feeling dizzy. I can't remember anything else." . . . This guard ended up in a psychiatric hospital and later is reported to have become very religious, sending one of his sons to be a monk after Stalin opened the Ivolginsk Monastery after World War II. (Mukhanov 2005: 199–200)

Stories about undying or disappearing lamas escaping Soviet anti-religious campaigns are widespread in Buryatia.[20] One lama who was arrested, beaten up, and thrown into a barred military car, was nowhere to be found on arrival. Instead, a Tibetan sacred book was left in his place. Arrested lamas are said to walk through walls of prisons right in front of their astounded guards, or they disappear into thin air while covering thousands of miles per second on their escape route to China and Mongolia.[21]

Besides miraculously preserved bodies and bodies that miraculously escaped, a variety of other Buddhist techniques, such as reincarnation and certain ritual practices involving the destruction of one's body, allow some Buddhist individuals a degree of control over their own mortality. The stories of escapes point to a certain kind of unauthorized mobility, which silently defies the logics of larger sovereignties, such as the Russian state, which, through all its incarnations, continues to be reluctant to see its Buddhist subjects cross borders. In this book, I use the data collected during my field and archival research across Buryat communities in northern and southern Asia to elaborate on several interconnected stories of the various Buryat border crossers who became key sites for the contemporary self-fashioning. Some of them have crossed borders between life and death, whether planning their own exhumations, like Itigelov (chap. 3), or engaging in practices of re-

20. Similar narratives are also widespread in other Siberian regions and other post-Soviet regions in general, where memories of violent repressions often found expression in stories of magical escape (Balzer 1997; Grant 2011).

21. Another story about damaging evidence that kept disappearing (Rus. *ischezaiushchii kompromat*) tells how every time after local NKVD (the Soviet secret police agency) authorities collected incriminating evidence about a lama and put it in a safe, the next morning the safe was either empty or contained blank sheets of paper (Mukhanov 2005: 199).

incarnation and tantric discipleship (chap. 2), or performing visualized self-annihilations and dismemberments in a chöd ritual (chap. 5). Others have crossed borders by secretly visiting distant lands (chap. 1) or by openly traveling to such lands in search of specific bodies (chap. 4). Yet others used far less spectacular means to insert themselves into contemporary global frameworks, bypassing the restricting idioms of the nation-state and even transnational religious communities (chap. 6). This study is thus intended as a contribution to the growing literature on postsocialist body politics (Gal 1991; Todorova 2009; Verdery 1999; Tumarkin 1997; Borneman 2004), cross-disciplinary studies of sovereignty that focus on the body as a site of sovereign power (Hansen and Stepputat 2004; Agamben 1998 [1995]; Foucault 1980), new developments in Buddhist studies, where issues related to the body and embodiment have recently become a central focus of inquiry (Faure 2003; Germano and Trainor 2004; Mrozik 2007; Strong 2004; Powers 2009), and the emergent field of the anthropology of religion under and after socialism (Rogers 2009; Balzer 1999; Buyandelger 2013; Steinberg and Wanner 2008; Lindquist 2000; Grant 2011; Humphrey 1999 [1983]; Luehrmann 2011; Pedersen 2011). Before I proceed to the detailed chapter outlines and organization, however, I would like to say a few words about Buryats and my field experience.

Buryats: Religion and Society

The majority of Buryats, a people of Mongolian descent, language, and culture, who number some four hundred sixty thousand across the Russian Federation, live in the Lake Baikal region of southeastern Siberia.[22] A further sizable community of about eighty thousand Buryats is found in Mongolia, and about six or seven thousand live in northern China.[23] The establishment of a Sino-Russian frontier in 1727 separated the northern Mongol communities, who found themselves on different sides of the border. According to Caroline Humphrey, the simple

22. 2010 Russian census data. This number includes all Buryats of the Russian Federation, where most Buryats live in the Republic of Buryatia and the Irkutsk and Chita regions. Of the total number, about 8,000 Buryats live in the Republic of Sakha, and between 4,000 and 6,000 live in Moscow and St. Petersburg. Of the post-Soviet states, 1,172 Buryats live in Kazakhstan, 849 in Ukraine, and several hundred in Uzbekistan and Kyrgyzstan (Zhukovskaia 2001: 510–511; Moscow and St. Petersburg numbers adjusted, according to the Russian census of 2010).

23. The numbers for Buryats living in Mongolia and China vary widely in different sources. The numbers cited above are referenced in Nimaev and Abaeva 2004: 11.

formula of "conquest," common to many other Siberian peoples and indigenous peoples worldwide, does not quite apply to Buryats, most of whom eventually became subjects of the Russian empire voluntarily, due to the lower tax burden and lighter state duties than those imposed on them in Khalkha Mongolia. Some voted with their feet, preferring the tsarist system of indirect rule to the internecine warfare in Mongolia (Humphrey 1999 [1983]: 27).[24] Thus, Humphrey suggests that Buryats can be defined as "those northern Mongol tribes which decided they wished to remain in the Tsarist Russian Empire" (1999 [1983]: 27–28).[25]

At the time of their annexation to the Russian empire, Buryat society was stratified in a semifeudal manner with a mostly pastoral economy. The predominant religion was shamanism of the Mongolian type, with a highly developed hierarchical shamanic pantheon.[26] Buryat chronicles traditionally designate the arrival of Tibetan and Mongolian lamas in the early eighteenth century as the official beginning of the spread of Buddhism (or, as it was called in Russian-language literature on Buryats until recently, Lamaism) in the Transbaikal.[27] Buddhism spread very unevenly between various Buryat clans: for example, Selenga and Khori Buryats were among the first to start practicing it, shortly after its arrival, while Tunka, Barguzin, and Alar Buryats did not have a significant Buddhist presence until the nineteenth century, and Irkutsk Buryats—until the beginning of the twentieth century (Galdanova, Gerasimova, and Dashiev 1983: 16).

The policies of the Russian imperial government created further distinctions among various Buryat groups. While until the mid-nineteenth

24. Although the official annexation (referred to in Russian-speaking scholarship as *prisoedinenie* [joining]) of Buryats to the Russian empire was relatively peaceful, a number of bloody conflicts between Russians and Buryats took place during the seventeenth century. Some Russian scholars consider that the annexation of Buryats to Russia started as early as 1629 and took about one century to complete. In 1629, Russians first attempted to impose the fur tribute (Rus. *iasak*) on the native communities to the west of Lake Baikal. Buryats, however, who themselves took tribute from the smaller tribes in the region, were not interested in ceding these privileges. Thus, from 1629 until the end of the seventeenth century, armed conflicts regularly took place between Buryats and Russians (Koreniako 2001: 172–181; Zalkind 1958: 15–46).

25. When exactly the ethnonym "Buryat" appeared is still a subject of much scholarly debate. What is at stake here is the controversial issue of whether various Buryat clans already had a certain unity before they became part of the Russian empire (Mikhailov 1998; Bertagaev 1970; Tsydendambaev 1972; Sanzheev 1983; Zoriktuev 1996; Shadaeva 1998).

26. For early Russian-language studies of Buryat shamanism, see Banzarov 1891; Khangalov 1958–1959; and Petri 1928. For Soviet and postsocialist scholarship, see Galdanova 1987; Gerasimova 1998; Skrynnikova 1997; and Zhukovskaia 1968, 1999. For English and French language studies, see Buyandelger 2013; Empson 2007; Hamayon 1990; Humphrey 1999 [1983]; and Quijada 2009.

27. See Lopez 1998: 15–46 on the history of the term "Lamaism" in Western scholarship.

century the tsars did not create significant obstacles to the spread of Buddhism in the Transbaikal, those Buryats who lived on the western shore of Lake Baikal were subjected to increasing Christianization and Russification. Buryats of the western shore, sometimes referred to in literature as "western Buryats," have predominantly Russian names, do not generally speak Buryat, and practice a mix of shamanism and Russian Orthodox Christianity.[28] In the Transbaikal, however, where the majority of Buryats lived, by the nineteenth century, Buddhism was firmly established, becoming a major community-consolidating factor. The growth in the number of Buddhist monasteries, which became centers of learning, written culture, and the arts, became cause for serious concern for the eastern Siberia administration (Pozdneev 1887a: 173).[29]

The new course toward cementing the main role of Orthodox Christianity in the Russian empire led the government to revise its policies toward non-Christian religions. In 1853, the tsarist government issued a decree entitled "The Statute on Lamaist Clergy in Eastern Siberia," which attempted to regain control of Buryat Buddhism by restricting the numbers of monasteries and lamas and imposing direct subordination of the Lamaist church to the government. The number of "approved" (Rus. *komplektnye*) monasteries was fixed at thirty-four with 285 "staff" (Rus. *shtatnye*) lamas. A newly centralized system of religious de-

28. According to the 1989 census, there are about seventy-seven thousand "western" Buryats (Zhambalova 2000: 9). Buddhism started to become established among western Buryats in the early twentieth century; however, it never quite took root due to subsequent socialist antireligious campaigns of the 1920s. (After the removal of administrative and legal obstacles, preventing western Buryats from converting to Buddhism in 1917, ten temples were quickly established in this region (Galdanova, Gerasimova, and Dashiev 1983: 26)). In the postsocialist period, many western Buryats are again becoming interested in Buddhism, due to its increased prestige as a "literary" Buryat religion and a potential factor that might finally unify all Buryats. As of 2009, six Buddhist communities belonging to the Buddhist Traditional Sangha of Russia and one Karma Kagyu community were registered in Irkutsk Oblast'. A major monastery is located in Ust'-Orda, and several more are currently under construction throughout the region. (Quoted from the official government website of the Irkutsk Oblast', http://www.govirk.ru/print.aspx?article=643dd522-f9bb-43d6–8056-98c3537ca4f9, accessed October 7, 2009.)

29. An interesting glimpse into nineteenth-century religious politics in Buryatia is provided by the records of the London Missionary Society, which spent considerable efforts and resources on a long-term conversion mission among the Buryats. The mission turned out to be a spectacular failure: after more than twenty years of work during the first half of the nineteenth century, only a few Buryats were converted and none were baptized by the missionaries. The Orthodox mission was more successful during the second half of the nineteenth century: while in 1851 there were nine thousand baptized Buryats, at the turn of the century there were as many as eighty-five thousand. The English missionaries, however, report that many of these conversions were nominal: "Becoming a Christian meant no more than changing a few habits—living in a house instead of a tent, wearing the hair short instead of in a pigtail, eating fish on Wednesday or Friday, making the signs of the cross and so on" (Bawden 1985: 245, 354).

grees and diplomas was directed to go through the Gusinoozersk Monastery (the seat of the Khambo Lama). Despite the new "triple" control system—building new monasteries was strictly prohibited without the approval of first the Buryat administration, then the Siberian governor general, and then the St. Petersburg Ministry of Internal Affairs—the number of monasteries and lamas continued to grow.[30] Likewise, many received their religious degrees outside Buryatia, in Urga and Lhasa (Galdanova, Gerasimova, and Dashiev 1983: 30).[31]

After 1822, Buryats were governed according to the Speranskii statute, which provided Buryats with a degree of local self-government, allowing them to retain much of their existing clan organization. Buryats were allowed to form their own "steppe duma," a kind of local council of elders, which represented all Buryats before the Russian provincial administration. By the end of the nineteenth century, the steppe dumas were abolished, bringing the administration of Buryats into line with that of Russian peasants. Shortly, Russian and Ukrainian peasants increasingly started settling on Buryat lands, which, together with the growing discontent about policies of Russification, eventually led to the development of the Buryat nationalist movement (Rupen 1964: 30–33).

By the end of the nineteenth century, considered today by many the golden age of Buryat culture and society, in addition to the clerical elite, there had appeared a sizable Buryat secular intelligentsia, Russian educated but often culturally oriented toward Mongolia and Tibet (Humphrey 1999 [1983]: 30). Many became advocates for native rights and cultural autonomy. Early twentieth-century Russian revolutionary politics divided the Buryat elites, with some advocating progressive tendencies and reform of the Buddhist church and others, staunchly conservative, resisting these reforms in favor of the Buryat "traditionalism" (Rupen 1956; Gerasimova 1964; see also chap. 1). The watershed events of the 1917 October Revolution and the subsequent civil war in Russia further divided native intelligentsia: some supported the Bolsheviks, while others supported the Whites. Still others joined the counterrevolutionary forces of Grigorii Semenov and Aleksandr Kolchak.

In 1923, the Buryat-Mongol Autonomous Soviet Socialist Republic

---

30 By 1910, there were fifteen thousand lamas and thirty-seven monasteries (Rupen 1964: 37).

31. For scholarship on the imperial politics toward Buddhism in the Transbaikal, see Gerasimova 1957.

was established. It included all the areas traditionally populated by Buryats, including what is today the Republic of Buryatia and large areas in the Chita and Irkutsk Provinces (Rus. *oblasti*). In 1937, however, fearing Buryat nationalism and pan-Mongolism, Stalin divided the Buryat Republic into three different noncontiguous administrative units, creating arbitrary borders. Subsequently, in 1958, the suffix "Mongol" was dropped from its name. The republic now included only some of the territory to the east and south of Lake Baikal. Two large areas in the Chita and Irkutsk Provinces were singled out and renamed Aga and Ust'-Orda Autonomous *Okrugs* (smaller territorial units within Russia), while the two other alienated territories were blended with the larger Chita and Irkutsk Provinces. Known by the striking corporeal idiom of "dismemberment" of the republic (Rus. *raschlenenie*), it is considered by many Buryats to be among the most traumatic events of the twentieth century, placed alongside the destruction of the Buddhist church and religious culture.

Socialist transformations such as the organization of Buryats into collective farms precipitated a rapid indigenous language loss. If, during the earlier centuries of cohabitation, Russians settlers were likely to learn Buryat, since the 1930s, Russian has been increasingly displacing Buryat. By the 1970s, almost all Buryats were fluent in Russian. Russian penetrated almost all spheres of life: work, school, administration, media, and the entertainment industry (Humphrey 1994a: 66–67). Despite the fact that the Law on the Languages of the Peoples of the Buryat Republic was passed in 1992, making both Russian and Buryat official state languages, the sphere of Buryat language use remains limited. Buryats generally speak and especially read Russian better than Buryat, and the number of Buryats who do not speak Buryat and those who name Russian as their mother tongue is still growing despite renewed attempts at language revitalization by the nationalist elites (Dyrkheeva 2003).

After perestroika, the Republic of Buryatia became one of the twenty-one republics that represented ethnic areas of the Russian Federation. During the 1990s, many Buryat nationalist intellectuals campaigned for the reestablishment of pre-1937 borders, where the two "dismembered" regions would be joined back with the Buryat Republic. However, instead of giving the "dismembered" regions back to the republic, the policy of "amalgamation" (Rus. *ukrupnenie*) of the Russian regions, started by former President Putin as a larger tendency toward the centralization of power, effectively dissolved them into Russia. The Aga

Autonomous Okrug ceased to exist in 2008, when it was joined with the Chita Province to form a new unit of Zabaikal'skii Krai, and Ust'-Orda Okrug was joined with Irkutsk Province in 2006.[32]

Due to the Christianization of the "western" Buryats and the subsequent destruction of the Buddhist church during the Soviet period, Buddhism did not become the consolidating factor that many prerevolutionary intellectuals had hoped for. Statistics are not reliable; many Buryats who call themselves Buddhists also go to shamans and some go to church (see also Quijada 2009). Other Buryats have remained atheists since Soviet times, while some have become skeptical of religion due to the clergy's involvement in some of the postsocialist "worldly" conflicts and politics. Still, an overwhelming number of Buryats, and a majority within the republic of Buryatia, either profess Buddhism as a religion or at least claim it as part of their cultural heritage. This number continues to grow. Thus, in 1996–1997, 35.2 % of Buryats identified Buddhism as a marker of their cultural difference, while only fifteen years later, in 2002–2003, 46.7 % expressed this view (Elaeva 2005).[33] How this Buddhist history and Buddhist present inform cultural politics and emerging geopolitical imaginaries in this region of northern Asia is the broad focus of this book.

The book deals primarily with Russian Buryats, the largest Buryat group, and their transnational links with Tibetan Buddhists in exile. The world of Inner Asian Buddhism, however, is not a smooth expanse, and in establishing their links with Tibetans in exile, Buryats have not entirely been leapfrogging a huge terrain of Inner Asia. In the postperestroika period, Buryats have also developed links with their kin across the Mongolian border (mostly concentrated in northeastern provinces across from the Russian border) and in Inner Mongolia, China, in the region of Shenehen in Hulun Buir Prefecture (referred to as "Shenehen Buryats"). These diasporas were formed in the early twentieth century, as thousands of Buryats moved south across the border in an attempt to escape the Russian civil war and subsequent Soviet repressions only to get caught by Soviet socialism that spilled over to Mongolia and later

32. Both okrugs kept their names within these larger units, with the key exception of the word "autonomous," which was removed.

33. Religiosity also appears to grow. In 1996–1997, 41% of Buryats said they were believers who follow all traditions and rituals; 22.2% identified themselves as believers, who did not follow rituals and traditions; 15.4% identified themselves as "hesitating"; 9.4% identified themselves as atheists; 11% found it difficult to choose an answer; and 1% did not answer. A 2002–2003 survey yielded the following results: 48.3%—believers, try to observe rituals and traditions; 30.5%—believers but do not observe rituals, 7.9%—hesitant, 7%—atheists; 5.3%—found it difficult to choose an answer; and 1% did not provide an answer (Elaeva 2005).

by the Sino-Soviet split. In the early 1990s, there were some efforts to create a structure for the formal repatriation of Shenehen Buryats to Russia, based on such models as the repatriation of Kazakhs to Kazakhstan; however, it was never established. Nonetheless, the local Buryat newspaper *Inform-Polis* reports that more than three hundred Shenehen families have moved to Buryatia and the former Aga Autonomous Okrug since the 1990s (Anonymous 2004a). A biannual cultural festival, Altargana, which unites various Buryat diasporas, regularly takes place in different locations in Russia and Mongolia. These links, however, do not play a significant role in the debates regarding cultural sovereignty, revival of Buddhism, and transnational journeys that are the focus of this book. Although many Buryats in Russia admire the ways in which these diasporic communities have preserved their traditional ways of life, such as shamanic practices and nomadic herding, and scholars studying Shenehen Buryats tend to treat them as a "unique laboratory" to study cultural preservation (Baldano and Diatlov 2008: 165), most active Buryat Buddhists do not look up to their "minority kin" as an ideal place for Buddhist development.[34] While some curious Buryats, including journalists and scholars, have visited Buryat communities in Mongolia and China, these locations have not become pilgrimage places and sources of long-distance authorizations for Buryat Buddhists. This role in the contemporary Buryat Buddhist imaginaries has been firmly filled by India, which, in Buryats' eyes, has acquired a double significance as a cradle of Buddhist civilization and, simultaneously, a "renewed" Tibet: the home of the Dalai Lama and thousands of Tibetan exiles, who have managed to re-create many important secular and religious institutions in a new context.

The Field, the Camera, and the Gift

My research with Buryat transnational Buddhist practices started in the spring of 2001, when I inadvertently ended up following the route of contemporary Buryat pilgrims to India. Originally interested in the life of the Tibetan diaspora in India as a master's student in visual anthropology at the University of Manchester, I was on a plane from London to Delhi, planning to head north to the Himalayan foothill town of Dharamsala, home to the Tibetan government-in-exile, to shoot my

---

34. On Buryats in Mongolia and China, see Buyandelgeriyn 2007; Empson 2011; Baldano and Diatlov 2008; Boronoeva 2003; and Namsaraeva 2010.

first ethnographic documentary. To offset the costs related to travel, I bought the cheapest ticket I could find, with the Russian state airline Aeroflot, which, due to its uneven reputation, was not especially popular with prudent British citizens. As a native Russian, however, who spent most of the 1990s shuttling between the United States and Russia in the uncertain state of a reluctant émigré, I felt at home in these slightly shabby cabins, famous for their rambunctious passengers and copious amounts of alcohol. As I comfortably stretched across a whole row of seats in a practically empty flight on the first leg from Heathrow to Sheremetyevo, I was entertaining myself by trying to imagine the various kinds of passengers who would join us once we stopped in Moscow. Would these be tipsy diplomats that I got used to seeing on transatlantic flights, New Age tourists in search of new gurus in exotic lands, or intrepid explorers bound for the ultimate wild nature adventure? What I saw, however, did not conform to any expectations, eventually changing my research and life course in ways I could not have ever predicted.

As the cabin doors were flung open, the cabin started filling up with maroon-clad Buddhist monks, sporting neatly shaved heads and identical yellow cloth shoulder bags with embroidered Sanskrit symbols. A far cry from the usual merry Aeroflot crowd, it was as if the exotic-looking photos of Tibetan monks I had spent so many months researching had suddenly come alive, albeit in rather unexpected, if surreal, surroundings of a Russian airplane. But why were these monks here, in my hometown of Moscow, instead of in the Himalayas, where I expected to see them? As the new arrivals settled in their seats, I was in for another surprise. These were no Tibetans, but Russian-speaking Buryat monks, who had to first cross five time zones westward from their home on the eastern shore of Lake Baikal in southern Siberia to get to Moscow only to board this Delhi-bound plane, now crossing four zones back eastward on their way to see the Dalai Lama. Like me, they also planned to save money by roughing it overland on a twelve-hour rickety bus, departing from the northern Delhi Tibetan enclave of Majnukatila and crossing the dusty plains of Punjab to emerge into the spring Himalayan air.

After this encounter, I became fascinated by the history and contemporary practice of Buddhism in Buryatia and its long-standing transnational links with Mongolia, Tibet, and, most recently, India. As I was working toward the completion of my short visual ethnography of exiled Tibetan monks in Dharamsala during this first trip, on more than one occasion, I ran into my new Buryat friends, many of whom contributed to this text. Starting in 2003, I became fully engaged with researching Buryat Buddhism, resulting in more field trips to Buryatia and culminating in an extended research year in 2007–2008, both in Buryatia and at the Drepung Monastery in southern India, where many Buryat monks currently receive their religious education. Besides these monastic networks, I have also followed lay religious practitioners both in Buryatia and across various sites in India, concentrating on the Buryat expatriate community in Dharamsala. This book is thus a result of eight years of research, travel, and collaboration with local scholars, learned monks, and laypeople.

A few words must be said about access and methodology. Some of this material comes from my archival research at the Buryat National Archives and the Institute of Oriental Manuscripts of the Russian Academy of Sciences. Most of the data, however, come from participant observation in Russia and India over four visits, between 2001 and 2008. I conducted a number of interviews with Buryat and Tibetan lamas and monks (a total of thirty-five interviews in Buryatia and India) and select, diverse members of the Buddhist community (a total of thirty interviews in Buryatia and India). I have also interviewed government officials in charge of religious affairs in Buryatia and Drepung Gomang monastic officials in charge of foreign monks. In addition, I have consulted city statistics and records in Buryatia to estimate the nature of religious participation and tracked public debates on the significance of the training abroad and representations of these debates in the popular press, including print and electronic media. All the interviews and participant-observation research with Buryats both in Buryatia and in India were carried out in Russian. Training in modern spoken Tibetan and a lesser knowledge of classical Tibetan, in turn, enabled me to conduct interviews with Tibetan lamas in both Buryatia and India and engage in the study of relevant Tibetan canonical texts with the monks.

The laypeople whose life histories I collected came from all strata of Buryat society: from advanced religious practitioners and active members of the Buryat intelligentsia to regular urban and rural Buryat Buddhists. The Buryat community in India cuts across class distinctions: while most of the monks and pilgrims come from the middle and lower middle classes, some come from poor rural families, who have been saving for these trips for years. Older pilgrims often receive these trips as gifts from their children. Almost none of the monks and very few of the pilgrims come from elite families. In Buryatia, I focused on those members of the clergy and laity who were most involved in local and transnational Buddhist politics and movements. While they may not be the most representative of the ordinary Buryat Buddhists, they most clearly articulate the issues that constituted the focus of my research. Most Buryat Buddhists who regularly visit temples and lamas for individual services, such as divination, personal advice, and health rituals, are often not aware of these politics, although Tibetan lamas evoke almost universal reverence and respect. Although there exist sharp distinctions between Tibetan lamas in exile in terms of their stance on issues of tradition, modernity, and Tibetan independence, the five lamas I worked with most closely in Buryatia and India were not actively involved with internal Tibetan politics. Such distinctions therefore are beyond the scope of this study.

Visual research, a crucial component of my methodology, turned out to be critical for matters of access. Between 2001 and 2006, I made two documentary films, *Join Me in Shambhala* and *In Pursuit of the Siberian Shaman*, on Buryat Buddhism and shamanism, respectively (Bernstein 2002b, 2006). These visual ethnographies received wide exposure and distribution both in Buryatia and elsewhere, being screened at more than a hundred ethnographic film festivals, museums, and public venues. As a result, both principal characters of the two films, Tibetan lama Yeshe Lodrö Rinpoche and Buryat shaman Valentin Khagdaev, were made into public figures on the transnational Buddhist, shamanic, and ethnographic scenes. One can say that for both of these characters my films were part of their own "skillful means."[35] In addition, the films inspired indigenous intellectuals from other Siberian republics to envision producing similar visual records of their traditions.[36] For me personally, these films established the relations of reciprocity that determined my successful access to many of the previously closed doors of each of the esoteric traditions.

As a scholarly tradition, canonical visual anthropology has long advocated that a researcher not start filming until the relationship with a community is firmly established. This could take months or even years and many repeated trips. My real-life fieldwork experience, however, kept thwarting these rules. In 2001, through a complicated network of contacts, I had finally secured a preliminary agreement from a Tibetan lama to be filmed. When I arrived in Buryatia, however, it was almost impossible to arrange a meeting with him in the city, since he was in

---

35. Many thanks to Faye Ginsburg for this observation. Yeshe Lodrö Rinpoche has used my sympathetic portrayal of his missionary activity to enhance his standing against his many detractors. The shaman Valentin Khagdaev now screens my film to tourists—a curious use of an ethnographic film analyzing shamanic tourism as a way of indigenous self-fashioning.

36. Ul'iana Vinokurova, personal communication.

high demand by the faithful. Finally, they agreed to let me follow them on a long trip around Buryatia and Yakutia (the Republic of Sakha). As I met them for the first time at the train station in Ulan-Ude with a blue *khata* (Buddhist ceremonial scarf) in my hands, against my best manners, I stuck the camera in front of their faces instead of an introduction. Not only did these first awkward moments of encounter later constitute some of the best footage of the film, but they also crucially defined my relationship with these men. While the camera in earlier ethnographic fieldwork constituted an intrusive alien object, which required some getting used to on the part of the local interlocutors, nowadays the filmmaker is an even more familiar "cultural character" than the ethnographer.[37] In turn, my being associated with the Rinpoche opened many doors for me, as I followed him with a camera around Buryatia. During these trips, I was able to meet local Buryats and start learning about Buryat Buddhism.

Fast forward seven years. I arrived in the Drepung Monastery in India as part of a yearlong research stay. One of the monks met me at the train station, helped me settle, and assisted in arranging a few formal interviews. However, I found it extremely difficult to strike up a casual conversation with the majority of the Buryat monks, which severely limited my participant-observation opportunities. One day the rumors about my films reached the Buryat dorm, and younger monks—less formal and more curious about me—invited me to screen my documentaries in their dorm.[38] In the middle of the film, during a rather solemn scene of a ritual service in a famous rural Buryat monastery, the room exploded with laughter. It turned out that a young monk, whom I diligently filmed in close-up beating the huge ritual drum, was sitting right next to me in the room! After this incident, my relationship with the monks improved dramatically. During my subsequent stints in various Buryat communities across northern and southern Asia, many a time I have used these films as an opening. I eventually ran out of blank DVD disks onto which I copied the films to be given out as gifts. The use of the camera drew me into a chain of social rela-

37. In fact, being without a camera among monks turned out to be more difficult. Had I been doing research in Buddhist studies and wanting to engage in the study of specific Buddhist philosophical or ritual texts, my presence at the monastery would have had some legitimacy. An ethnographer who wanted to study the monks themselves, however, appeared to them a rather odd character (and possibly a spy).

38. They were also very curious about my film on shamanism, although officially most of them did not approve of shamans. Later it turned out that most of them had never seen one and that shamans were as "exotic" for them as for their peers in the West.

tions, which had a crucial effect on my positioning and legitimacy as a fieldworker in a restricted social setting, while also facilitating practical issues of access.[39]

At Drepung Monastery, I was able to live in the monastery itself, first in the monks' quarters, and then in the little guesthouse on the premises. Living in the monks' quarters was a most unusual arrangement, as visitors, especially women, are normally not allowed into the monks' dorms. The exception was made due to an important event which coincided with my arrival—the Dalai Lama's visit to consecrate a new assembly hall of the Loseling Monastic College.[40] Along with hundreds of Tibetan, Ladakhi, and Sikkimese pilgrims hailing from all over India and even Tibet, and Western and Asian Buddhists, about fifty Buryat pilgrims arrived for this event. Unlike Dharamsala, Drepung Monastery is rarely visited by such large numbers of pilgrims, partially because of its location in the restricted area of India, for which a special permit is required in addition to a visa. As the two tiny guesthouses, for both Gomang and Loseling Colleges, were overbooked, pilgrims with substantial community connections were allowed to stay in the quarters of monks who came from their own communities. Thus, many Ladakhi pilgrims stayed with the Ladakhi monks, while Buryat pilgrims were allowed to stay in the Buryat monastic dormitory. During this time, monks themselves slept outside in makeshift tents while allowing their Buryat compatriots to occupy their cells. Upon my arrival, I was allotted a space in one of the monastic cells, with four other Buryat female pilgrims (one of them a nun). This fortuitous arrangement allowed me access to both the pilgrim and monastic communities.

In Dharamsala, I stayed in a guesthouse right by the residence of the Jebdzundamba and conducted trips to the Gyüto Monastery, where some Buryats also study. In Buryatia, I chose not to live at the Ivolginsk Monastery. Instead, I lived in an apartment with a local family in Ulan-Ude. Having made the city my base, I traveled almost constantly into various districts of Buryatia and the Transbaikal Krai to conduct interviews and participant-observation research. During my research stays in Ulan-Ude, I traveled almost daily to the Ivolginsk Monastery (about

---

39. Faye Ginsburg makes a similar observation in her book: the fact that she first arrived in the field as a producer of a documentary film, and only a few years later as an anthropologist, allowed her to establish rapport quickly with opposing social groups, each of which was seeking publicity (1989: 4–5).

40. Loseling is one of the four colleges constituting Drepung Monastery. Buryats usually study at the Gomang College.

one hour by bus from the city center), interviewed religious leaders, and conducted archival research.

Structure and Organization

I start this book by looking at the prerevolutionary history of Buryats' engagement with greater Eurasia, drawing on the legacies of the Russian Buddhological school and exploring the intellectual and political context of its emergence in the late nineteenth century. Chapter 1 explores the role of Russian Orientalists and political figures such as V. P. Vasil'ev and Prince E. E. Ukhtomskii, looking closely at the fieldwork of the first Russian-trained indigenous Buryat Buddhologists, G. Ts. Tsybikov and B. B. Baradiin. I demonstrate that this ultimately Eurasianist school of Buddhology was born out of conflicting sentiments toward Russia's cosmopolitanism, statehood, and imperial destiny in Asia, as well as representations of indigenous peoples of southern Siberia. The latter part of the chapter maps the emergent forms of what I call "Asian Eurasianism," linking it to contemporary debates about cultural sovereignty in Buryatia.

Chapter 2 proceeds to look at the early twentieth-century Buryats' engagement with Tibet and its recent legacies. Based on my field research in Buryatia and India, I introduce new materials on cross-ethnic reincarnation and apprenticeship practices between Buryat and Tibetan lamas in the context of these communities' expanding ties, despite the many restrictions on the circulation of Buddhist practices within Tibet. The reincarnated are, by design, highly mobile bodies imbued with an extraordinary status. In their status as border crossers, I am interested in how they have become sites for the competing claims to sovereignty in light of changing geopolitical consciousness. Similar to reincarnation, religious apprenticeship, which constitutes quasi-kinship ties between Buddhist masters and their disciples, is also analyzed in terms of emerging postsocialist geoimaginaries. Case studies for this chapter come from my field research with the Tibetan monks who are reincarnations of former Buryat lamas (at the Drepung Monastery in India) and naturalized Tibetan émigré lamas of Buryat "lineage" (in Ulan-Ude, Buryatia).

Chapter 3 shifts the focus back to contemporary Buryatia, taking a close look at the strategies used to reconsecrate the postsocialist Buddhist landscape and the production of new sacred geographies, historiographies, and cosmologies of time and space. While proposing to look at these phenomena in the context of the widely known Tibetan phenomenon of "treasures"—objects found underground that are accorded a revelatory status—I expand the understanding of "treasures" by highlighting the special role of dead bodies as quintessential objects of the post-Soviet treasure hunt. Among other cases, I look at the necropolitics that have developed around the fate of a famous lama who died in the 1920s and on whose "miraculously incorruptible" body, unearthed in 2003, the autonomy of Buryat Buddhism is currently said to rest. By claiming that this lama, believed to be a reincarnation of a long lineage of Indian sages, intentionally manifested himself in these troubled postsocialist times, Buryat Buddhists create a renovated cosmology that overwrites their otherwise seemingly peripheral location in the Mongol-Tibetan world.

Chapter 4 once again brings us back to the Drepung Monastery in southern India, where since 1989, many Buryat novices have traveled to receive their religious education. I focus on the older group of Buryat monks, who are now returning to Buryatia after spending about ten years studying at Drepung. These monks are expected to redefine and renovate the religion. However, as I demonstrate in this chapter, this task has not been completely attainable and in fact is fraught with contradictions. Having left as young adults and spent most of the turbulent final decade of the twentieth century and the first decade of the twenty-first away from the rapid transformations that shook postsocialist Russia, some are coming back to a country that has, in some ways, become more incomprehensible to them than tropical India. In the meantime, the competing claims to sovereignty described in the previous chapter, which have often put Buryat Buddhists at odds with their Tibetan coreligionists, leave the Indian returnees in a precarious position. This chapter looks at Buryat life in the Indian Drepung, focusing on the issues of gender and monastic body politics. It is argued that through travel, pilgrimage, and prolonged sojourning at Tibetan monasteries in India, Buryat monks acquire particular types of bodies, which, while granting them certain religious statuses and privileges, sometimes fail to correspond to indigenous understandings of religious authority, masculinity, and national loyalties. Although Buryat monasticism is predominantly male, exceptional cases of a few Buryat nuns are also considered.

The theme of bodies and gender is continued in chapter 5, where I join Buryat pilgrims on a journey from the Drepung Monastery in tropical Karnataka to the Himalayan foothill town of Dharamsala, which some Buryats have recently made their home. Here I am interested in their engagement with the ritual of chöd, which I propose to treat as a particular kind of biopolitical practice. Asking why this practice has become a contested issue in the Buryat Buddhist self-fashioning, I identify three reasons. First, I suggest that it provides an outlet for lay Buddhists, particularly women, to engage in a meaningful Buddhist practice, simultaneously indigenous and cosmopolitan, traditional and modernist, from which they were formerly excluded by the monastic establishment. Second, similarly to the relic treasures discussed in chapter 3, chöd evidences a certain kind of necropolitics, as the dead are being retheorized. By entering into a ritual economy with the deceased, Buryat adepts reconfigure entire universes of meaning, as the living and the dead become linked into one interrelated chain of causality. And finally, considered through the lens of gift exchange, chöd might reflect the changing notions of reciprocity, morality, and the market, characteristic of postsocialist societies. In other words, I suggest that the prominence of this particular ritual is related to the three broad shifts essential to postsocialism: the transformations of the ideas of gender, the dead, and exchange.

Chapter 6 continues the themes of gifts and exchange, looking at the changing discourses about money, religion, and morality in the new Russia. Using my ethnographic observations on the conflation of religious and economic practices through multilevel marketing and relating it to the broader Buryat discussions about the perceived Buddhist notions of wealth and private property, I argue that Buryats constitute themselves as new economic subjects and participants in global capitalist networks through particular interpretations of the Buddhist doctrine in light of the emergent postsocialist values.

While this is a varied portrait, it stems directly from my interest in knowing the specific paths taken by Buryat pilgrims a hundred years ago, as well as today, as they have struggled to articulate their place in broadly configured religious and political communities.

ONE

Pilgrims, Fieldworkers, and Secret Agents: Buryat Buddhologists and a Eurasian Imaginary

Since the end of the Soviet Union, Buryats have been renewing their traditional Buddhist faith while rebuilding transnational, post-Soviet ties across northern and southern Asia. In contrast to many scholars, who have seen Buryats purely as "native," "indigenous," or even a "fourth world" people, many Buryats have long viewed themselves as cosmopolitans, regarding the long history of Buryat Buddhist pilgrimages to Mongolia and Tibet as a prominent marker of southern Siberia's transnational history and identity. Today, Buryats make competing statements about a Eurasian future. Some view themselves as a truly cosmopolitan people spanning three major Eurasian states (Russia, Mongolia, and China) and extending their transnational religious practices into two more (Tibet and India); others express a more restricted understanding of their homeland within the Russian Federation.

From its early beginnings as the brainchild of Russian émigré intellectuals, to Lev Gumilev's poetic theories of "passionarity" (Rus. *passionarnost'*), to its contemporary political incarnations in Russia and the post-Soviet states, "Eurasia" is a shape-shifting notion today. At first sight, the word "Eurasia" refers to a geographic location, encompassing Europe and Asia. However, the complex of ideas to which it refers has its roots in an early twentieth-century quest to find Russia's unique character among the world's peoples, a quest that often incorporated a preoccupation with Russia's messianic role in world history. Politically speaking, in contemporary Russia "Eurasian" generally means "anti-Western," in Kazakhstan and Tatarstan it means "Western-friendly," and in Turkey it can mean either (Kotkin 2007: 497).

However, beyond its narrow political meanings, "Eurasia" has also been employed as an intellectual paradigm to encourage historical research beyond the notion of nation-state. In this chapter, I join with Mark Von Hagen and others by using the term "Eurasia" not in the sense of twentieth-century philosophical and contemporary political movements, but as a tool to analyze powerful and emergent geoimaginary formations, such as those now being asserted in and beyond Buryatia (Grant and Yalçin-Heckmann 2007; Ram 2001; Von Hagen 2004). This kind of approach shares the broad interest in new "Eurasianist" paradigms across the former Soviet Union but locates this issue foremost in arenas of contemporary religious practice. The goal is not only to uncover how varied communities of Buryats have understood their place vis-à-vis the imperial center, but also to describe the profound efforts to recenter Eurasian spaces at the end of the Soviet era.

Buryats have visited Tibet not only as modern pilgrims but also as some of the earliest scholars, like G. Ts. Tsybikov and B. B. Baradiin, whose acclaimed early twentieth-century monographs firmly linked Buryatia to the Tibetan religious universe. In postsocialist Buryatia, however, debates regarding the place of Tibet in the national imaginary have taken a different turn. Should Buryat Buddhism be understood as adhering to a "Tibetan" model, one most recently advanced through pilgrimages by monks and well-funded laypeople to Tibetan monasteries in India? Or, as nationalists argue, should it downplay its international ties to assert itself as a truly independent "Buryat" religion? Over the last decade, the official head of Buryat Buddhists, Khambo Lama Damba Aiusheev, has repeatedly expressed his dislike for the proliferation of Tibetan and other Asian Buddhist "missionaries" in the republic, arguing that Buryat Buddhism is fully autocephalous. That is to say, it should be allowed to develop independently of the influence of other traditions (Corwin 1999; Filatov 2007).[1] This is also Moscow's view on the matter, which has strongly discouraged Buryats' international connections, with Putin's 2000 National Security Policy calling for "coun-

---

1. Also author interview with the Khambo Lama Aiusheev, Ivolginsk, 2008.

teracting the negative influence of foreign religious organizations and missions" ("O kontseptsii natsional'noi bezopasnosti Rossiiskoi Feder-atsii" 2000).[2]

In contrast, other major Buddhist leaders have expressed incredulity toward the legitimacy of such notions as independent "Buryat Buddhism" or even "Mongolian Buddhism," considering both traditions indivisible from larger transnational Tibetan Buddhism with the Dalai Lama as its only leader. Asked if the notion of "Buryat Buddhism" has a right to exist, a leader of the opposition to the current Buddhist leadership, the ex-Khambo Lama Choi-Dorzhi Budaev, expressed his opinion as follows:

Journalist: In your opinion, does the notion of "Buryat Buddhism" have the right to exist?

Ex-Khambo Lama Budaev: What are you talking about! This is not a very intelligent claim. . . . The global Buddhist community does not even grant Mongolian Buddhism such a status, and Mongols have an ancient Buddhist history. If we look into history, we will see that Tibetan lamas were always helping in the development of Buddhism here in Buryatia. Even the first Khambo Lama, Zaiaev, studied in Tibetan monasteries. But some of us have forgotten about this, and now we go as far as promoting some "Buryat Buddhism." In older times, even the greatest of lamas could not take the liberty of making such claims. National pride is good, but not when unfounded, and by no means when it overlaps with religious issues. (Zhironkina 2006)[3]

In order to understand the new cultural and political orientations in a Eurasia present and future, marked by Buddhist transnationalism, one must explore the earlier pathways that lie beneath the surface of the current debates. This chapter examines the prerevolutionary history of Buryats' engagement with greater Eurasia, drawing on the legacies of the long-underappreciated Russian Buddhological school and exploring the intellectual and political context of its emergence in the late nineteenth century. An exploration of the role of Russian Orientalists

2. After 1992, the Dalai Lama was repeatedly refused permission to visit Buryatia, while he was granted a visa for a brief visit to Kalmykia in 2004. The Dalai Lama, however, has been able to visit Mongolia several times since 1990.

3. Contrary to some of these claims, Mongols themselves engage in very similar debates. For a fascinating discussion of what contemporary Mongols think about the issue of "Mongolian" versus "Tibetan" Buddhism and why there can be Western "Tibetan Buddhists" but no Western "Mongolian Buddhists," see Elverskog 2006. For historical precedents to creating "Mongolian" Buddhism see Atwood 1996, and on how Mongols have historically understood and interpreted the process of Tibetanization, see Elverskog 2007.

and political figures such as V. P. Vasil'ev and Prince E. E. Ukhtomskii, and a reading of the fieldwork of the first Russian-trained indigenous Buryat Buddhologists, G. Ts. Tsybikov and B. B. Baradiin, demonstrates that it was a tradition born out of conflicting sentiments toward Russia's own cosmopolitanism, statehood, and imperial destiny in Asia, as well as from representations of indigenous peoples of southern Siberia. This chapter concludes with an outline of the emergent forms of what I call "Asian Eurasianism," linking it to contemporary cultural debates in Buryatia, which are crucial for understanding the ways in which many non-Russians position themselves on the vast Eurasian continent.

Russian Orientalism and Ideologies of Empire

Edward Said's foundational work once defined Orientalism as a particular set of cultural assumptions about the "Orient" adopted by the "West," necessarily linked to an imperialist agenda (Said 1991). Scholars of other Orientalisms have produced extensive critiques of the universality of his thesis: it has been argued that German Indology was not linked to immediate imperialist interests while Japan was both a subject and an object of Orientalism without ever being colonized (Minear 1998; Pollock 1993).[4]

Scholars of Russia have often cited the case of Russian "Asianism"—an imperial ideology that privileged Russia's Asiatic identity as opposed to its European one—as a peculiar kind of identification, whereby the "Orient" was both of the empire and foreign to it (Bassin 1999; Schimmelpenninck van der Oye 2001, 2010; Tolz 2011). Asianism, which exerted a significant influence on Russian intellectual, artistic, and political circles at the turn of the twentieth century, and its later offshoot, Eurasianism, proposed an alternative solution to the endless debates between Slavophiles and Westernizers by positing an inherent spiritual, geographic, racial, and political affinity of Russia with Asia.[5]

Buddhism, as an object of Western knowledge and scholarship, came into focus during the latter period of the so-called Oriental Renaissance, a European "discovery" and subsequent engagement and fasci-

---

4. See also Bakic-Hayden 1995 for a description of "nesting" Orientalisms in the Ottoman-ruled Balkans.

5. Slavophiles and Westernizers were two influential groups of intellectuals who held opposing views regarding the nature of Russian civilization. Slavophiles contended that Russia's civilization was unique and defined by Russian Orthodoxy, autocracy, and the peasant community. Westernizers believed that Russia needed to follow Western Europe as a way to modernization.

nation with Oriental cultures and civilizations, comparable in its cultural impact to the rediscovery of ancient Greek texts in the fifteenth century (Schwab 1984). Buddhology or Buddhist studies originated as an offshoot of Indology, Sinology, philology, and archaeology in the early nineteenth century and, similarly to earlier forms of Orientalism, was inextricably linked to imperialist ideologies and the colonial context (Lopez 1995a). However, as Donald Lopez rightly notes, the "direct political role that Said describes for Orientalism . . . is not immediately evident in the case of Buddhist Studies," since unlike the Islamic world, which inspired fear and fascination due to its very proximity to Europe, the Buddhist world was far away and presented no such threat. Instead, Buddhologists' contribution to Orientalism was in the creation of the reified object called "Buddhism" (Lopez 1995c: 11–12). In certain strands of European Buddhology based on Indological scholarship, Buddhism—which had effectively disappeared from India by the time of the British rule—was safely considered a rational religion, often opposed to "idolatrous" Hinduism, with Buddha often portrayed as "an Indian version of Martin Luther," a social and progressive reformer struggling to cleanse the corrupted religion of ritualism and superstition (King 1999: 145).[6]

Unlike Europe, the Russian empire did not view the Buddhist world as an abstraction. By the mid-nineteenth century, more than half of Russia *was* Asia, with China arguably being the most important Asian neighbor and half a million Mongol subjects inhabiting the empire's borderlands. As early as between 1768 and 1774, Peter Simon Pallas, a German scholar invited to teach at the Academy of Sciences in St. Petersburg by Catherine the Great, conducted several expeditions in the Mongol regions of Russia. His remarkable observations of contemporary Buddhist practice were translated into English in a three-volume work entitled *The Habitable World Described* (Trusler 1788). Subsequently, when Buddhist studies appeared as an academic discipline in Russia in the mid-nineteenth century, it was not surprising that the first Russian Orientalists to engage in the study of Buddhism included Sinologist V. P. Vasil'ev and Mongolist O. M. Kovalevskii, as well as the

6. The importance of being socially progressive would also be prominent in postrevolutionary "reformist" Buryat Buddhist discourse. Buryat lama Agvan Dorzhiev argued in his *Autobiography* that Buddhism was fully compatible with "this newly established system of communism," stressing that both were based on compassion, insisting on helping the poor, and establishing basic justice. He also vehemently condemned corruption in both systems, explaining it by the fact that monks had abandoned the teaching of the Buddha, just as Bolsheviks had corrupted the "good" teachings of Lenin (Dorzhiev 1994 [1921]: 31–35).

German member of the Academy of Sciences Mongolist and Tibetologist Ia. I. Schmidt. The Academy of Sciences became a very important venue for the publication of early Buddhological scholarship.

Due to the significant presence of ethnic Buddhist subjects within the empire, Russia found itself in a unique position for the study of Buddhism. Stimulated by a growing rivalry with Great Britain for influence in Inner Asia, a powerful academic tradition of Orientalist Buddhist studies, represented by such scholars as F. I. Stcherbatsky, E. Obermiller, O. O. Rosenberg, I. P. Minaev, and S. F. Ol'denburg, had already emerged by the mid-nineteenth century. Like its European counterparts, early Russian Buddhology was mostly text oriented. As Russian scholars accumulated more knowledge about its subject populations, by the late nineteenth century the rumors that Buryats and Kalmyks were in regular contact with "mysterious" and "remote" Tibet generated enormous academic interest. Russian Buddhologists thus revolutionized the discipline in the sense that they turned their attention to the form of Buddhism known to them as "Lamaism," practiced in several regions of the Russian empire, including those inhabited by Kalmyks and Buryats.[7]

Russian Tibetology, as a late nineteenth-century branch of Russian Orientalism, is especially interesting in this regard, as it privileged the training of native scholars and fieldwork along with the study of texts. Due to Russia's own strong ethnographic situation, a certain line of Russian Buddhologists was among the first to use the classical methods of ethnographic field research, much earlier than more famous practitioners like Franz Boas or Bronisław Malinowski. By using native scholars as researchers of their own traditions, Russian Buddhology established its own kind of ethnographic authority, unprecedented in previous academic research.

Since Tibet was notoriously inaccessible, having sealed its borders to all foreigners with the exception of Asian Buddhist pilgrims in 1792, Russian Buddhologists turned their attention to Russia's own Mongol adherents of Tibetan Buddhism and soon discovered that they had regular relations with Tibet. Although Buryat and Kalmyk Buddhists, as Russian subjects, were also banned from entering Tibet, some pilgrims managed to enter Tibet posing as Khalkha Mongols. The rumors about

7. I would like to acknowledge my debt to Tatiana Ermakova's incisive and thorough analysis of Russian Buddhology, *Buddiiskii mir glazami rossiiskikh issledovatelei XIX–pervoi treti XX veka* (Ermakova 1998). Her research has greatly enhanced my understanding of this topic, and hence the development of the arguments I present below. See also Tolz 2011: 111–134.

Buryats crossing the border into Tibet were all the more surprising since, shortly after the establishment of Buddhism in Buryatia in the early eighteenth century, Count Raguzinskii's 1728 decree on border crossing had banned foreign lamas from crossing into the Buryat communities on the Russian side and restricted Buryats from excessive foreign travel. By declaring that Mongol lamas who came into Russia with Khalkha noblemen could stay, but that no new lamas from Mongolia or Tibet could enter the country, Raguzinskii made the first attempt to separate Buryats from the greater Tibetan Buddhist world, a trend that was subsequently pursued throughout the next two centuries.[8] Despite these efforts, the borders remained extremely porous through the 1920s, with Tibetan and Mongolian lamas entering all areas with relative ease and numerous Buryat pilgrims undertaking trips to Tibet and Mongolia.

By the time Russian scholars became interested in studying Tibetan Buddhism, it was already well established among Transbaikal Buryats, providing these academics with unprecedented access to a living Buddhist tradition. In a little more than one hundred years, the number of monasteries grew from a few yurt-temples to thiry-four monasteries, and the number of lamas grew from 150 in 1712 to 4,509 in 1846 (and 15,000 in 1910) (Rupen 1964: 37). This expansion became a serious concern for the tsarist administration, especially in light of the new ideology that attempted to cement the role of the Russian Orthodoxy in the empire (see the introduction). Thus, the study of Buddhists within the empire began to acquire immediate political relevance.

"If we were more familiar with the religion of our alien (Rus. *inorodnye*) subjects, we could have avoided the many difficulties we have encountered," wrote Russian Orientalist V. P. Vasil'ev on the subject of the rapid spread of Buddhism in Siberia (Vasil'ev 1873: 3). He also wrote the following in his review of the ground-breaking book on Buddhist monasteries by another famous Orientalist, A. M. Pozdneev, an expert on the Mongolian world, published in the *Journal of the Ministry of Public Education* in 1888:

Although we, in Russia, do not have special Buddhist provinces, given our confusion between cosmopolitanism and statehood, the Buddhist question becomes even more urgent. Influenced by cosmopolitanism and not knowing how to overcome even the mere shamanism of the Chuvash, Tungus, and other *inorodtsy*, we are even

---

8. For a detailed analysis of primary sources on imperial Russian politics toward Buddhism in the Transbaikal, see Gerasimova 1957.

more defeated when it comes to Lamaism. . . . Before the very eyes of our administration, our Buryats, who were still shamanists when they became our subjects,
came over, as if in silent protest against their masters, to the religion professed
by their fellow tribesmen in a neighboring country, subject to a foreign authority.
Before our eyes, Buryats started to influence our Kalmyks, who previously lived in
isolation. . . . Now they send them huge bundles of sacred books. While we were
convinced that with one more generation, the Kalmyks would turn into Russians,
instead they (who, in the beginning of this century, finally dropped their braids
and Mongolian costume) have turned even further away from us. (Vasil'ev 1888:
422–423)

For Vasil'ev, full citizenship is inextricably related to Russification,
which involves both conversion of "aliens" (Rus. *inorodtsy*) and the de-
nunciation of specific "alien" cultural customs (such as, in this case,
braids and Mongolian dress). To stop being an *inorodets* (literally "person of a different kin," a foreigner), one had to convert, which would
enable one to start paying taxes instead of tribute (Rus. *iasak*) and thus
acquire full rights of citizenship and participation in Russian society.
The "defeat" refers to the failure to convert Siberian peoples, often bemoaned in the nineteenth century.

Buryats presented a special case, because, as Vasil'ev notes, Russians
came to the Transbaikal at the same time that Buddhism was beginning to penetrate these lands. Instead of converting them, the Russian government concentrated on Irkutsk Buryats, being very careful
with those of the Transbaikal due to the strategic border area. Until
1841, the affairs of Lamaist Buryats were under the jurisdiction of the
Ministry of Foreign Affairs; later they were transferred to the Ministry
of Internal Affairs. While the Ministry of Foreign Affairs was mostly
concerned with the subordination of the Lamaist church to the tsarist
government (to prevent separate relations with Mongolia), the Ministry
of Internal Affairs concentrated on subordinating Buryat clergy to the
local administration. Before the mid-nineteenth century, the government began to regret its policies, which included helping lamas fight
shamanism with the help of local police. They issued a number of orders to protect shamanism, viewing it as an ideology that would not be
able to oppose Russification as strongly as Lamaism (Gerasimova 1957:
31–32).

Thus, tsarist policies encouraged the flourishing of Buryat Buddhism
until the mid-nineteenth century, when the government started to reverse its policies after repeated complaints from the synod and the Orthodox mission, which contended that missionary activity was being

completely undermined by the tsarist encouragement of Buddhism. This resulted in the important 1853 "Statute on Lamaist Clergy in Eastern Siberia," which directly subordinated all Buryat religious affairs, from the elections of the Khambo Lama to the administration of monasteries, to the state (Gerasimova 1957: 41).

In the passage above, Vasil'ev also exhibits the classical colonial view that ethnographic knowledge could be used to rule colonial subjects more efficiently. Writing about colonial ethnography in India, Nicholas Dirks noted that "by the late nineteenth century, ethnological knowledge became privileged more than any other form of imperial understanding" (Dirks 2001: 44). Good colonial rulers were those who "knew" India, exemplified by the character in Kipling's classic novel *Kim*, Colonel Creighton, who is both head of the Ethnological Survey and master spy in the Great Game. Despite this "imperial empiricism," Dirks notes, there was still a sense that India would ultimately remain inscrutable: "The more one knows about natives, the less can one say what they will or won't do" (Kipling, cited in Dirks 2001: 44). Similarly, Vasil'ev distances himself from his subjects by framing them in terms of an ultimate alterity, which can be overcome only through the assimilation or imitation of Russian culture.

Over the course of the nineteenth century, in order to understand how to facilitate work for the Russian Orthodox mission in the Transbaikal, the Russian government sent a number of functionaries and scholars to investigate Buddhism in this region, among them the Orientalist scholar Pavel Schilling von Canstadt, Levashev, an employee of the Department of Spiritual Affairs, Prince Ukhtomskii, and finally Professor Pozdneev himself (Gerasimova 1957 provides a detailed analysis of these documents). As Pozdneev commented on this government policy in an unpublished manuscript entitled "Buddhism in the Transbaikal,"[9]

If one looks closely into the history of the establishment of Buddhism in the Transbaikal, the mistakes made by the Russian government in patronizing paganism explain why and how Lamaism became so influential in our country. We can also learn how to artfully counteract it, using its own silly desires and weaknesses. . . . The contradictory government policy toward Buryats (especially most recently) turned out to be extremely corrupting for them. . . . Our Siberian Lamaists were and remain completely confused regarding why, on the one hand, the government

9. This manuscript, stored in St. Petersburg's Orientalist Archives, appears to be the source for Ukhtomskii's 1904 monograph.

required complying with impossible (from religion's point of view) regulations while applying to Buddhism the European notions of the freedom of conscience completely alien [Rus. *dikie*] to the nomads. (Pozdneev ca. 1888: 1, 18)

Like Vasil'ev, he laments the government policies in the region, which, in his view, have strengthened Buddhism. By "weaknesses" he means existing disagreements and enmity between different Buryat clans, which he recommends using to weaken Buddhism and facilitate conversion to Christianity. He concludes his manuscript by saying that "Europeans will have to act in a pagan country by the principle 'divide et impera'" (Pozdneev ca. 1888: 52).

If Vasil'ev's and Pozdneev's tone reminds one of Kipling's Colonel Creighton on the Russian side of the Great Game, the ideas of another Orientalist thinker, Prince E. E. Ukhtomskii, strike one as perhaps more uniquely Russian. Sometimes a poet, sometimes a government bureaucrat influencing Nicholas II's thinking on Asian foreign policy, Ukhtomskii was chiefly known as the publisher of the widely read and cited newspaper *Peterburgskie vedomosti*. He was a devotee of Buddhist philosophy and an amateur antiquarian whose collection went on to become the basis of the Hermitage's East Asian collection. One might see Ukhtomskii as simply a "sympathetic" kind of Orientalist akin to the Theosophists he admired, were it not for the fact that his ideology was categorically imperialist, albeit of a mystical kind. A proponent of Russia's role as a "natural leader" in Asia as opposed to the "crude" and "mercantile" imperialism of the British, supposedly incapable of relating to the spiritual traditions of their subjects, Ukhtomskii argued that Russian Orthodoxy possessed deep spiritual affinities with Buddhism, which would allow Russia's expansion into Asia simply to occur as a "natural fusion." He was strongly opposed to resorting to military means to conquer Asia. In fact, conquest was superfluous: "Russia in reality conquers nothing in the East, since all the alien races visibly absorbed by her are related to us by blood, in tradition, in thought. We are only tightening the bonds between us and that which in reality was always ours." "In Asia we have not, nor can have, any bounds, except the boundless sea breaking on her shores" (Ukhtomskii 1896–1900: 444).[10]

Ukhtomskii argued that Buryats were strategically crucial to Russian foreign policy in Asia: "Trans-Baikalia is the key to the heart of

---

10. See also David Schimmelpenninck Van der Oye for an analysis of Ukhtomskii's Asianism (2001: 41–62).

Asia, the vanguard of Russian civilization on the frontier of the 'Yellow Orient'" (Grünwedel 1900: ix). Due to Ukhtomskii's efforts, two ethnic Buryats became especially influential in St. Petersburg: Agvan Dorzhiev, a Buryat lama who studied in Lhasa for many years and later became a prominent adviser to the Thirteenth Dalai Lama and an intermediary between the Russian court and Tibet, and Petr Badmaev, a doctor of Tibetan medicine who had access to the Romanov court.[11]

Of the three lobbies in Tibet at the turn of the century—pro-Chinese, pro-British, and pro-Russian—the latter became very influential, as Dorzhiev urged the Dalai Lama to seek protection from Russia, when seeking patronage from an (arguably) Western power was unprecedented in Tibetan history (Andreyev 2003: 30–31). Badmaev, whose conversion to Christianity opened many doors for him, became a fashionable "Eastern" doctor at the time when occult beliefs were very much in vogue with the Russian aristocracy. Eventually he had become so influential in the tsar's thinking on eastern policy that he convinced Nicholas II of the possibility of detaching Mongolia and Tibet from China, eventually overthrowing the Qing dynasty. His plan centered on building an extension to the Trans-Siberian Railway from Lake Baikal to the Chinese city of Lanzhou across the Gobi Desert, where Buryat traders, herders, and pilgrims would use their connections in the region to agitate their fellow Tibetan and Mongolian Buddhists to come under the sovereignty of the Russian "White Tsar" (Semennikov 1925: 68–75).[12] His less grandiose projects included the first periodical in the Buryat language, intended to provide Buryats with "accurate" information about Russia, and, most important, a private gymnasium for Buryats in St. Petersburg, which many future Buryat intellectuals attended until they were required to convert to Orthodoxy.

Badmaev was crucial for the development of Russian Buddhology in that he brought Buryats into the spotlight of Russian politics and science, having initially sponsored two Buryat students, Gombozhab Tsybikov and Bazar Baradiin, to come to St. Petersburg. Later these two Buryat scholars went to study at St. Petersburg University under Rus-

11. Although Agvan Dorzhiev is a key figure for the contemporary Buryat imaginaries of Tibet, in this chapter I will mention him only in relation to other characters, such as Tsybikov and Baradiin, on whom very few published materials exist in English. For a detailed and informative study of Dorzhiev's life, see Snelling 1993. See also Andreyev 2001, 2003; Rupen 1956; and Dorzhiev's autobiography (1994 [1921]).

12. David Schimmelpenninck van der Oye also quotes from an unpublished memorandum from Badmaev to Nicholas II: "Peter the Great opened a window on Europe, and Petersburg became the symbol of Russian might. . . . [Now you] have opened a window on the Chinese East" (2001: 200).

sia's three internationally renowned Buddhologists: A. M. Pozdneev, S. F. Ol'denburg and F. I. Stcherbatsky.[13] Both Buryat scholars undertook successful two- and three-year-long field expeditions to Tibet disguised as Buddhist pilgrims, bringing back extensive fieldnotes, maps, and some of the first photographs of Tibet.[14]

Buryat Buddhologists in Tibet

Gombozhab Tsybikov in Central Tibet

Gombozhab Tsybikov is sometimes called the "Buryat Lomonosov" (after a famous Russian polymath of peasant origins), for he came from a poor nomadic Buryat family. His education was extremely rare for a Buryat at that time: he graduated from the Chita *gimnaziia* and later went on to study medicine at Tomsk University. Badmaev, who happened to pass by Tomsk, met Tsybikov there and convinced him to quit medicine and come to St. Petersburg to major in Oriental studies and diplomacy, promising financial help and essentially recruiting him for his future projects. When Tsybikov refused to convert to Christianity, however, Badmaev cut off his stipend. Fortunately, Tsybikov's countrymen managed to collect the money for Tsybikov to continue his education.

After he graduated from St. Petersburg University's Faculty of Oriental Languages, Tsybikov spent a year doing field research on land management in the Transbaikal. The idea of sending Tsybikov to Tibet occurred to his supervisor, A. M. Pozdneev, when he discovered and translated a manuscript written by the Kalmyk lama Baza-bakshi about his trip to Lhasa from Kalmykia from 1891 to 1894 (Pozdneev 1897). The manuscript is unique in that gives us glimpses not only of overland Buddhist pilgrimage routes but also of sea routes, since the lama took a boat back from Hankou through Singapore, Sri Lanka, the Suez Canal, Constantinople, and Odessa. Pozdneev, who himself had

---

13. See Vera Tolz for an informative discussion on how these imperial scholars came to play an active role in fostering nationalist movements among the minority groups they studied, including Buryats (2011: 111–134).

14. The trend of using Buryats as agents in Tibet continued in Soviet times: see Andreyev 2003. On the British attempts to penetrate Tibet by training Indian pundits in surveying techniques, see Waller 1990. On larger imperial Russian and early Soviet explorations of Tibet and Inner Asia, such as those conducted by Nikolai Przewalski and his student Petr Kozlov, see Andreyev 2006. None of them managed to reach Lhasa, being consistently turned away at the border.

conducted fieldwork and written a detailed study of Buddhism in Mongolia (Pozdneev 1887b), was nonetheless disappointed by the scarcity of details in the lama's diary, thinking that sending a trained native scholar to Tibet would make a more serious contribution to academic scholarship. Subsequently, Pozdneev recommended Tsybikov to the Russian Geographic Society, which sponsored his expedition to Tibet. The trip took three years, from 1899 to 1902.

In Tibet, Tsybikov played a double or even triple role—he was a pilgrim traveling with a group of fellow Buryat pilgrims, a dedicated fieldworker taking extreme risks to clandestinely use his camera and thermometer to collect data and scribbling fieldnotes between the lines of Buddhist sacred volumes, and a Russian secret agent whose goal was to expand geographic knowledge and gather as much information as he could about the political and socioeconomic situation in Tibet. However, he was also a Buryat nationalist, a member of the Buryat nascent intelligentsia who would later use his position to advance the Buryat cause in postrevolutionary times.

On his return to Russia in 1902, Tsybikov gave a lecture on his expedition at the Russian Geographic Society, to much acclaim. However, he did not publish the monograph based on his fieldnotes until 1919 (Tsybikov 1981 [1919]). Although Tsybikov was the first scholar from an (arguably) European empire to penetrate Tibet in the late nineteenth century, his work passed relatively unnoticed in Europe, since many other accounts of Tibet already had appeared in both the scholarly and the popular press in English in the early 1900s (Chandra Das 1902; Kawaguchi 1909; Waddell 1905).

Tsybikov's travelogue immediately impresses the reader with its rather dry and austere tone, without a hint of the sensationalism that so often accompanies accounts of Tibet. Given how romantically Tsybikov is viewed by many Buryat Buddhists today, his treatment of religion is surprisingly positivist. In the spirit of his progressive views, he goes to great lengths to describe the poverty and extreme social stratification in Tibet, proceeding to treat religion as a kind of ideology serving the interests of the ruling class and showing how class interests are indirectly expressed through religion. Other prominent themes include the corruption of Buddhist monasticism, which was to become an important issue in the Buryat Buddhist reform movement. He reports that the coveted Lhasa-issued diplomas of *geshe lharamba* (Tib. *dge bshes lha ram pa*), the highest master of Buddhist philosophy, so valued in Amdo, Mongolia, and Buryatia, could be bought for a few coins in central Tibet. The main concern during the *lharamba* defense is to provide a lavish feast for the senior monks (Tsybikov 1981 [1919]: 178–180). In Kumbum Monastery, drunkenness, promiscuity, and tobacco smoking are widespread, while many supposedly learned monks never learn how to read (Tsybikov 1981 [1919]: 48). Tsybikov's brief audiences with the Thirteenth Dalai Lama and the Sixth Panchen Lama are so absurdly ceremonious that their description acquires an almost comic quality.

As soon as we entered, the lamas started herding us in a hurry: they constantly pushed us forward, and if someone happened to linger or look aside, he was mercilessly pushed forward. We approached the Dalai Lama and hurriedly bowed to the ground three times. . . . After all the offerings, the Dalai Lama accepted my khadak [ceremonial scarf] and blessed me by touching my head with his right hand. During this time he was handed a silk ribbon; he made a knot, blew on it, and put it around my neck. . . . The Dalai Lama asked in his usual voice but very rapidly: "Did you have a good journey and do you live prosperously in your native lands?" According to the ceremonial etiquette, we were not supposed to answer, but only raise ourselves slightly and bow to the interpreter, who translated these words for us into Mongolian. The interpreter also silently bowed to the Dalai Lama. After this, cooked rice was brought, the Dalai Lama tasted a small amount from the cup handed to him and then rinsed his mouth from a special jug. We were also given quite generous portions of rice, which even overflowed the brim, but before we had time to taste it, we were told that the ceremony was over and we needed to hurry up and leave. The ending of the ceremony was not especially hospitable. Two enormous bodyguards with whips pushed us, yelling in the presence of the Dalai Lama himself: "Off you go, quickly!" We were naturally somewhat confused and ran off . . . and went home. The whole ceremony did not last ten minutes. (Tsybikov 1981 [1919]: 111)[15]

Despite his poorly hidden sarcasm, these scenes are nonetheless unique in providing an insider's glimpse at what the experience might have been like for a regular Buryat pilgrim. Most people who were able to meet the Dalai Lama and then write about it were European dignitaries, explorers, and scholars, so they were usually granted special privileges. Unlike Tsybikov, Baradiin did not have to hide his special status when he visited Tibet, so he was able to converse with the Dalai Lama on equal terms as a scholar. Tsybikov, on the other hand, had to hide under the guise of a humble Buryat pilgrim and thus received the typical "common person" treatment. At the meeting with the Panchen

15. All translations from Tsybikov and Baradiin are my own.

Lama, Tsybikov and fellow Buryat pilgrims were again most ceremoniously escorted into the audience rooms of the hierarch in Tashilumpo only to be rudely pushed out (as soon as the donations were offered) by frightening bodyguards who followed them with whips down the stairs yelling "off you go!" "We had to hurriedly run down the narrow staircase, which we were ascending with a certain honor just a few minutes ago" (1981 [1919]: 196).

In contrast to large scholastic monasteries, Tsybikov finds that very strict discipline was maintained in the tantric colleges (where monks specialize in ritual, magic, and esoteric techniques). In a characteristic tone, Tsybikov calls the exceptional discipline and incorruptibility of these monks the "miracle" of Tibet. He then proceeds to tell us that tantric faculties are in fact "nomadic monasteries," since entire faculties of monks are constantly traveling due to the high popular demand for the performance of exorcism and other rituals. While admiring their discipline, in his description, Tsybikov once again reinforces the impression that the population of Tibet is ignorant and steeped in superstition (1981 [1919]: 160–163). The true religion of Tibet, Tsybikov asserts, is money, interspersing his narrative with colorful examples of the "prayer business" in the main Lhasa temple: priests charging money for the reading of simple prayers, lamas selling ignorant believers corpses of the temple mice considered sacred, along with the pious veneration of Buddhist sacred objects and relics which Tsybikov calls "not so skillful" artworks (1981 [1919]: 81, 168).

Skepticism about folk religion, however, does not diminish the scholarly significance of Tsybikov's work. Besides being one of the first academic Orientalists to produce informed ethnographic descriptions of the Buddhism practiced in Tibet, he also expanded the Western tradition of Tibetan studies beyond an exclusive focus on Buddhism, ancient history, and art. His analysis of socioeconomic and political structures, and his assessment of the negative role of organized religion and élites, as well as his general "deromanticization" of Tibet, added complexity to the simplistic myth of "old Tibet" that persists to this day.[16] Other contributions to Buddhist studies included biographies of all thirteen Dalai Lamas and extensive details on the history, organization, and curricula of the major monasteries, as well as on contem-

16. The myth of old Tibet as a land of carefree peasants led by enlightened lamas promoted not only by Western Tibetophiles but also by Tibetans-in-exile who tend to romanticize their own past began to be questioned only recently and still provokes much controversy, having been called the "denial of history" (Shakya 1999: xxviii). The Shangri-La discourse started to be debunked in Western scholarship in the late 1980s (Lopez 1998; Bishop 1989).

porary iconography, pantheon, and rituals. Tsybikov also managed to produce some of the first photographs of Tibet and Lhasa and brought back three hundred volumes of Tibetan texts.[17]

Tsybikov's remarkable overland journey on camels and yaks, starting in the Transbaikal, crossing much of Inner Asia and ending in Lhasa, is one of the very rare sources on Buryat pilgrimage routes from Siberia to Lhasa. This evidence of earlier routes is crucial to our understanding of contemporary Inner Asian Buddhist mobility, as it already begins to tell us about the kinds of engagements Buryats had with the larger Tibeto-Mongol world. As we will see later in the chapter, Tsybikov's personality, as well as his emblematic journey and scholarly achievements, became a key site for contemporary Buryat political imaginaries, in which Tibet—whether real or imaginary—continues a play a prominent role.

Bazar Baradiin in Eastern Tibet (Amdo)

The success of Tsybikov's expedition inspired Russian Orientalists to send another Buryat scholar to explore Tibet. At this time, a new committee for the exploration of Central Asia was formed, directly subordinate to the Ministry of Foreign Affairs. This time, a special program of training was created for the young Buryat scholar Bazar Baradiin, for whom the Orientalists Ol'denburg and Stcherbatsky created a special four-year study plan: during the first three years they took the responsibility of teaching him Sanskrit, Buddhist philosophy, and history. During the fourth year, Baradiin was to undertake a trip to the two great Amdo monasteries Labrang and Kumbum (also visited by Tsybikov on his way to Lhasa) and then a second trip to central Tibet. Buryats are perfect for the study of Tibet, Ol'denburg writes in 1903, since they can become "real pundits" (Ermakova 1998: 102). "We are late!" wrote

17. The very first photos of Lhasa were made by another Russian subject, the Kalmyk Ovshe Norzunov, a year before Tsybikov. There is a widely circulating story in contemporary Buryatia that the publication of Tsybikov's photos of Lhasa in *National Geographic* saved the latter from imminent financial collapse. I was not able to verify the information about the financial crisis. What I found, however, was that indeed the publication of Tsybikov's and Norzunov's full-page photos of Lhasa in 1905 became a hallmark event in *National Geographic*'s history, which allegedly sparked its reinvention from a textual journal to a magazine famous for its photos. American studies scholar Susan Schulter writes that "most commentators trace the *National Geographic*'s photographic tradition to 1905, when a Russian explorer sent fifty unsolicited photographs of Lhasa to the magazine, offering them at no charge in exchange for acknowledgment of his authorship" (Schulter 2000: 18). The National Geographic Society's website gives the following account of the story: In January 1905, Gilbert N. Grosvenor "filled eleven pages of the magazine with the photos of Lhasa. Expecting to be fired, he was instead congratulated by Society members" (Anonymous 2010a).

Ukhtomskii in his famous polemical piece in 1904, "The English are about to invade the kingdom of the Dalai Lama." "If only we could understand the situation of the split Mongolia and establish a relationship with Tibet through our lamas . . . there would be a Russian emperor in Beijing instead of a Manchu one" (Ukhtomskii 1904: 3–4). Thus, when Baradiin set out for Tibet with a group of fellow pilgrims, the Great Game was still being played in the Russian mind.[18]

Baradiin never reached Lhasa, spending a year at Labrang Monastery in Amdo.[19] Unlike Tsybikov's account, his writing is characterized by a more sympathetic view of Buddhist religious practices and livelier and less caricatured portraits of Buddhist practitioners. Although still traveling as a Buddhist pilgrim, unlike Tsybikov, he never had to take extreme precautions to conceal his identity (Amdo was not closed to outsiders, as was central Tibet), enabling him to interact more freely with local Buddhist leaders, scholars, and regular folk, providing a better glimpse of the local culture. While Tsybikov's travelogue, following the conventions established by Pozdneev in his monograph on Buddhism in Mongolia, judged from the position of contemporary social science, was purely descriptive, Baradiin presents a more structured and focused attempt to analyze the institution of Buddhist monasticism.

In his brief report to the Russian Geographic Society published in 1908, and his full diary (not published until 2002), Baradiin weaves a fascinating ethnography of Labrang Monastery as well as a description of the pilgrimage routes commonly traveled by Buryat pilgrims (1908, 2002). Although Tibetan Buddhist studies produced an impressive amount of scholarly literature, surprisingly few ethnographic studies of monasticism exist to this day. As late as 1985, anthropologist Melvyn Goldstein lamented this gap in Buddhist studies, quoting only four works dealing with this issue (all from the 1960s to 1980). Thus, Goldstein writes, "Surprisingly little is known about the manner in which that philosophy [of the Buddha] was put into practice, that is to say, about how Buddhist monks actually live and work and how the monastic system functions" (Goldstein and Tsarong 1985: 14).

Well ahead of his time, Baradiin was addressing precisely this problem. First, he defines the state of contemporary Buddhology, establishing the separation between the study of the textual tradition and the

18. See Andreyev 2003 for the detailed historical context of Russia's and, later, the Soviet Union's relation to Tibet.

19. Baradiin was supposed to join the Thirteenth Dalai Lama, who fled to Urga before the British invasion of Tibet in 1904, on his journey back to Lhasa. The Dalai Lama, however, extended his stay in Mongolia, so Baradiin went to Labrang alone.

"study of the life of Buddhists themselves." Second, he argues that the study of the living Buddhist tradition has lagged behind due to the fact that only travelers and explorers (but not scholars) have thought it worthwhile to pay attention (Baradiin 1926: 109). While, like Tsybikov's, his tone is neutral and scholarly, his progressive views are sometimes revealed to the reader, as in his treatment of the Tibetan institution of reincarnation. While impressive in his very contemporary take on it—Baradiin relates the origin of the institution of incarnate lamas to the rights of inheritance of private property by monks—he nonetheless considers reincarnation an aberration and violation of what he imagines ancient Indian monasticism to have been, lamenting that this custom has now started to penetrate Buryatia (Baradiin 1908: 142–143).

His most innovative contribution to Buddhist studies, however, is his typology of contemporary Tibetan Buddhist monasteries based on firsthand ethnographic fieldwork (Baradiin 1926). He divides all the monasteries he explored during his trips to Buryatia, Tibet, and Mongolia into two large groups: scholastic (Rus. *shkol'nyi*) and anchoritic or hermitic (Rus. *otshel'nicheskii*) types. In turn, he divides scholastic monasteries into the ones with academic instruction or departments (Rus. *fakul'tety*) and those without them, while anchoritic monasteries comprise those where monks live in groups as well as single cells in the mountains for individual hermits. Baradiin also elaborates a classificatory scheme of Buddhist monks based on their personal trajectories, goals, types of monastic vows, ethnicity, social status, age, skills, and occupation.

A number of traits make his pioneering research methods similar to those of early ethnography. At the beginning of the monograph, Baradiin offers a theoretical justification for why the monastery should be the focus of the fieldwork-based Buddhist studies, arguing that monasteries, temples, and the artifacts within them present "ideal museums" while the observation of monastery life and interacting with "the living people," the monks, can provide the fieldworker with something that no library, museum, or armchair research could ever do (1926: 110). Having arrived in the field with a strict research plan elaborated in advance, Baradiin quickly abandons it in favor of what we now call participant observation: "My three-day loitering from house to house and chatting about all kinds of matters gave unexpected results: I am now firmly convinced that this is the only way, in addition to knowing the local language, through which one can really begin to understand the life of an unknown society. I now abandoned my previous system of collecting data according to a preconceived plan" (2002: 45).

His stress on the importance of the local language is also innovative for that time: until very recently Tibetologists were not well trained in spoken Tibetan, which differs considerably from its written form.

Another important contribution is that Baradiin was probably the first scholar to emphasize that Tibetan monasteries functioned as *multi-national* communities with various ethnic groups living together, evidence of Inner Asian Buddhist cosmopolitanism. In his words, Amdo served as a bridge for the spread of Buddhism from Tibet to Mongolia. Out of three thousand monks in Labrang, the majority of whom were Tangut,[20] there were about five hundred Mongols of various ethnic groups, including one hundred Buryats, several Tungus, and thirty Chinese (Baradiin 1908: 132, 140).[21] Similarly to the way students were organized in medieval European universities, monks in Tibetan monasteries were grouped by nation (Dreyfus 2003: 348). Baradiin, who stayed in the monastery with his fellow Buryats, provides unique insider descriptions of the functioning of the *kantsen* system (regional house, Tib. *khang tshan*, Rus. *zemliachestvo*) and of the Buryat *kantsen* specifically. He notices that the monasteries often develop what he calls "middle dialects"—a kind of *lingua franca* mixing diverse Mongolian and Tibetan dialects. The fact that Tibetan monasteries at the turn of the twentieth century were not homogenous entities, and that even Tibetans there often came from many different areas which barely had a common spoken language, is crucial for understanding contemporary Tibetan monasteries as convergence sites for transnational religious networks. Baradiin's account helps us to understand today's Tibetan monasteries in India, where many Buryats go for pilgrimage and religious training, not only as a postsocialist development but also as an extension of this ancient tradition.[22] As in the past, contemporary monaster-

20. Russian sources of the time often use the term "Tangut" for Amdo Tibetans.

21. Baradiin's report, *Puteshestvie v Lavran*, presented to the Russian Geographic Society in 1908, was republished as an appendix in Ermakova 1998. All citations and page numbers are from app. 5 in Ermakova 1998: 117–151.

22. Baradiin's travelogue is also an interesting example of proto-anthropological-relativist thinking. While criticizing Mongols for their complete dependence on the whims of nature, derived from their nomadism, he does not advocate that they become an agricultural or industrial nation. Like most of his contemporaries, Baradiin adhered to nineteenth-century social evolutionism (the belief that social development was an inevitable and determined process), claiming that sooner or later Mongols would have to deal with European culture, when "their free steppes will face a choice: either the death of a weak savage or the life of a cultured human being." However, he goes on to say that in order to become "cultured," they do not need to adopt specifically European economic ways, but to improve and perfect their own system (nomadic herding in this case). "An agriculturalist can be a savage, and a herdsman—a cultured person and vice versa." "Unfortunately," he laments, "this seemingly simple truth is still not recognized by many" (Baradiin 1908: 125). This view challenged the reigning evolutionary paradigm of ordering cultures

ies connect monks of various nationalities through notions of divine authority, tradition, and the transmission of Buddhist teachings.

As our material thus far has demonstrated, Russian Buddhology, or Buddhist studies in Russia, was understood as a special fieldwork branch of the Orientalist school and was born out of the conflicting ideas of seeing the "Orient" as an element in a shared political imaginary and as a domain of the empire's alien subjects. Both Asianists and Orientalists were united in their concern for foreign policy and expansion in Asia and, paired with the efforts of Buddhist studies scholars of the St. Petersburg school, produced the first fieldworkers in the study of Buddhism. Although romantic "Asianists" like Ukhtomskii, writing about "luminous expanses" of Asia, were influential in producing these Buryat scholars, the views they expressed were more in line with mainstream social science, with its positivist-evolutionary paradigms. The success of Buryat fieldwork Buddhologists within Russian academic Orientalism also established a new form of authority in ethnographic studies of Buddhism: an authority validated by previous scientific studies, the personal experience of fieldwork, and the fieldworker's being a "native." While the first two criteria correspond to what James Clifford (1988: 22–32) identified as a particular mode of "ethnographic authority" in the British anthropology of the 1920s, the importance of the identity and, thus, subjectivity of the fieldworker emerged as a particular feature in the Russian historical context.[23]

Buryat Buddhologists and the Buddhist Reform Movement

After their return from Tibet, both scholars were engaged in teaching and research, with Baradiin at the Department of Oriental Languages in St. Petersburg and Tsybikov as the chair in Mongol Philology at the newly created Orientalist Institute of Vladivostok, headed by Pozdneev. While Tsybikov limited himself mostly to scholarly pursuits, Baradiin also wrote prose and poetry and translated Russian literary classics into Buryat. It was around 1917 that both Buddhologists raced into the whirlwind of Russian and Buryat revolutionary politics in eastern Siberia. After the February 1917 Revolution, which established the Provisional Government in place of the tsar, Tsybikov quickly arrived in Buryatia

---

along the ladder of human cultural development, suggesting a relativistic methodology of treating cultures on their own terms. See Bernstein 2009 for further discussion of this point.

23. See Bernstein 2009 for further development of this argument.

from Vladivostok and joined Baradiin and Buryat intellectuals Tsyben Zhamtsarano, Mikhail Bogdanov, Elbekdorzhi Rinchino, and others to form the Buryat National Committee (Rus. *Buriatskii natsional'nyi komitet*, further referred to as *Burnatskom*), which supported the Provisional Government and promoted national autonomy. After the victory of the Soviets in Siberia, Burnatskom was eventually declared a "bourgeois nationalist" organization and attacked as anti-Soviet.

While asking for more freedom for Buddhism, Buryat intellectuals did not aspire to return to the prerevolutionary situation. Instead, they moved on from Burnatskom to create a drive for reform (known simply as the "reform movement," Rus. *obnovlencheskoe dvizhenie*) that was unprecedented in Buryat Buddhism and, in fact, in Tibetan Buddhism at the time. Baradiin and his close friend, Buryat scholar Zhamtsarano, were the most active members, while Tsybikov, perhaps disillusioned by the defeat of Burnatskom, again devoted himself to scholarly pursuits. Agvan Dorzhiev, on the other hand, actively participated on the side of the reformists (Rus. *obnovlentsy*). The reform movement advocated complete restructuring of the administrative system of Buddhism, the separation of church and state, the establishment of free elections of clergy, the elimination of excess wealth from monasteries, the adherence of monks to the Vinaya (the section of the Buddhist canon regulating monastic life), and the introduction of a system of examinations for various Buddhist degrees. They also called for the improvement of Tibetan medicine in accordance with modern medicine, the opening of secular schools at monasteries, the use of contemporary European literature on Buddhism, the nationalization of Buddhist sermons, and the abolishment of the cult of incarnate lamas and oracles.

Baradiin especially stressed the importance of harmonizing European science with traditional monastic education, opposing "vulgar and superstitious Lamaism" to "pure" Indian Buddhism and insisting on viewing Buddhism not as a religion but as an ethical philosophy with the Buddha not as god but as an ingenious thinker and philosopher (Gerasimova 1964: 160–162). If these ideas sound familiar today, it is because, in searching for a way to reconcile his beloved Buryat culture with his progressive views and the contemporary political situation in Russia, Baradiin turned to the ideas of European Buddhologists who also had a nostalgic vision of early Buddhism as a rational, and even atheist, religion.

While Buryat Buddhism was never able to implement these reforms, half a century later some of them have entered contemporary Buddhist imaginaries, especially Western ones, as many tend to think of Buddhism in precisely this way. An eager modernizer, Baradiin not only rejected certain "backward" aspects of Tibetan society as unsuitable for Buryatia, but also aspired to improve it in Tibet itself. As late as 1927, Baradiin made plans to be sent to Tibet with a Buryat expedition, for research, but also on an educational mission to improve sanitary conditions and introduce certain consumer goods, such as samples for farming, yeast, and typewriters with Tibetan script for Tibetans (Andreyev 2003: 333). Despite the reformists' seeming orientation to the "West," however, their ideas resembled early twentieth-century Russian Eurasianism in that, most important, they promoted Buryats' Mongolian heritage (language, religion, folklore) while being convinced that Buryats were on a special mission to combine the best in European/Russian and Mongolian culture. Of the three, Dorzhiev was the only one whose political program included a version of pan-Mongolism, which Robert Rupen called pan-Buddhism, promoting the idea of a Tibeto-Mongolian theocratic state headed by the Dalai Lama (Rupen 1956: 390).[24] All three of them—Tsybikov, Baradiin, and Dorzhiev—tried to collaborate with the Soviet government, but eventually all were accused of "bourgeois nationalism." Tsybikov was lucky to die what has been described as a natural death in 1930.[25] Baradiin was shot in 1937, and Dorzhiev died in a prison hospital in 1937 after being convicted of treason and counterrevolutionary activity.

Tibet and Contemporary Buryat Cultural Politics

The politics of the Russian imperial government toward Buddhism in Siberia was contradictory in that, on the one hand, it tried to separate Siberian peoples from their links to greater Asia and, on the other hand, used these links to advance its own imperial agenda. This need for exploration and expansion created a new generation of European

---

24. It has to be pointed out that Dorzhiev's "pan-Buddhism" embraced only areas of Tibetan Buddhism, such as Tibet, Mongolia, and Buryat and Kalmyk regions in the Russian empire. For a version of pan-Buddhism that established connections between such different traditions as Japanese, Chinese, and Tibetan Buddhisms, see Tuttle 2005: 68–72.

25. Russian Mongolist N. N. Poppe, who knew Tsybikov personally, writes that Tsybikov's biggest passion was cattle breeding and that he spent most of his salary on buying livestock, acquiring a huge herd by the end of his life. During Soviet collectivization in the 1930, his cattle were taken away and "he soon died of a broken heart. The Communists ignored the fact that he had not acquired his herd by exploiting the poor but by buying it with his earned salary." His widow and foster son were arrested and exiled to northern Siberia, where they died shortly thereafter (Poppe 1983: 99–100).

educated native scholars, who would later take an active part in advocating liberal reforms in Buryat Buddhism.

Today, while little known outside Russian scholarly circles, Tsybikov and Baradiin have acquired almost mythical status in Buryatia proper as national heroes. A monument to Tsybikov has been erected in Aginskoe, and a project of erecting stelae with bas-reliefs of major Buryat leaders, including Baradiin, has been proposed for Ulan-Ude. While their names are famous, until recently, their works were not widely distributed, so most people knew about them either by word of mouth or by the titles of their books. That said, Tsybikov, who was definitely more acceptable to Soviet authorities, possibly because he was so critical of religion, is much better known to the general public (both Buryat and Russian) than Baradiin. While both gained wide acclaim on the wave of the national revival, the titles of their works are somewhat misleading, as both Tsybikov and Baradiin come across as pious Buddhist pilgrims, rather than as academic scholars or intelligence gatherers. Upon familiarization with the texts themselves, some Buryats, especially Buddhist believers, express disappointment and dismay. Talking about Tsybikov's book, one young educated Buryat wrote in a post to a popular Buryat online forum:

> Honestly, I was disappointed by this book. Upon reading it, I saw an ordinary spy who did not hide his animosity toward Tibet and its spirituality and sacraments. So as a regular spy, he got this little medal around his neck, as a loyal lapdog of the tsarist administration [he is referring to the medal Tsybikov received from the Russian Geographic Society]. Personally, I prefer the writings of Bazar Baradiin—he is really the one who respects himself and his traditions.[26]

Equating respect for the sacredness of Tibet with respect for one's (Buryat) self and Buryat traditions, this comment assumes Tibet is an important aspect of Buryat culture.

However, the place of Tibet in the contemporary Buryat imagination is not uncontested. Ancient pathways and intellectual traditions have proved to be instrumental in shaping new alliances ahead: in some ways, contemporary debates in Buryatia mirror some of the important contradictions encountered by late nineteenth-century Russian Asian-

---

26. Discussion thread from Sait buriatskogo naroda, entitled "On the Famous Buryats and Kalmyks in the Recent History of the Mongols," http://www.buryatia.org/modules.php?name =Forums&file=viewtopic&t=3527&start=45&sid=39223cb894f7473c03bf19475f366628, accessed January 9, 2007.

ists and their intellectual successors, the Eurasianists. Yet, if Asianists like Ukhtomskii used Buryats to illustrate Russia's affinity with Asia and, ultimately, his mystical imperialist ideology, contemporary Buryats have a very different stake in the issue.

In the post-Soviet period, most Buryats tend to favor their own version of "Asianism," reclaiming with pride their membership in a larger Asian Buddhist civilization. And yet for many Buryats, despite being geographically located in Asia and being well-aware of their oft-invoked "Asian phenotype," "Asia" remains as exotic and mystical as it does for many Russians, and both invoke it whenever irrational qualities need to be named. Here we can trace the distinctions between the more extreme "Asianist" view (expressed by views that foreground Buryat Buddhism's derivation from Tibetan Buddhism) and the views of the Khambo Lama that stress the uniqueness of Buryat Buddhism and its blending of influences from East and West. The Khambo Lama's understanding could be considered a version of what we might call "Asian Eurasianism" in the sense that, in separating Buryats from their Tibetan and Mongolian heritage and linking them to Russia, it is belonging to "Asia" that is at stake here, not "Europe." Here I suggest that, contrary to Russia's preoccupations with defining itself against Europe, which resulted in the development of the Eurasianist ideology, Buryat "Asian Eurasianism" is invoking "Russia" to define itself against "Asia." While the extra "Asian" inflection may seem unnecessary to some readers, "Asian Eurasianism" is one political label that many Buryats could support.

While nationalist in its desire to create an "indigenous" Buryat Buddhism, the clergy's cultural orientation as expressed by the Khambo Lama is one that does not view Buryats as uniquely part of Asian civilization (the latter is the view of the pro-Tibetan opposition, such as the followers of ex-Khambo Lama Budaev and some secular nationalist intellectuals). In a way, he opposes them to the rest of Asia, stressing the benefits of their "blending" with Russia. Such a view, it has been pointed out, is useful to reconcile ideas about Buryats' distinctive identity with the fact of their existence within the Russian Federation (and to ascertain loyalty to the center) (Humphrey 2002a). In this we can see similarities to early twentieth-century classical Russian Eurasianists who saw Russia as a "bridge" between Europe and Asia, for this discourse also stresses Buryats' uniqueness, thus redefining the ideas of Eurasian center and periphery.

There is something different, however, about the Buryat Buddhist clergy's orientation, which suggests that "Asian Eurasianism" might be an appropriate explanatory term to advance a better understanding of contemporary Buryat cultural politics. While the Buryat clergy certainly have had to struggle with the same issues of asserting cultural difference from within the federation, there is another major issue at stake here: the Buryats' position in a larger Buddhist world, and, specifically, a Mongol-Tibetan world. What I suggest here is that many Buryat Buddhists are using Asian Eurasianism to define themselves "against" Tibet (and the Buddhist world in general), because the issue of their exclusion from or inclusion in "Asia" is as vital here as that of "Europe" has been for Russia over the centuries.

Buryats' relation to Mongolia is an uneasy one. As in the times of Baradiin, Mongols are looked down upon as being "primitive" and "crude" yet are admired for being independent, knowing their language, and for being unquestionably "Mongol." Tales of victimhood, however, abound, as it is often claimed that in the 1990s Buryats again (as in revolutionary times) took some of the leading posts in Mongolia, this time at the cost of having to conceal their origins in order not to be discriminated against (see Bulag 1998, for the detailed discussion of this issue).[27]

Yet, I would contend, it is still the relationship with the Tibetan world that polarizes Buryat Buddhists the most today. Buryatia is the center of the small but influential Tibetan emigration into Russia, to which many Tibetan lamas initially came at the invitation of the clergy to teach at the Ivolginsk Monastery, which they later left to start practicing privately, opening small temples and monasteries that popped up all over Ulan-Ude. The Khambo Lama finds such activities deeply offensive (his term for these temples is "kiosks"): "We Buryats went to Tibet to study and on pilgrimage but we never opened our monasteries there. Why do they think they have the right to do it here?" Of his opponents, like Budaev, he says that it is a shame that they have forsaken their own nation in order to "sweep the streets in Lhasa."

In turn, for Tibetans (and many Mongols), Buryats' association with Russia is confusing and implies that they are not fully Asian and not fully Buddhist. Tsybikov and Baradiin report that Buryats have been fighting against being called "Russians" in Lhasa, but today this trend still persists among Tibetan émigrés in India. The Tibetan for Buryat is *urusu sokpo* [Tib. *u ru su sog po*, Russian Mongol], but most just say *urusu*

---

27. For Buryats' involvement in revolutionary politics in Mongolia and Inner Mongolia, see Atwood 2002; and Rupen 1964.

[Russian].[28] On more than one occasion, I was bewildered to be asked by Tibetans in Dharamsala what the difference was between "Buryats" and "Russians." The fact that their Asianness is denied by their coreligionists, especially Tibetans, with whom they already have a problematic relation, must deeply affect Buryat self-perception.

Buryats' relationship to Tibet has always been one of marginality, and, since the Soviet repressions, many Tibetans (and Western Buddhists in the Tibetan tradition) have looked down upon Buryat Buddhism as "inauthentic," claiming that what Buddhists call "transmission" has been broken. Like all Buddhists, Tibetans base claims to authority largely on lineage, claiming that the Buddhism taught in Tibet and by Tibetan lamas abroad could be traced backward in an unbroken line to the eleventh century, when the founders of the major Tibetan schools traveled to India to receive the *dharma* from the great Indian masters, who were themselves direct recipients of teachings that could be traced back to the Buddha himself (Lopez 1997: 24). In the Buryat case, from this standpoint, current Soviet-educated lamas cannot possibly have authentic transmission, because the lineage has been broken and can only be restored through Tibetan teachers coming to Buryatia from India, or Buryat monks going to India to study with masters who do have the proper transmission.

In attempting to repair these tensions, Aiusheev and the Traditional Buddhist Sangha of Russia claim Buryat Buddhism's uniqueness in being a "bridge" between "Asian" and "European" Buddhism. While being a "bridge" is typical of the general Buryat identity discourse and not unique to the Khambo Lama, the Buddhist leader cleverly utilizes

---

28. Since the Tibetan term for Russians, *urusu*, is most likely derived from Mongolian *oros*, it demonstrates once again that it was Mongols who first marked Buryats as "other" (Johan Elverskog, personal communication, 2009). Language appears to be a crucial factor in these identification discourses. Many Buryats do not speak Buryat; others speak it on a very limited basis, which, for Mongols, is another proof that Buryats are not "really Mongol." That Buryats today consciously position themselves as distinct from Mongols is evident from the following incident described by a Russian journalist: "I was having dinner in an inexpensive restaurant in Ulan-Bator. Three of my compatriots—who looked Buryat—were sitting at the next table. They addressed the waiter exclusively in Russian. 'Why are you speaking Russian?' I asked them. 'I thought you wouldn't have problems with the language?' 'Out of principle!' they replied. . . . 'Why are you so surprised?' said another Buryat interlocutor. 'As we all know, Russians and Ukrainians also have the same origins. But I didn't notice much love between the two of you'" (Volkhonskii 2007). On the other hand, even a hundred years ago, when most Buryats did not speak Russian, the other Mongols treated them as "Russians." When Buryat intellectual Tsyben Zhamtsarano visited Inner Mongolia, China in 1909–1910, local Mongols—themselves Sinified—took him for a Russian: "a Russian who spoke perfect Mongolian, on a beautiful horse with a beautiful saddle of European manufacture" (Rupen 1964: 106).

it to stress his point that Buryat Buddhism's existence within Russia resulted in a unique indigenous Buddhist civilization, which is historically and presently autocephalous and distinct from its "purely" Asian counterparts.

As we have seen though, these configurations are fluid and prone to change. If an orientation to Russia (as "West") versus Mongolia and Tibet (as "East") was the defining factor in the reformist-conservative split in Buryat Buddhism after the Revolution of 1917, paradoxically, the distinctions between "progressives" and "conservatives" in Buddhism in terms of their orientation to "West" versus "East" have reversed. While conservative elements represented by the Buddhist Traditional Sangha of Russia (the leading Buryat Buddhist organization, headed by Aiusheev) now look more to Russia, the more progressive and liberal Buddhists tend to look toward contemporary Tibet, more specifically the Tibetan diaspora and the liberal ideology embraced by its leader, the Fourteenth Dalai Lama.

This chapter has traced the genealogy of Buryat Buddhology as a branch of Russian Orientalism, exploring the role that both Russian and Buryat scholars played in its development. Although the formation of this school was largely based on ideologies of empire, it produced important scholarship that transcended the boundaries of conventional area studies, offering evidence of a Eurasian world. Knowing the specific orientations and pathways taken by these Buryat pilgrims and scholars is a key to understanding new geopolitical forms of consciousness, as long-held Eurasian ties are now being revived in the wake of Soviet rule.

TWO

Sovereign Bodies: Death, Reincarnation, and Border Crossings in the Transnational Terrain

In the summer of 1927, five Buddhist pilgrims appeared in Lhasa, the capital of Tibet. Their formidable journey, which took more than a year of travel on foot, started in the Buryat-Mongol Autonomous Soviet Socialist Republic in Siberia and passed through Mongolian grasslands, the Gobi Desert, Tsaidam swamps, and the high mountain passes of the Tibetan Plateau. Despite their inability to communicate in the local language and their fatigue from the long trip, they immediately did what every pilgrim did on arrival in the holiest of Buddhist cities—they went to the main Lhasa temple, the Jokhang, and unloaded offerings of gold for the deities and parcels for monks.[1]

1. I have assembled the history of these early Soviet pilgrims in a somewhat piecemeal fashion from the following four sources: oral histories with Kentrul Rinpoche (the current reincarnation of one of the pilgrims) and Yeshe Lodrö Rinpoche (a disciple of one the pilgrims); the autobiography of one of the participants, Agvan Nyima; and a brief note by Buryat researcher G. N. Zaiatuev, who mentions a group of five monks sent to Lhasa by the Buryat lama and diplomat Agvan Dorzhiev. Nyima does not state the year of their departure in his narrative; however, the preface written by Yeshe Lodrö Rinpoche sets the date at 1923. Both Kentrul Rinpoche in an interview with me and Zaiatuev in his book set the date at 1927, which I have used here (Zaiatuev 1991: 42; Nyima 1996: 4). Other discrepancies in the sources include the number of monks who were part of this group: while Zaiatuev lists five, both Avgan Nyima in his autobiography and Kentrul Rinpoche in an interview state there were about ten of them.

A different kind of offering was intended for the hierarch of Tibetan Buddhism, the Dalai Lama. This was a box of guns. It was presumably sent with the pilgrims by Agvan Dorzhiev, a famous Buryat lama and diplomat who had once negotiated between tsarist Russia and Tibet, and now, between Soviet Russia and Tibet.[2] The lamas who brought the parcels were Buryat monks, who, like their nineteenth-century predecessors, often filled the double mission of overt pilgrimage and covert diplomacy. By the beginning of World War I, tsarist Russia had withdrawn completely from Tibetan affairs by recognizing Tibet as a sphere of British interests, thus ending the Anglo-Russian rivalry known as the Great Game. The situation was reversed with the victory of the Bolsheviks, when Tibet once again entered into the sphere of rapidly shifting northern Asian interests (Andreyev 2003: xiii).[3] The anecdotal evidence of a gift of guns reflects the aspirations of the Soviets in the 1920s, who viewed Tibet as a possible subject of the national liberation movement against "foreign oppressors" by an "awakening Asia." At the same time, the Buryat-Mongol and Kalmyk Buddhist colonies in Lhasa were used to spread a positive image of Soviet Russia, in the hope of drawing some of Lhasa's fragmented political factions into the Soviet orbit (Andreyev 2003: 107, 216–217).[4]

The lamas enrolled in Lhasa's famous Drepung Monastery and embarked on a multiyear curriculum in the Gomang Monastic College, where it traditionally took some twenty years to obtain the title of *geshe*, the highest degree awarded by Tibetan monastic universities (Tib. *dge bshes*).[5] It is not known whether they originally planned to stay in Tibet after receiving their degrees; it was likely upon hearing of the severe repressions over religion that started in Russia in the late 1920s that they made the fateful decision to remain in Tibet. Within a few decades, almost all these men held senior positions in the Tibetan monastic establishment. This expedition to Lhasa, and what it augured for its participants, already begins to tell us about the kinds of mobility

2. Interview with Kentrul Rinpoche, Drepung, Karnataka, India, 2008.

3. For Tibet's role in the Great Game, see Shaumian 2000; and Snelling 1993.

4. These lamas do not appear to have been an official part of the several Soviet secret missions to Tibet carried out during the 1920s. Most likely, they were genuine pilgrims, a part of an educational exchange program launched by Agvan Dorzhiev (Andreyev 2003: 210). They fulfilled a double mission, however, in the sense that they were naturally expected to join and collaborate with the "Russian" colony in Lhasa (including Buryats, Mongols, and Kalmyks), which was viewed as a platform for spreading Soviet influence in Lhasa. See Andreyev (2001) for more on the Russian presence in Lhasa from the nineteenth century to the 1930s.

5. Drepung, founded in 1416 by Jamyang Chöje, a disciple of Tsongkhapa, at its height was the world's largest monastery, with more than ten thousand monks. For more on Drepung, see Goldstein 1998. For more on Buddhist monastic education, see Dreyfus 2003.

that have long shaped the lives of Buryats across conventional political borders. The fates of these five men in particular, however, can tell us a good deal more about how Siberian Buddhism, as it has been known in the Republic of Buryatia in the Russian Federation, defines itself today.

Unlike many previous Buryat pilgrims with multiple missions, these lamas never made it back to Buryatia, or at least not, by their own telling, in their 1927 bodies. Escaping repression in one country did not prevent them from becoming victims of tragic events in another. In the aftermath of the 1959 Lhasa uprising followed by the Chinese crackdown in Tibet, the most prominent of them, Galsan Legden (Arzhigarov), who by then had become an abbot of the Gomang Monastic College of Drepung, was imprisoned, and he was reported to have died in custody in the mid-1970s.[6] Another pilgrim, Agvan Nyima, managed to escape to India, following the Dalai Lama, while his friend Thubten Nyima stayed in Tibet.[7]

Little or nothing was known of the fate of these men in Buryatia until the late 1980s, when the first Buryat lamas newly mobilized by perestroika began visiting Drepung again, by then relocated to and re-created in southern India by the Tibetan exile community, and a thriving home to about 4,500 monks. To their amazement, the first of the late socialist Siberian pilgrims were stunned to discover three of these original five monks alive and well in the tropics. Agvan Nyima was now more than eighty years old and a former abbot of the southern Indian Gomang, while Galsan Legden and another Buryat lama named Zhibalha also lived in the monastery, as they themselves professed, in their *new bodies*.[8] That is to say, the Galsan Legden and Zhibalha who

6. It is not exactly known when Legden was imprisoned and for how long. Oral sources state that he was the abbot of the Gomang College from 1955 to 1959 and died during the Cultural Revolution. The Cultural Revolution, which was devastating for Drepung, took place in China from 1966 to 1976. However, Goldstein writes that already in 1959, after the abortive Lhasa uprising, a group of Chinese officials had been sent to Drepung. These officials terminated the power of traditional leadership and appointed a new administration from poorer and more "progressive" monks. The new administration was called the Democratic Management Committee. By the end of the Cultural Revolution in 1976, only 306 out of 10,000 monks remained in Drepung (Goldstein 1998: 23–25).

7. According to his Tibetan disciple Yelo Rinpoche, Thubten Nyima did not want to escape to India, claiming that it would be harmful for his monastic vows. He was rather indifferent to the political changes in Tibet, which explains why he was arrested rather late, during the Cultural Revolution period (interview, Ulan-Ude, Buryatia, Russia, July 2001).

8. It is not clear when Zhibalha arrived in Tibet, so he might or might not have been in this group. According to his current incarnation's account, his predecessor was born in Aga region, went to Tibet to study in Drepung Monastery, and then went to teach in Litang in the Kham region of China, where he died around 1954 (interview, Drepung, Karnataka, India, January 2008). Agvan Nyima died in 1990, so only the very first pilgrims from Buryatia were lucky enough to see him.

were found in Drepung in the 1990s were young monks believed to be *reincarnations* of the former Buryat pilgrims. The bodies these Buryats acquired were ethnically Tibetan, one from Nepal and one from the region of Kham in the Sichuan province in China. These two monks subsequently visited Buryatia, had reunions with their Buryat "relatives," and became active members of the Buryat Buddhist revival.

Consider also Thubten Nyima, one of the monks who remained behind in Lhasa, for a different case of transnational religious ties. While Nyima did not seem to have a recognized reincarnation, during his life in Tibet, he served as a master to a young Tibetan incarnate lama named Yeshe Lodrö (Yelo) Rinpoche. In the early 1990s, Yelo Rinpoche, now in his sixties, had been invited to teach in Buryatia due to his being of "Buryat ancestry" through his master.[9] Today, Yelo Rinpoche, an ethnic Tibetan, resides in Buryatia, speaks fluent Buryat (although almost no Russian), and has acquired Russian citizenship. Rinpoche's status as a "naturalized foreigner," however, is contested by the distinction between Tibetan lamas with "roots" in Buryatia and those without them, prompting a relatively new discourse on "roots," which might seem incompatible with the otherwise apparent cosmopolitanism of Buryat Buddhists, who have long been conscious of their many border crossings in both time and space.[10]

With the exception of Agvan Nyima, who wrote an autobiography (1996), practically no published materials exist on these lamas or their fates, a puzzle given the dramatic means by which their lives traversed some of the most famous political and religious struggles of the twentieth century. To learn more about these men, and to consider their impact on Buryat cultural politics today, I aimed to re-create many of their same paths by traveling myself between monasteries in Buryatia and southern India. What follows is based on field research and interviews between 2001 and 2008 with the three Tibetan lamas whose lives are continued under new auspices: via the current reincarnations

9. One of Yeshe Lodrö Rinpoche's early teachers in Litang was also a Buryat, Zhibalha, mentioned above. According to Rinpoche, Zhibalha intended to go back to Russia after finishing his monastic education in Lhasa, but it turned out to be impossible due to the political situation in the Soviet Union. Rinpoche also mentioned that in the midseventies he was able to study under Agvan Nyima in the Indian Drepung (interview, Ulan-Ude, Russia, 2001). Crucially, this Tibetan lama had a total of three Buryat teachers.

10. Several Buryat scholars and lamas who had traveled to Tibet left detailed descriptions of their journeys (Baradiin 1904; Nyima 1996; Tsybikov 1981 [1919]). The first Buryat lama to compile a written account of his journey to Tibet was Damba-Darzha Zaiaev (1711–1776), the first Buryat Khambo Lama (several Russian translations of this text are available; see, for example, Sazykin 1986).

of Galsan Legden and Zhibalha residing in India, and Thubten Nyima's disciple Yeshe Lodrö (Yelo) Rinpoche in Buryatia.

This chapter looks at the institutions of Buddhist reincarnation and discipleship as distinctive technologies of the body aimed at cultural reproduction that have enabled certain kinds of border crossings within the context of the relatively restrictive authoritarian states of Soviet Russia and China. The reincarnated are, by design, highly mobile bodies imbued with an extraordinary status due to their ability to control their own mortality. In their status as border crossers, I am interested in how these bodies have become canvases onto which contemporary Buryat Buddhists inscribe competing claims to religious and cultural sovereignty in light of changing postsocialist geopolitical imaginaries. By looking at two cross-ethnic reincarnation and discipleship lineages

Chart 1. Mobile Bodies

Case of Reincarnation	Case of Discipleship
Russian Empire	
(ca. early 1900s) Galsan Legden (Buryat) born in Siberia	(ca. early 1900s) Thubten Nyima (Buryat) born in Siberia
Soviet Union → Pre-Chinese Tibet	
(ca. 1927) Arrived in Tibet (ca. 1950) Became abbot of Drepung Monastery in Lhasa	(ca. 1927) Arrived in Tibet (ca. 1950) Became a senior lama, served as a tutor to a young Tibetan *tulku* (incarnate lama) (b. 1943)
Chinese Tibet (1950–)	
(ca.?) Died in a Chinese prison	(ca. ?) Died during the turmoil in Tibet
China → Nepal (via Reincarnation) → India	Tibet → Exile to India
(ca. 1976) Reincarnation born in his friend's family in Nepal	(ca. 1959) Young disciple (Yeshe Lodrö Rinpoche) fled to India following the Dalai Lama
India	
(ca. 1980) Discovered in Nepal by Tibetan monks from the Indian Drepung, brought to India (ca. 1990) Discovered by first postsocialist Buryat pilgrims to India, became conscious of his "Buryatness"	(ca.1980) Yeshe Lodrö Rinpoche completed his formal monastic education (ca. 1990) Rediscovered his Buryat "roots," went to teach first in Mongolia, then Buryatia, learned Buryat, became a naturalized Russian citizen
India → Postsocialist Russia	
(ca. 2000) Started to visit and teach in Siberia, reunited with his Buryat "relatives"	(ca. 2000) Opened his own monastery in Buryatia, became a major competitor to the official Buryat religious establishment

that began in 1920s Soviet Siberia, crossed over to Tibet, Nepal, and India, and eventually came back to postsocialist Russia, I argue that it is the ability of these reincarnated bodies to cross various boundaries, both physical and metaphorical, that has given them their prominence in the current debates on authority, tradition, and religious sovereignty (see chart 1). Such fusions of religious and political consciousness, I suggest, have allowed Buryats to preserve a careful balance between a greater Asian Buddhist universe and their loyalties to Russia.

Reincarnation: Bodies in Flux

Buddhists view a single human lifetime as simply one stage in a much longer, complex project, which involves endlessly taking new forms, both human and nonhuman. The ultimate goal of the Buddhist path is to understand the nature of reality, which, once fully realized by an individual, stops the cycle of birth, death, and rebirth (Skt. saṃsāra), achieving a state known as nirvāṇa (literally "extinction"). According to the Mahāyāna tradition followed among the Buryats, the highest goal is to achieve buddhahood oneself and then teach the path to enlightenment to others. Those who have advanced far along the path to buddhahood, called bodhisattvas, as well as those who have achieved buddhahood, are said to appear compassionately in the world in human form. While regular people do not remember their previous lives and are not able to control their rebirth, these individuals, designated in English *incarnate lamas*, can choose their place of birth and usually leave clues for the rest to where they will be reborn after their death.

Early Buddhist theology postulated that the Buddha had two bodies—the physical body (*rūpakāya*) and the transcendent body "of virtuous qualities" that was not subject to sickness and death (*dharmakāya*) (Lopez 2002b: 61–62). Later doctrines developed a tripartite scheme of the Buddha's bodies: the *dharmakāya*, in which the supramundane qualities of the Buddha evolved into a kind of transcendent principle of enlightenment, the *sambhogakāya*, a celestial body of the Buddha, and the *nirmanakāya* or "emanation" body, which might be assumed for the purpose of instructing and saving beings in our world, most famously in the form of the historical Buddha himself (Williams 1989: 167–185). In Tibetan, the Sanskrit term for "emanation body" is translated as *tulku* (*sprul sku*), suggesting that, at least technically, these beings are emanations of a buddha. According to common understanding, they are also considered to include advanced bodhisattvas. Since the fourteenth century, all Tibetan Buddhist schools have been identifying the successive rebirths of famous teachers. Incarnate lamas—the most famous of whom today is the Dalai Lama—are believed to be a line of individuals, who are in a sense the same person, returning to the world in lifetime after lifetime. In Mongolian and Buryat, the term for an incarnate lama is *xubilgan*, which is related to the word for "change" or "metamorphosis." The Fifth Dalai Lama (1617–1682), whose predecessor was a Mongol, was the first Dalai Lama to assume political control of Tibet, with the support of Mongol troops in 1642.

The most famous of these incarnate lamas are identified with specific buddhas and bodhisattvas. Thus, the Dalai Lama is understood to be the human incarnation of the bodhisattva of compassion, Avalokiteshvara, and the Panchen Lama an incarnation of the buddha Amitabha. The Bogd Gegeen (Jebdzundamba Khutugtu of Mongolia) is considered an emanation of Vajrapāṇi. Transferring the notion of emanation into the secular realm, Tibetan Buddhists have proclaimed sacralized historical figures to be manifestations of deities: Chinggis Khan is considered a manifestation of the fierce bodhisattva Vajrapāṇi, the Qing emperor Qianlong an emanation of Manjusri, while the Russian emperors are widely believed to be the emanation of the goddess White Tārā (Andreyev 2003: 7–8; Rawski 1998: 248). Secularizing the idea of reincarnate lineages even further by combining it with the Chinese notion of *zhengtong* ("political descent"), Inner Asian rulers often proclaimed themselves reincarnations of their charismatic predecessors, with Altan Khan identifying himself as a reincarnation of Khubilai and many other rulers claiming descent from Chinggis Khan (Rawski 1998: 210, 249). Although, unlike Tibetans, Buryats never developed a formal institution of reincarnation whereby a child is identified as a reincarnation of a previous lama, some prominent lamas were posthumously referred to as incarnates of past masters. (We will encounter some of these lamas in chap. 3.)

The identification of the successive incarnation of high lamas, an institution that developed in Tibet as early as the eleventh century, ensured the inheritance of leadership and property from one generation to the next at a time when celibate monastic communities replaced noble families—previously the primary patrons of Buddhism—to became centers of Buddhist power and governance. Taking a Weberian view of authority, Turrell Wylie suggested that the institution of reincarnation facilitated the "transition from charisma of person to a charisma of office: a change essential to the establishment of a hierocratic form of government that could survive as an institution regardless of the charisma of any individual" (1978: 584). Focusing on the role of reincarnation in the transfer of property, Melvyn Goldstein (1973) demonstrated how features inherent in reincarnation transformed the Tibetan political system itself, resulting in what he called a "circulation of estates," large blocks of arable land intermittently held by incarnate lamas in power. Besides high incarnate lamas, most dramatically exemplified by the Dalai Lama, the Tibetan tradition had also developed hundreds of minor lineages, in which incarnate lamas are associated with a particular monastery or local region. The personalities whom we encounter in this chapter belong to this category of incarnate lamas.

Reincarnation has often crossed ethnic boundaries and forged political ties, especially among Tibetans, Mongols, and Chinese, moving even to the West in the late twentieth century (Lavine 1998: 105–110). A folk story that I have often heard from Buryat adepts about the origin of the lineage of Mongolian Jebdzundamba Khutugtus tells of the Tibetan scholar Tāranātha (1575–1634) who, at the end of his life, asked his disciples where he should be born next. One of them, a Mongol, cried out, "Please be reborn in Mongolia!" Tāranātha was reborn in the noble Mongolian family as Zanabazar (1635–1723), who was recognized as the first Jebdzundamba and subsequently inserted into the lineage of Chinggis Khan and Khubilai Khan.[11] Several decades prior to this (in 1588), in a similar diplomatic move, the Fourth Dalai Lama was identified in a great-grandson of the Mongol leader Altan Khan, becoming the first and only non-Tibetan Dalai Lama at the time when Buddhism was once again starting to take hold in Mongolia (Snellgrove and Richardson 1995 [1968]: 184–185). Thus, beyond the issues of leadership and property succession identified by Wylie and Goldstein, reincarnation appears to have been crucial for the spread of Tibetan Buddhism to new regions, most notably its transmission into Mongolia.

Discipleship: Lineages in Motion

Reincarnation can be understood as an innovation to create extrakin and extraterritorial lineages in Tibetan Buddhism. Another quasi-kinship practice, known as a master-disciple relationship, serves a similar purpose (Mills 2000: 23–25). Incarnate lamas inherit not only property but also disciples, with whom they enter into a special ritual

---

11. For more on the lineage of Jebdzundamba Khutugtus, see Bawden 1961; Humphrey 1994b; and Sanders 2001.

relationship through which the master's power is transmitted to the student. One of the central rituals of tantric Buddhism is the process of the transmission of ritual power known as "initiation," or, literally, "empowerment" (Tib. *dbang*; Bur. *van abishig*; Buryats use a combination of a modified Tibetan term, *van*, from Tib. *dbang* and a modified Sanskrit term, *abishig*, from Skt. *abhisheka* to signify "empowerment"; contemporary Buryat Buddhists also use a Russian term, *posviashche-nie*). Through "empowerments" the disciple is initiated into the practice of a particular deity, which sometimes includes obtaining a new name. During this ritual the disciple must imagine his master as the deity, and fellow disciples who attended the initiation led by the same master are called "vajra brothers" and "vajra sisters" (Skt. *vajra*, or "thunderbolt," being the central symbol of indestructibility). In some initiations, such as the Kālacakra cycle, disciples must visualize the master in sexual union with a female consort, subsequently visualizing themselves as entering the mouth of the lama, passing through his body to the vagina and then on to the womb of his female consort, from which they are ritually reborn (Dalai Lama the Fourteenth 1999: 94–95; Mills 2000: 24).

Thus, tantric initiation rites create alternative "kinship-like structures" based on religious lineages, with descent taking place from deities to incarnate lamas to novices (Mills 2000: 25). While Martin Mills described initiation ceremonies taking place in the context of rural monastic Tibetan Buddhism in the Indian state of Ladakh, I have observed many tantric initiations in lay, urban, transnational contexts, where they increasingly take place today. Kālacakra initiations, for example, fairly regularly conferred by the Dalai Lama in India (as well as Europe and North America), are gigantic public spectacles attended by thousands of believers from all over the world.[12] Such initiations often become a focal point for lay Buryat and Tibetan pilgrims to India who then become "vajra brothers and sisters" (Rus. *vadzhrnye brat'ia i sestry*) with thousands of fellow coreligionists from Brazil to South Africa.

For those who cannot afford long-distance travel, Tibetan émigré lamas living in Russia and visiting lamas from India regularly conduct such tantric initiations in Buryatia. Since Buryatia does not have its own currently living lamas, who would be considered reincarnations of great past masters, in the postsocialist period such rituals have become the domain of Tibetan incarnates. As demonstrated in chapter 1,

12. For a behind-the-scenes ethnographic account of the staging of a Kālacakra initiation in New York, see McLagan 2002.

however, their authority is not uncontested, and certain lamas are considered by some Buryats to be more suitable than others to confer such initiations. Enter a new kind of a contemporary Tibetan teacher: the Tibetan of "Buryat ancestry" (literally, of Buryat "roots," Rus. *s buriat-skimi korniami*). Those Tibetan lamas who happen to be either the reincarnations or disciples of an important past Buryat master are considered better for this role than those with no direct ties to Buryatia.

In order to understand why Buryats today might prefer to receive empowerments from their own "kin," let us first consider the practices that make Tibetan lamas of "Buryat ancestry" possible, forging transnational ties between the two peoples. While the notion of reincarnation may have been developed in order to ensure the proper succession of religious authority, it also became a means of social mobility. Highly educated and talented monks sometimes became great masters, and after their death, a search for a successor might be initiated, thus founding a new lineage. This was the case with the two Buryat lamas mentioned at the beginning of this chapter, Galsan Legden and Zhibalha, who, by having achieved high status in their previous lives, forged the beginning of two new transethnic lineages.

Reincarnation and tantric discipleship both serve as nonbiological reproductive technologies, creating all-male transnational "families" and lineages. The fact that these Buryat lamas have exercised control over their own death and rebirth while engaging in unauthorized crossings of borders between hostile nation-states makes their bodies into powerful tools for the contemporary political imagination. Similar to classical sovereign bodies, such as those of the two-bodied kings (possessing the immortal body politic and mortal body natural) (Kantorowicz 1957), incarnate lamas derive transcendent authority from the perpetual nature of their reincarnated essence. This bodily duality has undoubtedly enhanced incarnate lamas' status as sovereign rulers of central Tibet since the seventeenth century, producing a characteristically Buddhist political theology. What is unique about the two Tibetan lamas considered in this chapter is that their very rebirth is due to and at the same time bypasses tumultuous events of the twentieth century, such as the Russian and Chinese revolutions and subsequent secularization campaigns. While Tibetan incarnate lamas are often considered the source of the highest authority in Buryatia, the fact that some of them turn out to be of "Buryat descent" allows them to be detached from the usual Tibetan orbits and incorporated into the Buryat body politic.

The belief that these Buryat lamas were able to use reincarnation and tantric mastership to literally "father" descendants beyond the borders of their immediate nation-states reverses the traditional cultural hierarchy with Tibetans on top as the more developed and ancient Buddhist culture. Instead, for some of the contemporary proponents of the autocephality (autonomy) of Buryat Buddhism, these Tibetan incarnate lamas embody a classical kind of sovereignty not only by virtue of their human-divine nature but also through being viewed as essentially "ours" (Rus. *nashi*).[13] How are we to understand the impact of these reincarnated bodies on the indigenous cultural politics in Buryatia? The biographies of two incarnate Tibetan lamas with "Buryat roots" will demonstrate that it is their ability to cross boundaries—between nation-states, but also between bodies, between life and death, and between conventionally defined lines of kinship and ethnicity—that makes them central to the contested notions of sovereignty in Buryat political imaginaries.

Buryats in Tibet: The Story of Galsan Legden

We met Galsan Legden earlier, when he was a Buryat pilgrim arriving in Tibet in 1927, only to die later in a Chinese prison during the Cultural Revolution. The present incarnation of Galsan Legden, now known as Kentrul Rinpoche ("ken" means "abbot," and "trul" signals "tulku"), was born in 1976 in Nepal. As is very common in reincarnation narratives, from the time he started talking, he always said he wanted to join the monastery.[14] When he saw monks, he tried to follow them, and when he saw red or yellow fabric, he often tried to grab it and put it on himself. When he was four, monks from Drepung Monastery appeared on his doorstep, claiming that the boy was a reincarnation of their former abbot. It turned out that when Galsan Legden was imprisoned in China, he shared his prison cell with a Tibetan monk who was planning to escape to Nepal. Knowing that his death was near, Legden asked his fellow inmate if he could visit him in Nepal. Thinking that he was talking about coming to his house in Nepal after the release

13. Cf. also Sahlins's notion of the "stranger-king" who gets absorbed and domesticated by the indigenous people (1985). I thank Giovanni da Col for bringing this to my attention (personal communication, 2011). See also da Col 2012b. The crucial difference in the Buryat case, however, is that these lamas are a particular kind of a "stranger," one that can claim religious descent from past Buryat masters.

14. For accounts of reincarnation and procedures related to the identification of tulkus written by incarnate lamas themselves, see Dalai Lama the Fourteenth 1997 [1962]; Norbu 1986 [1960]; Trungpa 2000.

from prison, Legden's friend responded, "Yes, of course, you can visit me, and I will do everything to make your stay comfortable." Thus, two lifetimes got conflated in the same conversation. Galsan Legden died in prison and was reborn into his friend's family in Nepal.[15]

The parents of the present Galsan Legden, a well-off Tibetan refugee family in Kathmandu, owners of a carpet factory, did not want their son to become an incarnate lama, perhaps unwilling to commit him to the lifelong monastic vocation. They did, however, agree to send the boy to Drepung in India. As for many parents, it was a unique opportunity to educate their son for free; thanks to the streamlining of Tibetan Buddhism in exile, monasteries now provide both conventional and classically religious education. The boy did not know he was an incarnate lama and lived as an ordinary monk. In a few years, however, he became very sick. The boy's chaperones addressed the Dalai Lama, whose assistants, after doing a divination, declared that the boy was sick because he was refusing to accept his reincarnation as a living deity. It was only in 1985, when he was nine, that the boy's parents finally agreed to enthrone him as an incarnate lama, after which he quickly recovered. This inevitability of accepting one's spiritual vocation related to the embodiment of divinity reminds one of "shamanic illnesses" in Siberian shamanism (Basilov 1984: 138–169; Eliade 1964 [1951]: 33–34; Novik 2004 [1984]: 195–196), where it is often explained as the rejected spirits' causing havoc in the reluctant shaman's body, which can only be cured by a proper initiation. In the case of Tibetan tulkus, the illness of the unrecognized tulku is often explained as disrespect to the divinity which his body is manifesting.[16] A tulku, and thus the divinity whom he manifests, not properly treated as such might bring about a "ritual pollution."

In many cultures, past lives constitute a vital part of one's identity, with newborns conceptualized as complex beings, far from being a simple tabula rasa. The idea of children being inhabited by their ancestors' thoughts, gestures, and dispositions is linked to indigenous notions of temporality, historicity, memory, and social reproduction (Balzer 1999: 175; Gupta 2002; Empson 2007; Humphrey 1992). While, in some contexts, there is often no agreement on whose rebirth a particular child is (Empson 2007: 73), in other contexts, establishing one's "real" identity vis-à-vis the past is a crucial stage in one's life: misrecognition may

---

15. Interview with Kentrul Rinpoche, Drepung, Karnataka, India, February 2008.

16. For an analysis comparing reincarnate Buddhist lamas with shamans, arguing that tulkus manifest a sort of "permanent" spirit possession, see Aziz (1976).

lead to negative consequences for the people in question, as their improperly identified souls work against them in the course of their lives (Willerslev 2007: 51).[17] The difference between ordinary rebirths and Tibetan reincarnations of high lamas, however, is that the tulku is seen as linked to the entire monastic community by the ties of Buddhist kinship. Such a misrecognition, for example, could affect not only the incarnate himself, but the monastic community as a whole, such as in one case of leprosy brought upon an entire monastery, when, through a variety of mishaps, an incarnate lama was not properly identified (Mills 2000: 26). Similarly, anthropologist Peter Moran has argued that since tulkus (the emanation bodies) have always "pointed to something beyond themselves," in the transnational terrain, Tibetan tulkus have become the "allegorical bodies" of the Tibetan nation. He also notes that contemporary tulkus have been some of the most mobile of their countrymen, often bringing and representing Tibetan Buddhism to Western audiences (Moran 2004: 14–34). Thus, tulkus emerge as a literal "body politic."

While simple rebirths usually happen within ethnic groups, and most often within the same genetic kin groups, reincarnations are not impeded by national borders.[18] From 1977 to 1980, Agvan Nyima, one of the original five Buryat pilgrims and the only one to escape Tibet, served as the abbot of the Gomang College of the Indian Drepung.[19] During his term, in the late 1970s, he initiated a search for the re-

17. Here, not only the awareness of past lives is crucial, but also the enactment of this recognition in everyday life, such as calling a child by the appropriate name. Willerslev's example describes the case of a child who was not called by the name of his great-great-grandfather, of whom he was a reincarnation, resulting in the child's unruly and offensive behavior (2007: 51). In a parallel case among another Siberian people, Balzer also notes that Khanty women say that babies will not stop crying unless it is properly determined of whom they are a reincarnation (a divination procedure done shortly after birth). In a more broad way, she argues that reincarnation beliefs among Siberian peoples served to counteract the Soviet ideology in this "crucial, identity-reproducing realm." Thus, ancestral Khanty names divined during the ceremony of reincarnation identification were kept in secret, while regular Russian names were given as "cover names." Russian names here serve a similar purpose, as nicknames like Rubbish or Insect were often given to babies during the first few years of life with the intention to divert the interest of evil spirits and thus conceal the child's true identity (Balzer 1999: 173–177, 265 fn6). Similarly, Empson states that in Mongolia, the practice of lay rebirths runs counter to secular memories. While prohibited from communicating with their ancestors through shamanic rituals, Mongolian Buryats continued relations with the deceased through rebirths (Empson 2007: 77).

18. Anthropological literature abounds in references to notions of rebirth in various cultures, from native North America to Africa to Melanesia. For a synthesis of many of these sources, see Obeyesekere 2002.

19. After retiring from his post as the Gomang College abbot, Agvan Nyima taught and worked in Switzerland and Holland. For more on Agvan Nyima (1907–1990), see his autobiography (Nyima 1996).

FIGURE 4. Kentrul Rinpoche (Galsan Legden) conducting an empowerment, Russia, 2008. Photo courtesy of Igor' Iancheglov.

incarnation of his old friend. Following all the standard procedures,[20] the search party from Drepung identified a Tibetan boy in Nepal as Galsan Legden (fig. 4), the Buryat from the Tunka region of southern Siberia who had served as the abbot of the Gomang College of the Drepung in Lhasa during the time of the Chinese takeover. Thus, due to the efforts of his countryman Agvan Nyima, Legden became the originator of a new lineage, which has so far spanned four countries and two nations. What might such ethnic fluidity, resulting from transnational reincarnations, signify? In 2008, I lived in the southern Indian Drepung Monastery for several months and sought out this young man to ask how he himself understood this reincarnation process. "When I was told I was a reincarnation of Legden, I was glad, but I didn't feel anything special. It was only when they showed me his picture, I felt something . . . unusual. When they told me my predecessor was a Mongol—I did not know about the difference between Mongols and Buryats at the

20. The standard procedures for the search for a reincarnation include performing a series of divinations to determine the location of the candidates and then examining the candidates' ability to demonstrate some knowledge of their predecessors' identities. The tests include having young boys choose objects belonging to the past incarnation among various objects presented to them.

time—I felt a sense of 'us' and 'ours.' A sense of pride for being a Mongol, even a feeling of some kind of patriotism. A Mongol patriotism."

It was only in the late eighties, when Kentrul Rinpoche saw the first Buryat monks and pilgrims who started arriving at Drepung from Russia, that he learned about this difference. The first Buryats who arrived in Drepung, the now renowned ex-Khambo Lama Choi-Dorzhi Budaev and the late lama Fedor Samaev, having heard of the reincarnation of their celebrated Legden, immediately treated him as a high lama, although he was only a teenager at the time. The word about the reincarnated master spread, and eventually, visiting and getting blessings from Kentrul Rinpoche and another former Buryat incarnate living in India, Zhibalha lama, became part of the pilgrim routine on visits to Drepung (see fig. 5).

While visiting Indian monasteries, most Buryat pilgrims engage in a number of ritual activities, one of the most important being securing audiences with as many incarnate lamas as possible. While seeing the Dalai Lama is of utmost importance but not often possible, it is considered especially valuable to visit their fellow "Buryats," Kentrul

FIGURE 5. Kentrul Rinpoche with Buryat pilgrims, Drepung Monastery, Karnataka, India, 2008. Photo by the author.

FIGURE 6. Zhibalha Rinpoche, another Tibetan lama with "Buryat roots," with Buryat pilgrims in India, Drepung Monastery, Karnataka, India, 2008. Photo by the author.

Rinpoche or Zhibalha Rinpoche, while in southern India (see fig. 6). (In the north, getting an audience with the traditional leader of Mongolian Buddhists, the ethnic Tibetan Jebdzundamba Khutugtu the Ninth, was another major goal until his death in 2012.) During such brief audiences, power can be transferred not through elaborate initiations but as a blessing through a simple touch by the incarnate to the devotee's head, a gentle blow on the face, or the holding and reciting of consecrating verses over various souvenirs purchased from street vendors. After these haptic engagements, the pilgrims are viewed as spiritually charged, and on their return home, many people, in turn, want to touch them to partake of their accreted power. The distribution of consecrated souvenirs, from more elaborate altarpieces bought for close friends and kin to simple threads blessed by the lamas to be worn on the wrists and necks, given as tokens of attention to other acquaintances, is often the central ritual upon a pilgrim's return.

When asked of his impressions of Buryatia, Kentrul Rinpoche said he was surprised by how many people wanted him to conduct the rituals of tantric empowerment. His surprise is understandable, for, until recently, most rituals of this kind had been restricted to the monastic establishment. It is with the spread of Buddhism to the West and modernization of Tibetan Buddhism in exile by the Fourteenth Dalai Lama that it had become common practice for laypeople to be initiated into the tantric "families."[21] Kentrul Rinpoche bemoaned the fact that some lay Buryats seemed to be more interested in receiving high-level initiations than getting a good grasp of Buddhist fundamentals, which he addressed in his public lectures. While he ascribed it to the "shamanistic" Buryat obsession with ritual, I would suggest the Buryat interest in receiving empowerments from a Tibetan lama with "Buryat roots" hinges on their belief in its greater efficacy precisely because it is articulated on both transnational and local levels. On the one hand, through empowerments, laypeople become incorporated in the Buddhist kinship-like structures, becoming part of global families of deities, incarnate lamas, and monks. On the other hand, by receiving empowerments from someone whose body itself acts as a link to the Buryat prerevolutionary golden age, they reconnect with specifically Buryat Buddhist kin and ancestors.

Yet the "us" feeling expressed by Kentrul Rinpoche in the above quote reveals a sense of belonging, distinct from both purported ecumenical religious and narrowly defined nationalist allegiances. While anthropologists have long argued that ethnicity is processual, relational, and situational, the experience of incarnate lamas both enhances and undermines this notion. On the one hand, the example of incarnates throws a relatively fresh light on contemporary social scientific understanding of ethnicity as existing at the intersection of descent, genetics, and cosmology. Existing in multiple temporal and spatial regimes simultaneously, Kentrul Rinpoche is obviously a Tibetan in regular worldly time, but when he switches to what might be called, in Benjaminian fashion, "messianic time" (Benjamin 1969: 263), manifesting his body as a link between past and present, he is a Mongol and a patriot. He is simultaneously himself, a Tibetan from Nepal, a Buryat from the Tunka region in Siberia who died in a Chinese prison, and an emanation of a divinity. At the same time, however, as in any folk usage (as in the Buddhist practice), reified ethnicity figures as a "thing," something fixed enough to be reincarnated from one life to

---

21. One exception is the Kalachakra initiations, which were public in traditional Tibet.

another, along with the usual array of habits and dispositions, despite the traditional doctrinal denial of any kind of permanent reincarnating "self."[22]

To revisit the central premise of this chapter, then: the bodies of the incarnates, which cross geopolitical borders, as well as transcend the borders between life and death and between classically ethnic identifications, became productive sites for inscribing Buryat competing notions of belonging in the postsocialist period. Since the eleventh century, the existence of incarnate lamas who were able to transcend site-specific allegiances or, in more recent times, literally "think and feel beyond the nation" (Cheah and Robbins 1998) has played the crucial role in making Tibetan Buddhism a translocal religion, reaching far beyond its Himalayan homeland. During the early Soviet socialist period, these transnational flows were mostly unidirectional, flowing outward from the USSR to allow Buryat pilgrims to cross borders and perhaps even recruit coreligionists into the Soviet fold. These ties were discontinued around the beginning of the 1930s, when Soviet internationalists abandoned their efforts to draw Tibet into its orbit (Andreyev 2003: 385–395). Today this Buddhist transnationalism has resumed in both directions, with the locus of authority for Buryat Buddhists relocated from Lhasa to Dharamsala, the current seat of the Dalai Lama and Tibetan government-in-exile, and to southern India, where three main Geluk monastic seats have been re-created. While thousands of Buryat pilgrims visit Tibetan communities in India every year, since the mid-1990s, Buryatia has become the center of Tibetan emigration to Russia. Tibetan lamas have had great success in postsocialist Buryatia as religious teachers, promoting an array of cosmopolitan and transnational subjectivities in an already pluralist Siberian republic. Below, I consider how specific notions of Buddhist kinship, arising from institutions of reincarnation and a particular form of religious discipleship, facilitate the renovation of Buddhism in Buryatia while having to negotiate postsocialist religious and ethnic politics. These processes are well illustrated by Yelo Rinpoche, whom we met earlier, the Tibetan incarnate lama residing in Buryatia.

---

22. For lack of a better term, I use the word "folk" to remind the reader that in the classical Buddhist doctrine, of course, there is no soul or self to be reincarnated, let alone a specific ethnicity. The Buddhist theory of personhood denies the existence of the fixed "self," arguing instead that the individual is the combination of five "aggregates" (Skt. *skandhas*)—physical form, sensation, perception, habits and dispositions, and consciousness—which are in constant flux. Conceptions of the process of rebirth vary among different Buddhist schools.

Tibetans in Buryatia: The Story of Yelo Rinpoche

Yelo Rinpoche was born in Litang in eastern Tibet in 1943. At the age of three, he was recognized as a fourth incarnate lama in the Yelo lineage. One of his early teachers was the Buryat Zhibalha mentioned earlier in this chapter. When Yelo was thirteen, he entered the original Drepung in Lhasa, where one of his main masters was Thubten Nyima, one of the five original Buryat pilgrims. Later he escaped to India, where he completed his monastic education under Agvan Nyima, who proved to be his next major Buryat teacher. After the collapse of socialism, he expressed interest in being sent to teach in Mongolia, where he spent a year mastering the Mongolian language.[23] At the same time, in the early 1990s, Buryats started asking the Dalai Lama to send them a master to teach at the Ivolginsk Monastery. Ivolginsk was built in 1945 near the village of Ivolga about thirty kilometers south of Ulan-Ude, in a postwar attempt to demonstrate freedom of religion in the Soviet Union. Ivolginsk served as one of only two Buddhist monasteries in Russia until the period of postsocialist renovation (Zhukovskaia 1997: 5; Chimitdorzhin 2008: 434). It now houses the largest monastic university in Buryatia and serves as the seat of the Khambo Lama.

Yelo Rinpoche arrived in Buryatia with his Tibetan disciple Tenzin, received Russian citizenship, and permanently settled in Ulan-Ude (see fig. 7). He was initially sponsored by the Sangha to teach at Ivolginsk; however, due to the ongoing conflicts with the local religious establishment, he dropped out and opened his own monastery on the outskirts of the city in 2004, along with several lay "dharma centers" in major Russian cities.

The cornerstone of the tensions between these two major figures in Buryatia lies in the Buryat relationship with the Tibetan world and the Buddhist world in general. To revisit my discussion in chapter 1, there is a deep schism between various religious leaders in the republic over issues of the identity and future of Buryat Buddhism. While some are convinced that it should be modeled as much as possible on

23. Yelo Rinpoche first visited Mongolia in the early eighties, trying to see the birthplace and find relatives of his "root" teacher, Thubten Nyima, who, he thought, was a Mongol. It was at that time, in Mongolia, that he was told that his teacher's native land was across the border to the north, in Siberia, and that he was, in fact, a Buryat (interview, Ulan-Ude, Buryatia, Russia, July 2001). See also my ethnographic documentary devoted to his life in Buryatia, where he reiterates many of the same ideas (Bernstein 2002b).

FIGURE 7. Yeshe Lodrö Rinpoche and his disciple Tenzin, Ulan-Ude, 2001. Photo by the author.

contemporary Tibetan Buddhism, others vehemently resist any foreign involvement or influence. The Khambo Lama, for example, advocates "indigenous" Buryat Buddhism, which, in his view, is equal (or in some versions of this argument, even superior) to but separate from Tibetan and Mongolian Buddhisms. Other leaders, in contrast, resist the appellation of "Buryat," arguing that there is only one Buddhism and that such distinctions are based on erroneous nationalist feelings, incompatible with the true Buddhist doctrine. To make matters more complicated, the Russian central government, from Catherine the Great to President Medvedev, always fostered notions of ecclesiastical self-government, since having a religious community on the former empire's borderlands subordinated to foreign leadership would complicate borders and loyalties. As we shall see, the ways in which these political allegiances manifest themselves through religious forms are manifold and complex.

Because he is one of the most powerful and respected religious figures in contemporary Buryatia, Yelo Rinpoche's extraordinary status as an incarnate lama presents challenges for the Khambo Lama, who, on many occasions, has expressed resentment of the fact that Tibetans open their monasteries in Buryatia. While both Yelo Rinpoche and the Khambo Lama are widely popular religious leaders in the republic, interestingly, the Khambo Lama has emerged as a truly populist leader who works and speaks for the nation and evokes feelings of Buryat pride, while Yelo Rinpoche is mostly favored by the Buryat intelligentsia in search of esoteric teachings.[24] Due to his status as the only incarnate lama residing in Russia (the Khambo Lama, by contrast, is not a reincarnation but an elected leader), Yelo Rinpoche is in high demand for conducting tantric empowerments. Because Buryatia does not have an institutionalized tradition of incarnate lamas, the status of Yelo Rinpoche is technically higher than anyone else in the republic, which intensifies the tensions already present in Buryat religious politics.

While tulkus have an extraordinary status everywhere in the Tibetan Buddhist world, in Buryatia, even regular Tibetan lamas are usually viewed by laypeople as charismatic, possessing special powers via a certain fetishization of Tibetan mystical "otherness." Tibetan lamas in Buryatia often enjoy a strong following, even if their reputation becomes questionable.[25] Unlike laypeople, some members of the Buryat clergy, especially those who have spent many years in India with Tibet-

---

24. Yelo Rinpoche, however, is also in great demand for his presumed ritual efficacy. On the days when he receives believers at his temple (twice a week during my visit there in 2008), who come to seek his advice on anything from health to children's education to marital abuse, lines form at 5:00 a.m. and do not dissipate until his working hours are over. A historical precedent of rivalry between Mongolian and Tibetan hierarchs that might be interesting for comparative purposes is well documented. When the Thirteenth Dalai Lama fled to Urga in Outer Mongolia to escape the British in 1905–1908, his relationship with the Eighth Jebdzundamba deteriorated, because the latter seemed jealous that Mongolians accorded the Dalai Lama enormous respect (Ya 1991: 253). A fascinating firsthand account of this growing rivalry by a Mongolian lama close to the Eighth Jebdzundamba is available in Bawden (1997: 35–46).

25. Perhaps the most famous lama in Russia, the Tibetan Geshe Tinlei, was recently involved in a number of scandals regarding "inappropriate" behavior, money, and relations with women, ending up disrobing and losing all his priestly privileges (according to unconfirmed rumors he was disrobed by the Dalai Lama himself during his visit to Kalmykia in 2004). This, however, did not affect his enormous following, with dharma centers set up in almost every major city in Russia, as he is believed to be intrinsically holy and continues to be venerated as a teacher despite his recently lay and married status (Anonymous 2004b).

ans, sometimes express skepticism and even cynicism regarding their fellow coreligionists. These views pass unofficially through rumors and private conversations, which in a tightly knit Buddhist community of Ulan-Ude quite quickly become public, creating a resentment that undermines Tibetan monastic emigration in Buryatia. A common view of some of the monks is that Tibetans have "failed" in Buryatia, understanding "failure" in terms of the impossibility of introducing the Tibetan model of monastic education in Buryatia and educating the public appropriately. Celibacy and monastic discipline are usually at stake, and the absence of these in Buryatia is often explained by the incompatibility of Buryat and Tibetan "mentality," with Buryats jokingly describing themselves as "wild nomads" who are impossible to discipline (cf. Herzfeld's 1997 notion of "cultural intimacy"), in opposition to Tibetans, who are locally viewed as rigid and rational. But perhaps most crucially and most commonly, the Tibetans are thought to be bound to fail in Buryatia because they do not have "roots" there. In this particular view, Tibetans are not great teachers and bodhisattvas, but alien intruders out to profit from the ever-growing religious marketplace and are almost genetically incapable of understanding local realities.

The pervasiveness of the biologistic discourse on "roots" is especially striking given that the Buddhist transnational and transcultural model of kinship is specifically designed to undermine this very ideology. In the remainder of this chapter I will examine how the debates around one particular ritual during the summer of 2008 became an arena through which competing notions of "roots" were expressed. Yelo Rinpoche's "Buryat ancestry" through his master Thubten Nyima, however, placed him in a special position in the "roots" debate, thus exemplifying the significance of religion-specific notions of kinship for indigenous cultural politics in the region.

Buddhist Ritual Wrought Anew

Some of the central seasonal rituals in Buryatia are ritual offerings called *oboo*. An oboo refers to a cairn usually built on a mountain top to mark the residence of the so-called land master spirits (Abaeva 1991; Humphrey 1999 [1983]: 422–423; Humphrey and Sneath 1999: 123–124). Land master spirits are linked to both kinship and territorial groups, with all residents of adjacent villages often gathering for a communal ritual. Oboo rituals are rarely missed by Buryats, even the

FIGURE 8. Oboo ritual, Buryatia, 2008. Photo by the author.

ones not actively involved in any kind of religious practice. Many, especially those who reside outside Buryatia, time their summer vacations
to correspond with these events. During the months of May and June,
Buryats come back to their native villages to attend the ritual and reconnect with numerous relatives. While oboo rituals can be performed
by shamans and knowledgeable elders, here I focus on the rituals performed by Buddhist lamas (see fig.8).

The lama is supposed to perform a certain tantric visualization,
generating himself as the wrathful buddha Yamāntaka or the wrathful bodhisattva Vajrapāṇi, and then, as Yamāntaka or Vajrapāṇi, ad-
dress land master spirits, asking them for protection, help in worldly
affairs, and various blessings. People attending the ritual bring copious
offerings of various foods and drinks, which are offered to the deities
according to an established ritual scenario and are consumed during
the communal feast that follows while the remains of sacrificed foods
are taken home and given to the relatives and friends who were not
able to attend. It is widely believed that successful oboo rituals bring
rain, much needed during the usually dry months of May and June. Yet
what happens if a ritual fails? During the summer of 2008, when I was

in Buryatia, June was extremely dry despite all the oboo rituals that had been performed.

The pro-Tibetan faction immediately declared that the oboo rituals performed by Buryat lamas had failed because they had made the *wrong* kinds of offerings, offerings that were not considered to correspond to "true" Buddhism. Meat and alcohol as food sacrifice became the most contested issues in this debate. Personal consumption and ritual consumption of meat and alcohol have always been controversial in Buddhism and vary widely between different schools and national traditions. As far as monastic rules go, while alcohol is explicitly prohibited in the early vinaya, meat eating is not prohibited as long as the animal was not slaughtered to feed the monk.[26] Despite the fact that there is no direct prohibition of the use of meat in early sources, there is a contemporary tendency to view those who abstain from meat as "better Buddhists," particularly widespread in modernized and Western interpretations of the "nonviolence" doctrine.[27] Although offerings to wrathful deities, both in Tibet and Mongolia, typically include meat and alcohol, some modernist Buryats seem unaware that the practice exists in those places and think of it as only a *Buryat* tradition that somehow perverted more authentic forms of Buddhism due to the influence of native shamanism. This particular construction of Buddhist authenticity built on an imagined earlier, purer version recently provoked controversy regarding the ritual use of meat and vodka in Buryatia (including animal sacrifice in shamanic rituals). Oboo rituals, especially notorious for the copious amounts of vodka brought, offered as libations, poured on the ground, and consumed in what often turns into a post-oboo ritual drunken revelry as soon as the presiding lamas leave, became the highest stake in this debate.[28]

"When Bakula Rinpoche, a famous Buddhist master from India, came here, he was stunned to see all this vodka poured into the ground. He said, 'Look, your spirits are all drunk! No wonder you cannot get any help from them. How can a drunken spirit help anyone?'"

26. Tibetan monasteries never served any food to monks, other than tea and tsampa. In the Indian Drepung, this is still the case, except that they now also serve noodles, rice, vegetables, and yogurt. Meat is not proscribed, however: monks who have the means to buy it from local vendors sometimes cook it in their dormitory kitchens.

27. For an informative overview of the various Buddhist attitudes to vegetarianism, see Harvey 2000: 156–165.

28. In a similar fashion, Ravina Aggarwal described the controversy between the Ladakh Buddhist Association, a reformist youth Buddhist organization, and Ladakhi villagers, over the use of *chang* (barley beer) during ritual occasions (2001: 558–561). Earlier, Appadurai referred to such conflicts as *gastro-politics* (1981).

FIGURE 9. Oboo offerings, Buryatia, 2008. Photo by the author.

one Buryat Buddhist lama related to me.[29] Similarly, a Buryat nun who currently lives in India commented that when she attended such an oboo ritual, she had a vision, in which she was able to communicate with the land master spirit to whom the offerings were being made. "The spirit told me that he had been a vegetarian since Buddhism was established in this area; however, no one had brought him his favorite cottage cheese [Rus. *tvorog*] for a long time. The spirit complained that all they brought him was meat, which he did not eat." The spirit asked the nun to kindly call her relatives who were going to attend an oboo during this season and make sure that the rules of vegetarianism be more strictly followed.[30]

29. The late Bakula Rinpoche, a prominent incarnate Buddhist lama from Ladakh in northern India, worked as a minister for the Indian government under Indira Gandhi. In 1990, he had been appointed an Indian ambassador to Mongolia, which enabled him to visit the USSR and later, postsocialist Buryatia.

30. One can trace these ideas to the fact that this Buryat nun, who had been living in Dharamsala, India, for several years during my visit in 2008, was influenced by the modernized Buddhism widespread in the Tibetan exile communities. The scene that she described happened during one of her visits to Buryatia. It is through cosmopolitan Buryat travelers like her that what has been called "modern Buddhism" (Lopez 2002a) is making its way into local rituals.

The "anti-Tibetan" faction represented by some lamas whom I interviewed during this period, however, insisted that offering meat and alcohol was a "Buryat tradition." They claimed that, unlike shamanist oboos, what they offer is not "really" vodka, but a special substance referred to as "nectar," into which vodka is transformed through appropriate prayers and visualizations.[31] The real reason for the failure of the ritual, they claimed, was that local spirits would not "take instructions" from "foreigners" (Tibetans) who tried to meddle in their affairs. (The obstacles here to the performance and efficacy of the ritual are constructed specifically in blood kinship terms as opposed to those of spirits' linguistic competence, since the ritual is always conducted in classical Tibetan.) Interestingly, the Tibetan incarnate lamas with Buryat "roots" discussed above are perhaps the only ones who have been somewhat exempt from these accusations, because, according to the Buddhist view of kinship, they "are" Buryat via their quasi-kinship relationship with their respective Buryat predecessors.

Indeed, the ability to establish peaceful relationships with local spirits is central to any lama's legitimacy in Buryatia, both Buryat and foreign alike. When Zhibalha Rinpoche, another Tibetan lama with Buryat "roots" mentioned earlier in this chapter, visited Buryatia and the Aga region in 2004 (the native region of his previous incarnation), the elders informed him of the lack of rainfall. He conducted several offerings to local spirits on the mountaintop and near the river, and within a couple of days there was a heavy downpour. "I felt that the local spirits [Tib. *yul lha, gzhi bdag*] were favorably inclined to me," he said when I interviewed him in his residence in Drepung Gomang in India in 2008.[32] Buryat elders also took Zhibalha's capacity to pacify the local spirits to be a sign of his legitimacy to act as a lama in Buryatia. Thus, his journey has been locally understood as a visit not by a foreign lama but by a "Buryat" lama finally arriving in his "homeland."[33] While Zhibalha Rinpoche (who still resides in Drepung Gomang and visited Buryatia only once) is still relatively unknown to the wider Buryat public, Yelo Rinpoche is a very public figure, and his every step is subject to scrutiny.[34]

31. Although lamas invoke this fact as a "Buryat tradition," this is true for Tibetan Buddhist tantric ritual in general.

32. Interview with Zhibalha Rinpoche, Drepung Gomang Monastery, India, January 2008.

33. Ibid.

34. Interestingly, Zhibalha Rinpoche became a key figure in the Buddhist revival in Tuva, regularly visiting the Tuvan Republic since 2004. His "Buryat" connection is very important for Tuvans, who also view him as "ours" (Ksenia Pimenova, personal communication, 2011). Al-

Thus, exempt from blame on the oboo front, Yelo Rinpoche was still reproached by his detractors for doing too many "flashy" tantric empowerments as opposed to the unglamorous work of spreading the dharma through regular teachings. However, since there are currently no Buddhist teachers of such high status in Buryatia, with all the appropriate initiations (a lama must have received an initiation in order to confer it), Yelo Rinpoche remains the most qualified lama for these empowerments. As mentioned above, Kentrul Rinpoche from India, another incarnate lama with Buryat "roots," was surprised by how many people approached him to conduct empowerments when he visited Buryatia. Since empowerment rituals structure the Buddhist community in kin-like ways (Mills 2000), I suggest that these lamas are sought out by Buryats not only because they are internationally renowned and qualified masters, but also because by acquiring these Tibetan lamas as their symbolic kin, Buryats also reclaim and reincorporate their own past masters into the current body politic. In other words, these incarnate Tibetan lamas with "Buryat roots" are in particularly high demand in Buryatia not only for their "reproductive" ritual capacity, but also because of their connection via the institutions of discipleship and reincarnation with their Buryat predecessors. Yelo and Kentrul Rinpoches' bodies serve not only as the crucial links in bringing Buryats into the new transnational and pan-Asian "vajra families," forging post-Soviet religious ties and transforming geopolitical imaginaries; these bodies also reconnect Buryat believers with specifically Buryat key religious personalities of the past. [35]

Due to their extraordinary status, incarnate lamas' presence blurs the lines of political and ethnic alliances. Despite being an ethnic Tibetan, the present Kentrul Rinpoche, by virtue of being a reincarnation of a Buryat monk, has become a key site for Buryat self-fashioning. Not only was he the only Buryat to preside over a famous Tibetan monastic college, he mastered the process of death and rebirth to be reincarnated outside of Chinese-occupied Tibet in order to eventually engineer his "return" to Buryatia, relinking ordinary Buryats with Buddhist deities.

---

though Tuvans are a Turkic group with strong Mongolian influences, Zhibalha himself (similarly to other Tibetan lamas familiar with the Buddhist peoples of the Russian Federation) believes Buryats, Kalmyks, and Tuvans to be "people of Mongolian ethnicity" (Tib. *sog po mi rig*) (interview with Zhibalha 2008). Since 2008, he has been residing in Tuva for half a year and regularly visiting Buryatia.

35. Cf. also Caroline Humphrey's idea of postsocialist reincarnations in Mongolia as a type of "embodiment," theorized as a form of engagement with the past, where people or actions in the present are identified with those of the past, even though they may not look similar (Humphrey 1992).

Incarnation here emerges as an empowering technology for mobility and border crossing. It also reveals a particular kind of sovereign body that is able to control the processes of both death and rebirth as well as more mundane state-imposed restrictions of mobility. In the case of Yelo Rinpoche, who is an apprentice of not one, but three Buryat lamas,[36] this link emerges from the Buddhist institution of the master-disciple relationship, which creates kin-like structures between the master and his disciples through tantric ritual. In this context, it is inevitable that these bodies have become important sites for competing ideas of religious and cultural sovereignty. While some proponents of Buryat autocephality resent these lamas' superior status and consider it detrimental to indigenous self-determination, others view them as "ours," descendants of the great Buryat lamas Galsan Legden and Thupten Nyima, who transcended both death and Soviet and Chinese controls of mobility only to reemerge in postsocialist Buryatia to renovate the religion in these troubled times.

Indeed, some twenty years after the collapse of socialism, the return of the dead is what seems to dominate social life in Buryatia. Some famous dead people have come back in the form of monuments and memorials, while others are believed to have returned in the flesh; yet others reappear as disembodied spirits to haunt the living. In the Buryat context, coming back in the flesh is made possible by specific Buddhist techniques of the body, namely, reincarnation and tantric discipleship, which allow the blurring of identities, the compression of times and spaces, and the crossing of a variety of boundaries, from those of nation-states to those between life and death. Besides these technologies for cultural reproduction that are characteristically Buddhist, other ways in which the Buryat dead reappear are a particular mix of postsocialist and Buddhist necropolitics. In the next chapter, I investigate another case of the dead returning in the flesh, setting in motion a particular chain of events whereby not only dead bodies, but also sacred objects literally begin to spring from the depths of the earth.

36. As a young boy in Litang, Yelo Rinpoche received basic Buddhist instruction from Zhibalha Rinpoche. He also received teachings from Agvan Nyima at the Indian Drepung Monastery (interview, 2001, Ulan-Ude).

THREE

The Post-Soviet Treasure Hunt: New Sacred Histories and Geographies

"You should not have come back here," the Khambo Lama Dashi-Dorzho Itigelov is reported to have said to Agvan Dorzhiev around 1921.[1] "You should have stayed abroad. Soon they will start arresting lamas. If they capture you, you will not get out of it alive." "What about you, why don't you go abroad yourself?" Agvan Dorzhiev asked him. "No need for this: they will not manage to capture me," Itigelov replied (see fig. 10).

As he himself predicted, Itigelov did not live to see the mass arrests of 1937, the deadliest year of Stalinist repressions, the year when Agvan Dorzhiev perished in prison and Bazar Baradiin was shot on the day of his trial. Instead, ten years earlier, in 1927, the Khambo Lama sat in a lotus position and asked his disciples to read a special prayer for the dead on his behalf. The disciples were at first reluctant to read this prayer while their master was still alive, but Itigelov insisted. This incident already starts to tell us about the remarkable ease in crossing not only state borders, but also the boundaries between life and death that many Buryat Buddhist adepts considered here have thus far demonstrated. "Come visit my body in thirty

1. As introduced earlier, Dashi-Dorzho Itigelov (1852–1927) was the last Khambo Lama elected during the time of the Russian empire (elected in 1911, stepped down in 1917).

FIGURE 10. Dashi-Dorzho Itigelov. Photo courtesy of the Archives of the Center of Oriental Manuscripts and Xylographs of the Institute for Mongolian, Tibetan, and Buddhist Studies of the Siberian Branch of the Russian Academy of Sciences.

years," he advised his distraught disciples and passed away (Dondokov 2002a, 2002b).

In September 2002, the body of Dashi-Dorzho Itigelov was exhumed for the third time. While the first two exhumations, which allegedly took place in 1955 and 1973, were held in secret (the body was exhumed, checked, and then reburied), this one was a media event performed in the presence of lamas, journalists, and forensic experts.

As expected by the lamas, the body did not decompose. The lamas installed the body in a glass case in the Ivolginsk Monastery, which very soon became an international and domestic sensation, with articles appearing in the *New York Times* and with Russian politicians and oligarchs rubbing shoulders with droves of pilgrims and tourists to catch a glimpse of the lama.

While Itigelov is perhaps the best-known lama kept under glass after his return to the land of the living, similar exhumations were performed for most of the previous Khambo Lamas, although no other "incorruptible" bodies were found. Instead, subsequent excavations revealed various objects, such as Buddhist ritual implements referred to as "treasures" (Rus. *sokrovishcha*) and accorded revelatory status. Treasures were found in places as diverse as ruins of former monasteries and remote areas of the forest. Sometimes such findings would trigger other miraculous events, such as the appearance of religious imagery in natural phenomena, accompanied by visions and prophesies. What all these phenomena had in common was their perceived connection to certain charismatic Buddhist personalities of the past: for example, the treasures would spring up near their former places of residence or supposed burial. Furthermore, in the local object ideology, the treasures were believed to have a certain kind of agency in the sense that they "chose" when to reveal themselves. Not only was Itigelov believed to have "come back," but also statues, books, lamps, and other attributes pertaining to religious life were thought to have "returned." In this chapter, I propose to examine this hunt for treasures as a kind of postsocialist *necropolitics* that aims to reconsecrate the post-Soviet landscape and create renovated cosmologies of time and space. I argue that, for participants, this effectively shifts the locus of "authentic" Buddhism from India and Tibet to contemporary Buryatia, strengthening assertions of cultural sovereignty.

Various objects such as relics of famous monks, auspicious images found on rocks, and ritual implements interred during Soviet times create new sacred geographies and historiographies. These recent geoimaginary formations serve to inscribe Buddhism physically into the land, as evidenced in the continuing search for and discoveries of treasures. Given that treasures are believed to be objects with a certain kind of *agency*, defined here in its primary philosophical sense as the capacity to act in the world, Buddhists approach these objects as potential expressions of past intentions, such as those of previous lamas. Translating these emic beliefs into the language of anthropological theory, one can say that treasure objects possess what Alfred Gell called "distributed personhood," where the object is viewed as an extension of a person (Gell 1998: 21; cf. Strathern 1990 on partible persons). Gell provides us with a famous example of one of Pol Pot's soldiers who distributes elements of his own agency in the form of land mines, and Gell argues that the mines present an example of a "second-class agency which artefacts acquire once they become enmeshed in a texture of social relationships" (1998: 17). Nonetheless, Gell makes a clear distinction between the "primary intentional agents" (humans) and their "secondary artefactual forms" (objects) (21). Buddhists, on the other hand, who already seem to have their own object ideology in place, locate agency in the space between the deeds of enlightened beings and the capacity of the devout to perceive them. Buddhist treasure objects—in particular, relics, which in this case include both the actual physical remains of a prominent lama and objects that came in contact with him—are invested with some of the intentionality of their owners. While some Buddhist elites have instrumentalized the treasures to strengthen their own political platforms, the pursuit of buried treasures has been important for many in Buryatia in being seen as part of their effort to move from a position of marginality in the Buddhist world to one of greater prominence, and to strengthen sovereignty claims within the Russian Federation and in the transnational Tibetan world.

During my field research I came across many kinds of treasures. They can be classified by type (ritual object, text, body) or by their location (ruins of former monasteries, caves, forest, hollows of trees). Some were "anonymous" in the sense that, at the time of their discovery, their importance was unclear. The treasures that gained great national fame were those linked to the agency of famous Buddhist personalities believed to have predetermined their appearances. While Itigelov's body is viewed by many as the ultimate repository of Buryat Buddhist sovereignty, in more specific ways the stories of his multiple incarnations and reincarnations authenticate a direct transmission of Buddhism from India to Buryatia, lengthening Buryat religious history and creating new ways to conceptualize time. Other discoveries reorder space, as evidenced by the discovery of a ritual object related to the famous lama Soodoi, which, as I will explain, transformed one of the most remote "shamanic" Buryat regions into a prominent pan-Buryat and, arguably, international Buddhist pilgrimage site. Finally, ruins, a particular kind of place in the midst of which treasures often "reveal" themselves, become dramatic instances of places that condense temporalities with crucial links not only to the past but also to the future.

Timeline Reedited

Scholars of socialism have observed that many post-Soviet historical re-visions reveal an interesting conception of time in which history may be visualized as a timeline that can be edited, with certain time periods snipped and discarded, while other, disparate periods, such as the pre-communist 1900s and postcommunist 1990s, can be "pasted" together. Such excisions go beyond simply emphasizing one period over another and reveal a new understanding of time as no longer fixed and irrevers-ible (Verdery 1999: 112–116). In a similar vein, many Buryat religious adepts now view the Soviet period as nothing but a brief intermission in the otherwise triumphant Buddhist march northward, often citing the Tibetan example of Buddhist decline during the ninth and tenth centuries. While this might seem to be a linear progression, on a larger scale postsocialist Buryats reject the linear timeline of socialist progress in favor of a more cyclical, messianic conception of time, viewed as an alternation of global Buddhist declines and revivals, advents and departures of various buddhas—most commonly, the "historical" Bud-dha is viewed as the fourth, while the fifth one, Buddha Maitreya, is eagerly awaited—as well as births and deaths of prominent enlightened beings.[2] The socialist suppression of Buddhism in Buryatia is viewed as part of this cyclical trajectory. Excisions of time produce what Erik Mueggler called an "oppositional practice of time" that undermines of-ficial temporalities (Mueggler 2001: 7).[3]

"Have you heard that there was only one single monk left in Tibet for almost two centuries?" one Buryat monk questioned me. "And yet they recovered. We only had seventy years of atheism and suppression, and some of our lamas survived the purges. We *will* recover. Many to-day blame us for not being what proper monks ought to be. In that sense, we are not really monks, we are builders. A foundation should be laid before proper Buddhism can take off. We are just the ones who cre-ate the necessary conditions [Rus. *predposylki*] for the future." This self-presentation by monks as "builders" and not "proper monks" is worth pausing over, since it displays a particular politics of time advanced by postsocialist Buryats in response to challenges from the transnational Buddhist establishment. Buryats' international coreligionists often

2. See Nattier 1991 for other ways of counting the Buddhas.
3. See Makley 2007: 96–97 for the application of this notion in another Tibetan Buddhist context.

look down on them for having a "corrupt" version of Buddhism. The Geluk school of Tibetan Buddhism, established in Buryatia in the early eighteenth century, is based on celibate monasticism. However, for various reasons beyond the scope of this chapter, celibate monasticism never took root either in Mongolia or Buryatia, and its lack presents the greatest challenge to Buryat Buddhist legitimacy; they must "catch up" in order to reach an ideal state of Buddhist development. Many contemporary Buddhists blame the Soviet period for this state of affairs, producing this distancing discourse that is a curious inversion of the characteristic Soviet discourse of time and development.

In a recent work, Susan Buck-Morss argued that the Russian Revolution challenged the notion of space (territory) as the single determinant of sovereignty and produced a discourse of time, which in socialist states became a distinctive arena for the exercise of sovereign power (2000: 38). The revolution was understood as an advance in time, supposed to conquer backwardness, reversing the European geopolitical understanding of history as "space over time." As Lenin famously proclaimed in 1918, commenting on his willingness to sign the treaty of Brest-Litovsk, which ceded Ukraine to the Germans, "I want to concede space . . . in order to win time" (Buck-Morss 2000: 24). Space was for socialist regimes only a means to an end: the territorial isolation provided a possibility to "catch up" with the industrial West. In Stalin's famous iteration, what had taken Western Europe one hundred and fifty years the USSR had to cover in just ten. While everyone in Russia had to speed up time, "tearing along on the fast locomotive of history," indigenous peoples in particular had to "race like the wind," skipping entire historical eras (conceptualized as evolutionary stages in the development of mankind) in order to emerge from their "backwardness" into socioeconomic modernization (Slezkine 1994: 200).

This formula, Buck-Morss notes, was somewhat reversed in the latter years of socialism, when indigenous peoples started questioning Soviet logics of sovereignty. These claims fashioned alternative discourses of time in which Soviet modernization was judged as reckless and destructive for both the environment and native cultures (Buck-Morss 2000: 39). While many former Soviet republics advanced their claims to sovereignty on a territorial basis, that was impossible in Buryatia, where by the fall of the Soviet Union Buryats were outnumbered by the Russian majority, constituting only 24% of the population.[4] Although

4. According to the Russian census of 2010, the percentage of Buryats in the Republic of Buryatia grew to 29.5%. Analysts quote two reasons for this increase: the out-migration of Rus-

Buryat elites seem to have abandoned the idea of political sovereignty in the early 1990s (Hamayon 2002), assertions of cultural sovereignty—understood as self-determination, rights to land and resources, language preservation, and the more general desire to be fully in control over their own cultural politics—are increasingly vital in this age of Russian authoritarian revival and centralization of power.

For many religious leaders and adepts, such sovereignty hinges on their Buddhist religion, which many view as the most important indigenous heritage. While Buddhism has been officially recognized as one of Russia's four official religions, international recognition of Buryat Buddhism as a distinctive tradition has lagged due to Buryats' marginalized position within the transnational Tibetan Buddhist world, which often regards them as "backward" Buddhists steeped in superstition and shamanism. This lack of recognition in the transnational arena, in turn, undermines Buryats' claims to cultural sovereignty within the Russian Federation. It is in response to these challenges, I suggest, that Buryats developed a distinctive practice of time to advance and justify their assertions of religious and cultural autonomy. It is similar to pre-revolutionary socialist discourse in that it acknowledges its own "backwardness" ("we are not proper monks"), although the desired ideal is no longer that of modernization but that of "traditional" Buddhist societies (often associated with Geluk celibate clergy). Yet the blame for this backwardness is placed on the "communists," who impeded Buryat Buddhist development at the peak of its glorious age in the early twentieth century. To "catch up" in time therefore requires spatial isolation and the exclusion of more established "foreign" religious traditions.

This discourse also emphasizes a radical shift in spatial arrangements of the Buddhist world in general. The phenomenon of treasures is locally viewed as proof that, with time, the Buddhist center of gravity will move north to Buryatia and Mongolia as Tibetan Buddhism is marginalized due to the unfavorable conditions for Buddhists in Chinese Tibet and exile settlements in India. In other words, given time for development, world Buddhism will be *recentered*.[5] These geoimaginary formations are materialized through the agency of objects that began bursting forth from the earth, thus grounding these seemingly abstract space-time cosmologies.

---

sians and the in-migration of Buryats from the former autonomous Aginskii and Ust'-Ordynskii Okrugs into the republic (Anonymous 2012).

5. This observation is inspired by Katherine Verdery's analysis of "recentering" of world Christianity (1999: 55–95).

The fact that my ethnographic consultants were inclined to think in these specific historical terms prompted me to consider the history of the decline and revival of Buddhism in medieval Tibet. At first glance this seems an unlikely intertext for postsocialist Buryatia, but a closer look at some of the interpretations of that period convinced me that following my Buryat interlocutors in thinking about this geographically and historically remote case might provide an insight into the transformations of time and space in contemporary Siberia. When my monk interlocutor drew a parallel between the current Buryat Buddhist revival and the similar period in medieval Tibet, what I found most striking was the prominence in the latter of the Tibetan "treasure" movement, which also emerged during a renaissance following a period of decline. What specific forces propel these objects to emerge from the ground during periods of religious renovation?

The Deepening of History

Analyzing the rebirth and reformation of Tibetan Buddhism after the catastrophic collapse of the Tibetan empire in the ninth century, Buddhist studies scholar Ronald Davidson (2005) raises the question of how it is that Tibet, until then an extremely peripheral place in the Buddhist world, managed to displace India itself as the source of ideal Buddhist practice and become a premiere destination of pilgrims from much of Eurasia, as well as Indians themselves. Davidson focuses on the several centuries of cultural flow among Tibet, India, China, and the Mongols in the period known as the "Tibetan renaissance" (950–1200 CE) and unravels how complex historical interactions between Tibetan indigenous spirituality and innovations brought from the more developed Buddhist countries resulted in development of what is now taken for granted as "original" Tibetan Buddhism. Especially interesting in relation to the Buryat situation are the indigenization strategies adopted by Nyingma (literally, "ancient"), the tradition of Buddhism dominant in Tibet before its collapse. Faced with the challenge of the new religious influences that inundated Tibet during the renaissance period, the older school employed particular strategies of authenticity that simultaneously allowed for a production of new religious forms while linking them to imperial legacies and lineages (Davidson 2005: 210–244). The most distinctive feature of the Nyingma school is the tradition of "treasure texts" (Tib. *gter ma*), texts believed to have been written at an earlier time but buried underground until the time to reveal them has come, like time-release capsules guided by destiny. The discovery events are believed to be predetermined by the concealer of the treasures and are performed by a particular kind of religious practitioner known as a "treasure discoverer" (Tib. *gter ston*), who then "translates" them into forms comprehensible to his contemporaries.

Treasure texts are usually seen by scholars to be a strategy for producing new legitimate indigenous texts while avoiding the conundrum of mandatory Indic origin for all authentic Buddhist scriptures (Gyatso 1993). Texts, however, should be viewed in relation to other kinds of treasures (hoards of precious materials buried during the time of unrest) commonly found at Tibetan imperial sites during the time of Tibetan renaissance, such as statues, bones, and ritual implements (Davidson 2005: 213).[6] As the Tibetan popular imaginary came to conceive of the empire as the golden age, the link between the found treasures and fascination with old dynastic realms became a major, additional source of legitimacy. With the end of the Cultural Revolution in China in 1976 and the start of the revival of Tibetan Buddhism, the treasure movement has also been revitalized by the contemporary Nyingma leaders in present-day eastern Tibet, as artifacts and scriptures have started appearing during excavations of ruined temples (Germano 1998).[7]

As I perused these accounts of imperial collapses, religious declines and revivals, and border crossings, I was struck by their resonance with present-day Buryatia. The Buryats' own hunt for treasures such as relics, ritual objects, and texts buried during the Soviet times relates the present to the imperial past, especially the golden age of Buryat Buddhism believed to have been achieved under the late Russian empire, when many important indigenous intellectuals and religious leaders came to prominence. Similar to the "old" school that, viewing itself as a legitimate heir to the glorious imperial Buddhist period, launched the treasure movement in medieval Tibet, in Buryatia the organization that claims legitimacy from the golden age of Buryat Buddhism—viewed by many as the early years of the twentieth century—is the Buddhist Traditional Sangha of Russia, henceforth referred to as "the Sangha." Just

---

6. Gyatso notes that, with time, the reasons for concealment had changed: rather than trying simply to protect the texts from present adverse conditions, the concealers of treasures refocused their concern on the future times of hardship, when these teachings would be particularly needed (1996: 152).

7. See also Terrone 2008 for a more recent account of contemporary treasure revealers in Tibet.

like the Nyingma school, which felt threatened by the new influences coming directly from India, the Sangha feels endangered by the modern Tibetan currents coming to Buryatia through traveling Tibetan lamas and Buryat pilgrims and monks visiting India. Tellingly, it was the Sangha that launched the postsocialist Buryat treasure hunt.[8]

One important difference between Tibetan treasures, or *terma*, and Buryat treasures is that terma were believed to be hidden by an Indian master: in this sense they are not really "indigenous," but a case of magically discovering a foreign source in the native soil. In Buryatia, however, treasures are connected to famous local lamas. Still, the Indian connection is of utmost importance, and, as will be shown, it is usually produced through viewing these local Buryat saints as incarnations of Indian masters. What both Tibetan and Buryat treasures also have in common is that upon their discovery both are viewed as if they were meant to be found at that particular time, and therefore are accorded revelatory status.[9] Similar to terma, Buryat treasures are believed to act as time-delayed mechanisms that activate during particularly "dark" times to deliver messages from the past. Specifically, in Buryatia, the agency of these treasures manifests itself as calls to action related to the spread and revival of Buddhism in a particular area. For example, if a treasure is found at a particular time at the ruins of former monasteries, these monasteries then get restored in an extremely efficient manner. Treasures are also often found near the former residences of particularly significant religious personalities of the past, near important shamanic sites or areas that, for one reason or another, are not yet controlled by the Sangha. The treasure finds not only signal that the time for restoration is ripe but also serve to authenticate new religious institutions through their physical link to the past. In what follows, I demonstrate how these treasures serve as an important factor in the Sangha's consolidation of power, as it attempts to bring the whole of Buryatia under its control, reawaken the faith lost under socialism, and assert the authenticity of Buryat spirituality.

8. Here it must be noted that the Sangha does not intentionally imitate strategies employed by the Nyingma school, and they do not make this connection. My point is that Buryats found a way to produce new legitimate sacred objects and sites in a structurally similar context of religious revival, as new strategies of authentication are being developed.

9. Another interesting parallel is that the phenomenon of Tibetan treasures came into full flower after the demise of Buddhism in India. That is, it was no longer possible to go to the source to retrieve the dharma, so the foreign source was discovered "at home," much as Buryats found treasures in Buryatia after the possibility of going to Tibet was lost. Also, just as Indian masters went to Tibet to escape Muslim persecution, so, too, are Tibetan lamas "escaping" to Buryatia.

Itigelov Comes to the Rescue

Much has changed in Buryat Buddhism since the exhumation of Itigelov's body in 2002. First, a popular cult immediately developed around his body. Itigelov is believed to grant one's most intimate wishes and instantaneously correct one's karma. It is said that diseases are healed upon touching his hands, and people are reported to have left their crutches at the temple. He has been compared to the famous room in the Zone depicted in Andrei Tarkovskii's film *Stalker* (adapted from the novel by Boris and Arkadii Strugatskii)—a place everyone is trying to reach, where only one's deepest subconscious desires are fulfilled. Pessimists worry that all sorts of unbalanced persons and "saviors of humanity" might try to abuse Itigelov's powers. These anxieties are compounded by paranoid fears that either the Kremlin or a mad scientist in search of the Nobel Prize for understanding immortality might buy or steal Itigelov's body. Until recently, it was held on the second floor of the main temple at Ivolginsk and was brought into the main temple area on major Buddhist holidays. During other times, temple visitors could touch a thread tied to his body that descended through the ceiling. In 2008, a new temple called the Palace of Itigelov opened, and it is now considered his residence. The construction of this palace, which started in 2003, is referred to as "people's construction" (Rus. *narodnaia stroika*), since it was built with private donations and volunteer labor (Basaev 2008).

While for most believers Itigelov's body is a vehicle of hope and enthusiasm, for the Sangha it became a new foundation of its legitimacy, which especially strengthened the institution of the Khambo Lamas.[10] To make sense of this phenomenon, let us take a closer look at the history of the Sangha. Although it claims to be heir to the Buryat Buddhist golden age, technically the Sangha is a successor to the Central Spiritual Board of Buddhists (Rus. *Tsentral'noe dukhovnoe upravlenie buddistov*), a Soviet-era organization formed in 1922 and reorganized in 1946. During the early 1990s, when Buddhist structures began to be reestablished in Buryatia, Munko Tsybikov, a lama from the older generation

---

10. My understanding of these issues has benefited from discussions with Nikolai Tsyrempilov, who used the Weberian idea of "routinized charisma" to juxtapose the authority of elected Khambo Lamas to the "pure charisma" of reincarnated lamas (Tsyrempilov, personal communication, 2004; Weber 1933 [1922]). Justine Buck Quijada further develops these ideas (2009: 189–190).

of Buddhists who was imprisoned in Stalin's camps, was elected the Khambo Lama. After his death, the Board of Buddhists was ridden with conflicts, with two Khambo Lamas in four years elected and then dismissed due to their "unsuitability to the office held" (Zhukovskaia 1997: 10). In 1995, a conflict arose among the Buddhist clergy when Khambo Lama Choi-Dorzhi Budaev was removed from office on charges of embezzlement. In his place, a little-known young lama, Damba Aiusheev, a former physical education teacher who had subsequently studied in Mongolia to become a lama, was elected the Twenty-Fourth Khambo Lama and the head of the Board of Buddhists (see fig. 11).

At first, no one expected this inexperienced but eager lama to keep his office for more than a few years. At this time also the Board of Buddhists' authority was being greatly undermined among lay Buryats by widespread corruption and financial scandals. The 1990s were characterized by public disillusionment with the behavior of the Buddhist clergy, which diminished the lamas' authority and led to widespread rumors about their inappropriate behavior. For example, the belief in the immortal soul that can leave the body at will, widespread among Buryats, is often criticized by more orthodox Buddhists as a shamanic

FIGURE 11. Khambo Lama Damba Aiusheev, Ivolginsk Monastery, 2008. Photo by the author.

"superstition," and one story warned believers against selling their last possessions to visit the monastery only to be told by a moody lama that his or her soul had "jumped out" (Rus. *vyskochila*) of the body. Another told of a lama who hit a grandmother on the head with a dry sausage (Rus. *kolbasa*, akin to a salami) instead of touching her head in blessing.[11] By the late 1990s, Buryat Buddhism needed not only a new leader, but also entirely new grounds for legitimacy.

Once elected, Aiusheev took all the monasteries under his personal financial control and began rebuilding monasteries and stupas all over Buryatia. Even his most vocal opponents, in interviews with me, admitted that not only had he proved himself an excellent *khoziaistvennik* (Rus. for "executive manager") and *prorab* (Rus. for "construction site supervisor"), but he was also merciless in fighting corruption and embezzlement. Aiusheev reformed the Board of Buddhists and changed its name to the Buddhist Traditional Sangha of Russia, which became legitimated as the main organization representing Buddhism in Russia. Subsequently, a schism (Rus. *raskol*) occurred in Buryat Buddhism, as several Buddhist communities declared their withdrawal from the Sangha and elected an alternative organ, which claimed the older name of Board of Buddhists. Lama Nimazhap Iliukhinov was then elected the head of that board, which conferred on him the title of Khambo Lama. Thus, there appeared two different Khambo Lamas in Buryatia. In addition, in 1998 the Khambo Lama Aiusheev entered a protracted confrontation with Buryatia's government (see Bernstein 2002a, on the conflict over the so-called Atlas of Tibetan Medicine). Tibetan lamas began leaving Buryat monasteries and opening their own temples, attracting large local followings.

By 2002, when Itigelov was exhumed, the reputation of Aiusheev and the Sangha had been significantly compromised, and the future of Buryat Buddhism was increasingly uncertain. The discovery of Itigelov, however, would soon radically reverse this situation. Why did his body produce such a dramatic difference in the Sangha's status? Writing about the circulation of relics in medieval Europe, Patrick Geary notes that relics, which he refers to as "person-objects," are high-prestige items that served as tools for creating community identity, status, and central ecclesiastical control. Smaller monasteries competed fiercely to

---

11. The touching of the head is a standard Buddhist blessing in classical Buddhist contexts determined by the rank of the believer. In pre-Chinese Tibet, while lamas touched high-rank believers' heads with both hands, less important people received a blessing with one hand or a finger, and they touched those of the lowest status with a short stick with colored ribbons.

get certain relics due to the enormous benefits they brought in terms of revenue, prestige, and pilgrimage traffic. The exchange of relics established bonds between givers and receivers, particularly relationships of dependency and subordination (Geary 1986). Below I demonstrate how Itigelov's body began to redefine relations between the Sangha and other Buddhist organizations in Russia.

Beyond its legitimacy problems in Buryatia proper, the status of the Buddhist Traditional Sangha of Russia headed by Aiusheev has been highly contested throughout Russia. First, the Sangha includes mostly Buryats, but not all Buryat Buddhist communities. Second, other "ethnic" Buddhists prefer to have their own, independent *sanghas*. For example, Kalmyk and Tuvan Buddhists do not officially recognize the sovereignty of the Sangha. However, the Sangha's possession of Itigelov's body is subtly pushing these relationships from equality toward subordination. For a case in point, in 2009 the president of Kalmykia, Kirsan Iliumzhinov, asked to "borrow" Itigelov's body for the celebration of the four hundred years of Kalmykia's "voluntary annexation" (Rus. *prisoedinenie*) to Russia. Iliumzhinov argued that Kalmyk believers also wanted to worship Itigelov but could not travel thousands of miles to Buryatia to do so. The Sangha "politely declined" this request, as reported in a Buryat newspaper article under the poignant title "Nevyezdnoi Itigelov" (Rus. *nevyezdnoi*, literally "banned from travel," a Soviet-era term often applied to dissidents denied foreign visas) (Makhachkeev 2009b)[12]. Furthermore, today the Sangha is the only Buddhist organization that has a direct relationship to the president of Russia's administration. Aiusheev is the only Buddhist representative at the Interreligious Council of Russia in Moscow and a member of the Public Chamber of the Russian Federation.[13] That the Sangha now possesses Itigelov is an example of how such person-objects work to structure social relationships and hierarchies, in this case mediating rivalry between the two Sanghas.

While the Sangha's deployment of Itigelov to boost its legitimacy is hotly debated in the republic, I do not wish to describe this phenomenon exclusively in strategic terms. Aiusheev's devotion to Itigelov is no different from that of ordinary citizens. A monk close to the Khambo

12. Aleksandr Makhachkeev is a journalist for a local weekly newspaper *Inform-Polis* who often covers Buddhist issues in the republic.

13. The Interreligious Council, an important organization for interreligious dialogue created in 1998, includes leaders of Russia's four traditional religions. It works to develop relations between the government, religious groups, and society.

Lama told me that Soviet atheism dies hard even among lamas. But thanks to Itigelov, he contended, the Khambo Lama has become a believer, perhaps for the first time in his life. As he has gained piety he seems also to have gained confidence. "Ha, no one criticizes us anymore," Aiusheev said to me with his usual mischievous smile, when I stopped by his residence at the Ivolginsk Monastery one day. "They respect us. Or maybe they are afraid. Either way, no one dares anymore to say anything against us. And you know why? Because Itigelov won't forgive them." Indeed, shortly after Itigelov was found and established, after many years of bitter conflict, the president of Buryatia for the first time paid a visit to Ivolginsk Monastery. Around the same time Aiusheev paid his first visit to the Ministry of the Interior of Buryatia to reconcile with the "people in uniforms" (Makhachkeev 2004b).[14] Did Itigelov indeed come back so that everyone would make peace and live happily ever after? What was it about his body that turned it into such a powerful religio-political symbol? Quoting instances of a post-socialist "parade of corpses," Verdery contends that while being central to the rewriting of history, dead-body politics can reveal shifts in the conceptions of time and space themselves (1999: 25–26). It is to this reordering and reconfiguring of Buryat spatial and temporal universes after Itigelov's 2002 "coming" (Rus. *prikhod*) that I now turn.

Buddhism Marches North: Itigelov's Past Lives

In one of his field diaries, Buryat Buddhologist Bazar Baradiin writes about a particular prophesy that circulated in Lhasa around the turn of the twentieth century and spread to the Transbaikal through lamas returning from Lhasa and Tibetans who visited. The prophesy talked about the possible demise of Central Tibet (which Baradiin places in the context of the 1904 British invasion), with the center of Buddhism moving northward to the monastery of Labrang in Amdo (Baradiin 1904). The contemporary popular rendering of this story goes as follows:

14. The rapprochement started in 2004, when, for the first time since 1998, high-ranking government officials visited the Ivolginsk Monastery, presumably due to their interest in Itigelov (Makhachkeev 2004c). During the visit to the Ministry of the Interior, Minister Mikhail Tsukruk told the Khambo Lama that his young men who serve in Chechnya always have Itigelov's picture on the windscreens of their Ural military trucks. "The Chechens ask them: 'Who is it?' And our guys reply, 'With him, no landmine can hurt us'" (Makhachkeev 2004b).

Buddhism has already met its demise in Chinese Tibet.

With the death of the current Dalai Lama and with India increasingly pressed by China, Buddhism will be marginalized in India, too.

The center of Tibetan Buddhism is now shifting north to Mongolia, the only sovereign country which has Tibetan Buddhism as a state religion, and possibly Buryatia, where Buddhism is also one of the official state religions.

While these geopolitical imaginaries have a role in reordering Buryat cosmologies of space, Buddhists hold the issue of transmission to be crucial to the religion's authenticity, and the fact of Itigelov's return alone has not established the lineage. Buryatia might now be the center, but how to restore the link between the undisputed Indian origin of Buddhism and its current Buryat version? Treasures, I suggest, are very effective agents for establishing such a link due to their ability to shorten the path between past and present, connect them, and thereby authorize the present. They provide focal points, where the painful recent past unfolds into a deeper, more glorious golden age, and they simultaneously announce the future by way of their present discovery. Treasures connect Buryatia to India by linking local lama bodies to important Indian personalities.

Itigelov's body shares important characteristics with classically known "treasure" objects. First, it serves as the physical link to the past while being oriented toward the future. This is perhaps true for all relics in general. More crucially, however, and similarly to the other treasure objects, whose concealers designed them to benefit the future generations during times of hardship, Itigelov is believed to have engineered his own burial and exhumation during a particular time after his death, thus being a kind of *self-concealing* treasure. Being one link in the endless "rosary of bodies," Itigelov's body not only stands for the authenticity of Buddhist transmission and continuity with older religious forms, but also embodies multiple temporal regimes. He is simultaneously himself and a reincarnation of the first Khambo Lama, Damba-Darzha Zaiaev (1711–1776) (see box 1), credited with introducing Buddhism into Buryatia. Itigelov, as one Buryat told me, is "two in one" (Rus. *dva v odnom*).

Drawing on Gregory Schopen's work, Buddhologist John Strong notes that Buddhist relics are "alive," since they can "own property, perform miracles, inspire devotees" and are "filled with various buddha qualities" (Schopen 1990; Strong 2004: 4). Unlike other scholars of Buddhism, who have treated Buddhist relics as "indexical icons" and "sedimentation of charisma" (Tambiah 1984: 5, 335ff), or as "memory

---

1. Damba-Darzha Zaiaev

The First Khambo Lama, Damba-Darzha Zaiaev (1711–1776), a Buryat from the Tsongol clan, is considered to be the founding father of Buryat Buddhism. Having received his monastic education at the Drepung Monastery in Lhasa, he started active propagation of Buddhism among the Selenga Buryats, having built the first monastery in Buryatia, called Baldan Braibun (the Buryat pronunciation of Lhasa's Drepung), also known as the Tsongol Monastery. In 1764 Empress Catherine the Great granted him the title of the first Pandito Khambo Lama of the Transbaikal, after which this date became known as the beginning of the formation of the official Buddhist church in the Russian empire. In 1768, at the request of the empress, who was fascinated with his stories about Tibet, Zaiaev composed one of the first Buryat written works, describing his journey to the "Land of the Snows." This unique document provided an early glimpse into Buryat pilgrimage routes through the Gobi Desert to Tibet (Russian translations are available in Vanchikova 2006; Sazykin 1986).

---

sites" and the "ultimate embodiment of a commemorative consciousness" (Charles Hallisey, quoted in Strong 2004: 4), Strong (who concentrates on the relics of the historical Buddha) suggests that instead of focusing on the "presence" or "absence" of the Buddha in the relics, relics should be viewed as "expressions and extensions of the Buddha's biographical process" (see 2004: 4–5 for Strong's comprehensive overview of the scholarship on Buddhist relics). Biographies of Buddhist saints do not start with their births and do not end with their deaths; they include the masters' previous lives (incarnations) and posthumous existences (of which relics are only one aspect). More than just being "two in one," incarnate bodies have the capacity to embody multiple temporalities, as Itigelov attests. Worshippers who come to touch Itigelov are touching much more than his present body. His relics embody a history that is longer than his life, reaching back to the time of Zaiaev, more than two centuries ago. Itigelov's body, however, does not merely evoke the past. Since he is believed by many to be "alive" and in meditation, he embodies the "slow" time of the present, unaffected by the normal rhythms of everyday life. Like other treasures, he also indicates the imagined future temporality of Buryatia's permanent reentry onto the Buddhist scene. And if, as Strong suggests, relics are extensions of the biographical process, in this case it did not take long for such biography to materialize, again in a mysterious way.

In 2005, a five-page text attributed to Itigelov was discovered among the thousands of manuscripts in Ivolginsk Monastery. No one was able to tell me where this text had been before, and the consensus was that it had intentionally revealed itself through the agency of Itigelov. In it, he described how in one of his previous lives as Zaiaev, he had offered gifts to the Dalai and Panchen Lamas who passed to him the information about his past lives. The document provided a list of what are interpreted as his former lives, which include five Indian, five Tibetan, and two Buryat incarnations.

Upon the discovery of this text, the Khambo Lama declared that this piece "largely explains the subsequent history of Buryat Buddhism" (Makhachkeev 2005). After the discovery, the Khambo Lama, in a provocative interview, minimized the role of Tibet:

Journalist: Considering the complex situation in Tibet and uncertainty regarding the future reincarnation and the institution of the Dalai Lamas on the whole, can we definitely say that there is a decline in the influence of Tibetan religious leaders on the minds of Buryat believers?

Khambo Lama: Buryat Buddhism has been quite self-sufficient for several centuries and reached incredible heights. The example of the Khambo Lama Itigelov, as well as our other great lamas, speaks for itself. One should not feel like a second-rate person.

Journalist: Venerable Khambo Lama, do you mean that it is a manifestation of some kind of cultural or religious colonialism when one prefers imported ideals over his native ones? But, as we know, Buddhism has reached Buryatia from the south—through Tibet and Mongolia?

Khambo Lama: Buryats received Buddhism from Damba-Darzha Zaiaev, who, in turn, received it in his first incarnation from Buddha Kasyapa, and in his second incarnation—from Buddha Sakyamuni! Remember this. (Makhachkeev 2008b)[15]

Many people took this statement to mean that the Khambo Lama was denying the fact of Buddhism's historical transmission from Tibet to Mongolia to Buryatia.[16] When I visited the Khambo Lama in 2008,

15. Kasyapa is known as the buddha who preceded Buddha Sakyamuni, who is known as the "historical Buddha."

16. Some advanced Buddhist adepts maintain that Aiusheev's take on the role of Itigelov's past lives in establishing the authenticity of Buryat Buddhism is egregiously ill informed, noting that Tibetan Buddhism holds authentic transmission in *this* life to be crucial. That is why, they point out, it is so important that all Tibetan *tulkus* receive all the teachings *again*, despite the fact

I asked him to clarify this statement. He offered me the following interpretation:

One peculiarity of Buryat Buddhism is that we took it ourselves. Russia was baptized by Prince Vladimir. Mongols accepted Buddhism on the orders of Khubilai and Altan Khan. It was all coming from above. In Tibet they had Padmasambhava and missionary-pundits from India. The same in China. We Buryats received Buddhism thanks to the son of our people Zaiaev, who studied in Tibet against the will of his parents. The phenomenon of Zaiaev allowed for the spread of Buddhism after his return from Tibet. Subsequently, Buryat Buddhism received autocephality and its own institution of Khambo Lamas, because when Catherine the Great met Zaiaev, she understood that he was a great man.[17]

Almost three centuries after Zaiaev's trip to Tibet, his reincarnation as Itigelov, who never traveled abroad, is becoming a sign that long-distance authorizations may soon be considered obsolete. One *no longer* needs to go to distant lands to become a great master, since by the early twentieth century Buryat Buddhism had already reached its golden age. "Why do we Buryats always try to bow in front of foreigners? Look at Itigelov—he never went anywhere," the Khambo Lama likes to say.

Itigelov's exhumation set in motion the search for other treasures. Not only were other Khambo Lamas unearthed in an attempt to discover other incorruptible bodies, but also all over Buryatia ritual objects, old scriptures, and other attributes of pre-Soviet Buddhist life started bursting from the ground (see fig. 12).

Ruins and Treasures as Geomantic Agents

An important place where treasures are often found is the ruins of former monasteries, which assumed special geomantic significance during the postsocialist period. They literally served as portals into worlds past. One of the first major finds after Itigelov were 450 identical Buddha statues buried in the vicinity of the ruins of Aninsk Monastery. Three of the statues were found under a stone slab in August 2002, about a month before Itigelov was exhumed. By November 2002, fifty more had been found, and by February 2004 the number had reached

---

that they might have already received them countless times in their previous incarnations (interview with Bair, an advanced Buryat lay adept, Dharamsala, India, 2008).

17. Interview with the Khambo Lama, Ivolginsk, Buryatia, 2008.

FIGURE 12. Treasures found at the Aninsk Monastery. Photo by Aleksandr Makhachkeev. Reprinted with permission of the Editorial Office of the Inform-Polis Newspaper.

203. After a religious ceremony was held devoted to the Buddhist New Year, about 150 more statues were unearthed at a spot where they had not previously been seen. In fact, it is said that in the late 1990s metropolitan archaeologists had looked for treasures at the same spot but had found nothing. "Before starting the dig, we conducted a ceremony and asked the main protector of the Aninsk Datsan, Gombo [Skt. Mahākāla], for blessings and guidance," said Legsok Lama, the head of the dig. "It is not we who found these buddhas; they revealed them-

selves to us. It is not a coincidence that they revealed themselves to the world now, when Khambo Lama Itigelov arrived! Itigelov studied and lived in the Aninsk Monastery for twenty years. We see a deep mystical connection between the advent of the incorruptible body and the appearance of the buddhas" (Makhachkeev 2004a) (see fig. 13). It is said that one thousand buddhas were buried here, and a search for the remaining 550 statues continues. While rumors of a rich collector having visited the monastery some years ago provoked much anxiety that the rest might be long gone, those 450 buddhas at the Aninsk Monastery promoted a flow of pilgrims, donations, and volunteers, whose efforts eventually enabled its full restoration.

The buddhas of Aninsk—the first widely publicized treasure to appear after Itigelov—seem to have set other treasures in motion. During the initial cleaning of the ruins of the Dzhida Monastery, destroyed in the 1930s, an abandoned well covered with earth was discovered. The lamas decided to clear it in order to have access to water and discovered a colony of frogs in the state of anabiosis, with many rusty ritual Buddhist implements buried underneath. The frogs were taken away and

FIGURE 13. Legsok Lama with one of the buddhas. Photo by Aleksandr Makhachkeev. Reprinted with permission of the Editorial Office of Inform-Polis Newspaper.

eventually came to life, which was taken as an auspicious sign for the monastery's full restoration.[18]

These finds reveal a particular Buddhist object ideology, wherein objects are imbued with partial personhood and agency of past lamas (see Gell's "distributed personhood," 1998: 21), as in the case of Aninsk treasures, where the statues were believed to be linked to Itigelov's intentions. In this complex system of social relations among humans, objects, and enlightened beings, monasteries themselves are invested with partial personhood. They are viewed as indices of past lamas' agency and often serve as channels for the discovery of treasures.

The agency of ruins is not always viewed as benevolent, however. Abandoned monastery ruins are viewed as especially dangerous places that are to be treated with extreme caution and respect (see fig. 14). Take, for example, the case of the Alar Monastery, built in 1815 in the region of Ust'-Orda. Although it was completely razed in the 1930s, its former territory has been twice reported to be the site of mysterious and sometimes tragic events. Once someone tried to dig a vault there but lost his crowbar when it was "swallowed" by the earth. In a second occurrence, a large poplar tree was toppled by strong wind. One man, despite warnings, decided to take it home and chopped it up for firewood. The next day he got into a motorcycle accident that left him handicapped (Sanzhikhaeva 2004).

What makes these ruins places of geomantic significance? After the Soviet period, with all thirty-six monasteries destroyed (and two rebuilt after World War II), ruins became an integral part of the Buryat landscape. Since prerevolutionary monasteries were almost never built in towns or villages but rather at some distance from them, their ruins often appear to be blended with, and are perceived as a part of the natural landscape. A rich Western tradition of thinking about ruins, however, prompts one to reconsider ruins as a particular kind of place where multiple historical layers overlap. Ruins have been perceived as places where "history is physically merged into the setting," which in turn casts history as a process of "irresistible decay." Ruins thus become an allegory of history itself (Benjamin 1998: 177–178). Other scholars have interpreted ruins as focal points of remembrance that possess "multiple temporalities" (Edensor 2005), as the material debris that enables the persistence of imperial formations (Stoler 2008: 194), or, as in the case of abandoned churches in various states of disrepair in

---

18. Nikolai Tsyrempilov, personal communication, September 2008.

FIGURE 14. Aninsk Monastery ruins. Photo by Aleksandr Makhachkeev. Reprinted with permission of the Editorial Office of Inform-Polis Newspaper.

Soviet urban contexts, as ways to both encode political change and undermine the socialist masterplot of progress (Schönle 2006: 665–666). Buryat monastic ruins became dramatic instances of places that condense temporalities, with crucial links not only to the past but also to the future, through the agency of treasures that "reveal" themselves in their midst.

Unlike some of the more static modern ruins that continue to fascinate cultural theorists, Buryat monastery ruins, as objects cast off by socialist modernity, are undergoing a dramatic change in trajectory. As they are gradually being turned into replicas of their former selves, what is taking place is a certain reconfiguration of not only space but also of time, expressed in the virtual excision of time periods, visions of cyclical time through incarnations and reincarnations, and the "deepening" of the timeline, which changes the perception of one's place in time and history. Many monasteries are restored to be exact copies of the prerevolutionary structures, while others are built in a different style that nonetheless always displays linkages to specific historical occurrences. Itigelov's new palace was built based on a photograph of a temple found in the Museum of the History of Buryatia (see fig. 15).

FIGURE 15. Itigelov's new temple in Buryatia, still under construction during my visit of 2008. Photo by the author.

That former temple, a part of the Iangazhinsk Monastery destroyed in the 1930s, is said to have been built by Itigelov himself when he served as an abbot at Iangazhinsk. Ianzhima Vasil'eva is the spokesperson for the Institute of Itigelov, a nonprofit organization devoted to promoting the heritage of the lama, and is said to be his grandniece. She empha-sized that the new structure was not just a temple, but a palace, be-cause a palace was also built for the first Khambo Lama, Zaiaev. "This way, the tradition is observed, and Khambo Lama Itigelov is moving *back* into his palace. As you understand, the Twelfth Khambo Lama, Itigelov, is no one else but the Khambo Lama Zaiaev in his twelfth in-carnation!" (Basaev 2008; my italics). The number twelve here presum-ably refers to the document of Itigelov's past lives, which states that he had five Indian and five Tibetan incarnations, with the eleventh being his first Buryat incarnation, as Zaiaev. She deploys the deepest sense of "Buryat" history, starting with ancient India, and thus time, space, and one's place in them are being reconfigured. Unlike Tibet and Mongolia, Buryatia never experienced the establishment of the institution of the incarnate lama—with successive generations of great teachers identi-fied while they were children. However, some lamas have been posthumously proclaimed to be embodiments of previous masters, as in the case of Itigelov being proclaimed an incarnation of the first Khambo Lama, Zaiaev.[19] Many in Buryatia today wonder whether Aiusheev himself might eventually be proclaimed an incarnation of Itigelov. This would not only link Aiusheev to the beginnings of Buddhism in Buryatia, but would also open the doors to conceiving origins in multiple ways: from the birth of the Buddha in the fifth century BC, to the renaissance of Buddhism in Tibet in the eleventh century, to the return of Zaiaev from Tibet in the mid-eighteenth century.

So far as the reordering of space is concerned, a key function of both treasures and ruins is that they allow for the production of the new sacred geographies while also preserving a necessary continuity with the past. Buddhist sacred places never appear on neutral lands. In twelfth-century Tibet, sacred mountains were redefined as tantric Buddhist pilgrimage sites through the process of "mandalization," whereby mandalas were imposed on the landscape as the organizing principle (Huber 1999). Similarly, Tibetan historiographers have interpreted the placements of early temples in Tibet as having "nailed" to the ground the "supine demoness," who inhabited this land prior to the advent of Buddhism, at various parts of her body (Davidson 2005: 87; Gyatso 1987). In Buryatia, both treasures and ruins serve as geomantic agents, indexing qualities of the landscape into which Buddhism reinscribes itself. While treasures found at the ruins of former monasteries allow for the restoration of these religious structures to their former glory, treasures found in the landscape with the dead bodies of famous personalities are a necessary element for the expansion of Buddhism into new territories. While the treasures discussed up to this point were used to reconsecrate former sacred spots, in what follows I give an example of how treasures are used for the development of *new* sacred geographies to demonstrate that the post-Soviet revival of Buddhism goes beyond a simple restoration of the past. A treasure found in a remote Barguzin forest, paired with a powerful dead body, set off a chain of magical events and eventually transformed this rugged region, still known for its powerful shamans, into arguably the second-most-important focal

19. Unlike in Tibet and Mongolia, in Buryatia, the institution of reincarnation was an initiative from "below," through which especially popular lamas were believed to be reincarnations of previous charismatic lamas (Belka 2001: 125–126). According to the current Khambo Lama, the particularity of reincarnation ideas in Buryatia was that one's reincarnation was often established *after* his death. In his view, this system is superior to the Tibetan one, because it "does not allow for the development of pride that some incarnate Tibetan lamas might have due to their extraordinarily status" (interview, Ivolginsk, Buryatia, 2008).

point on the map of the newest Buddhist sacred geography, rivaled only by the current location of Itigelov.

Ianzhima Reveals Herself

The Barguzin Valley is an attractive region with dense taiga forests, snowcapped mountains, and crystal-clear blue lakes. It received Buddhism about a hundred years later than other Buryat regions, after a famous lama named Nimalain won a magical contest with shamans. Nonetheless, up to the destruction of Buddhism in the 1930s, shamanism remained quite strong in this region. During the Soviet period, in the absence of organized religion, shamanic traditions grew still stronger. They remain so today: whenever a problem arises, local custom requires people to visit a shaman first before heading to the monastery. It is shamans who are in charge of the preliminary ritual of "opening the road," without which any services conducted by the lamas are deemed ineffective. The Khambo Lama, the most outspoken opponent of shamans, appeared to be less than pleased with this situation. Moreover, during the 1990s, Kurumkan, the only Buddhist monastery in the valley, served as a retreat base for the popular Tibetan teacher Geshe Jampa Tinlei, and this made the region a sort of Mecca for esoteric devotees of all stripes, many of whom were metropolitan Russians. In other words, by 2005 the Barguzin Valley stood out like a sore thumb on the otherwise triumphant map of the Sangha's consolidation of power. It was at this time that the Sangha lamas, headed by the Khambo Lama himself, determined to rectify this situation and conducted an arduous journey to Barguzin to look for an appropriate place to build a new monastery.

Construction of new Buddhist monasteries is a highly ritualized affair that involves a number of complex procedures leading to the determination of the proper site. Steps include astrological divinations and "taking possession" of the land, which is often referred to as "taming" (see Gardner 2006). Therefore, upon arrival in the valley the Khambo Lama immediately inquired whether there were any auspicious places or events in this region. Locals recalled that in 1996 Buryat hunters had found in the pine forest above the village of Iarikto a *tsa tsa*, a miniature Buddhist votive clay-relief, pyramid-shaped figurine of one thousand buddhas of the kind used in large numbers to fill up the inside of a stupa. Aiusheev with his lamas immediately headed to the spot and searched for more treasures but could find nothing. What then happened is already a canonical story: Tired from these unsuccessful searches, the

FIGURE 16. The stone with self-arisen Ianzhima, Buryatia, 2008. Photo by the author.

Khambo Lama sat down under a tree and entered a deep state of mediation, reciting the mantra of Itigelov. When he opened his eyes, he saw
clearly the face of a deity that appeared on a large stone right in front
of him. This was a self-arisen image, common in the Tibetan Buddhist
and Hindu traditions, an image considered to be of nonhuman origin.
The Khambo Lama pronounced in Buryat, "Endemnai Burkhan suuzha
baina!" (Oh! A Buddha is sitting here!). His lamas and accompanying
locals now also saw what he saw—a big stone covered with multicolored
mineral stains, which could vaguely resemble a deity if one tried hard
to fill in the blanks (see fig. 16). Later, iconographers were invited to determine which deity this was, and it was pronounced to be the goddess
Ianzhima (Skt. Saraswati, Tib. Yangchenma) since she appeared to hold
a lute and to stand with a raised leg, a characteristic pose recognizable
from her iconography. A colorful booklet published by the Sangha soon
after this discovery and sold at the site contextualized its meaning:

Everyone understood then that the ritual pyramid-shaped figurine was left here
by the great son of the Barguzin Valley, Tsyden Sodoev [Soodoi Lama], who was
meditating in this place. . . . Barguzin Buryats believe that the treasures from the
Barguzin Monastery are buried around this spot. . . . The Khambo Lama often says,

115

"There are no coincidences in Buddhism." Now we understand that the goddess of Art and Wisdom Ianzhima was the main meditational deity of Soodoi Lama, and it is not a coincidence that she revealed herself to the Khambo Lama Damba Aiusheev himself. (Budaeva 2006: 5)

The evocation of the famous lama-prophet of the region, Soodoi Lama (1846–1916) (see fig. 17), who is locally believed to be an incarnation of

FIGURE 17. Soodoi Lama. Photo courtesy of the Archives of the Center of Oriental Manuscripts and Xylographs of the Institute for Mongolian, Tibetan, and Buddhist Studies of the Siberian Branch of the Russian Academy of Sciences.

the famous Indian Buddhist master Nāgārjuna, and his promotion to the level of a national saint are crucial to the processes of space-time making and religious authorization considered in this chapter. A rare cosmopolitan in his times, Soodoi Lama was a prophet, a person with special powers to access a range of temporalities not only through his ability to read the future, but also, and perhaps most crucially, due to his being considered an incarnate lama. Like Itigelov, Soodoi Lama's persona compresses different temporal and spatial regimes. Through the initial treasure find, the *tsa tsa* pyramid, believed to have been left there by Soodoi Lama himself, the unique and miraculous event of a

---

2. Shamans Defeated: Buddhism Arrives in Barguzin

Once upon a time, a mysterious illness struck the villagers of the Barguzin Valley. Local shamans could not help, so it was decided to send for the strongest shaman, named Gombon, known to reside in the distant Aga steppes. After many days of travel on horseback, upon arrival in Aga, to their dismay, the search party was informed that Gombon was a very capricious person and would never agree to travel that far. "Why don't you ask a lama from the Tsongol Monastery instead? His name is Nimalain, and he is very skilled in these matters," suggested the locals. Barguzin villagers had no idea what a "lama" was, since Buddhism had not yet reached this remote mountainous area, but decided to give it a try. They set out on their return journey with the lama; however, as they approached their village, the local shamans, having heard that the great shaman was not coming, got suspicious and hostile toward the lama. The main shaman met the lama before the last river crossing, took three grains, whispered something upon them, and threw them on the other side of the river. The lama's horse fell dead. The lama, in his turn, whispered something, making his horse come back to life, and threw the grains back across the river. The grains turned into arrows, flying toward the shaman, who, in turn, turned into a bird and started flying away. The arrows almost reached him, as the shaman turned into a fish while the arrows turned into three big fishes and almost got him. Having turned into a fox, the shaman again tried to run for his life, but the arrows turned into three wolves, at which point the shaman admitted his defeat and barely escaped with his life.

Before returning home, Nimalain Lama predicted that a famous lama and prophet would be soon born in this region. In 1846, Soodoi Lama was born. (Oral histories collected by the author, Kurumkan, Buryatia, August 2008)

> ## 3. Tsyden Sodoev (Soodoi Lama) (1846–1916)
>
> Born in 1846 after the prediction of Nimalain Lama, who had defeated Bar-guzin shamans, Soodoi Lama became famous for his powers of predicting the future. He is said to have predicted many key events of the twentieth century, including the death of the tsar's family and the launching of the first spaceship. Famously, he told his fellow villagers not to accumulate wealth, for soon "people in leather jackets" would come and make all possessions communal. According to the oral tradition, he was educated in Drepung in Lhasa from 1881 to 1886, becoming an abbot of the Barguzin Monastery in 1894. He traveled widely, including pilgrimages to Mongolia, Tibet, Nepal, and Sri Lanka, and also making a trip to St. Petersburg to attend a ceremony of the coronation of Nicolas the II, about which he composed a poem in Tibetan, written in the style of Buddhist descriptions of paradise lands (Tsyrempilov 2008b: 282–283; 2008a). It is also widely believed that at some point during his travels Soodoi Lama befriended the Russian writer Anton Chekhov.[21] The Soodoi Lama is popularly believed to be a reincarnation of the Indian philosopher Nāgārjuna, the founder of the Mādhyamaka school of Mahāyāna Buddhism believed to have lived around 150–250 CE.

self-arisen Ianzhima is now firmly linked with his ineffable presence: the lama's body is thought to be buried in the vicinity, while his "spirit has been flying invisibly over the valley for 160 years" (Budaeva 2006: 6).[20] Thus, powerful dead bodies of pre-Soviet Buryat personalities not only help establish new postsocialist religious cults and practices, but also are instrumental in creating new timelines and alternative histories. Soodoi Lama's past lives as Nāgārjuna allow once again for the minimizing of Tibet's role in the Buryat Buddhist lineage by establishing a second line of transmission directly from India, in addition to Itigelov's.

While the discovery of Itigelov reordered Buryat cosmologies of time, the discovery of Ianzhima turned out to be crucial for the reordering

---

20. See Makley 2007: 33 on establishing certain regions as "fields of action" of specific incarnate lamas.

21. The sources are very contradictory. Some say Chekhov mentions Soodoi Lama in his Sakhalin diaries while others claim the writer met the lama in St. Petersburg. I was not able to locate any mention of the lama in the writer's Sakhalin diaries.

of space, since both events are locally seen as proof of Buryatia's newly acquired status as the emerging center of the Buddhist world. Lamas invoke the fact that in Hindu mythology Saraswati was also a sacred river, worshipped as much as the Ganges. However, due to the coming of "dark times" the river disappeared underground and was expected to come back at a better time. The coming of Saraswati-Ianzhima to Buryatia is regarded as a sign that the locus of authentic spirituality had definitively moved northward from its Indian origins, once again reconfiguring the notions of religious centers and peripheries.

The Goddess and the Gaze

Finds such as Ianzhima demonstrate that the worlds reconfigured and reimagined are to a large extent structured by the Buryat practices of visuality, which, in turn, are influenced by the political and social dynamics in the republic. In an interesting twist, the goddess of art and wisdom soon became known to locals as the patron of motherhood, as Barguzin villagers have interpreted her lute as a big, round stomach signifying pregnancy. The realization that the goddess was facing the village of Elysun, which reportedly boasted the highest number of mother-heroines (*mat'-geroinia*)[22] in the former Soviet Union, was soon followed by reports of successful treatments of infertility in women after visiting the site. Dolls and baby clothes were soon heaped all around the site, while stories of formerly reproductively challenged women getting pregnant with the help of Ianzhima started to circulate and make it to the local and national press (see figs. 18, 19). At the moment of my field research in 2008, Ianzhima was considered a principal fertility site, second in importance only to a similar site on Alkhanai Mountain in the Transbaikal (formerly Aga Buryat Autonomous Okrug; after the 2008 amalgamation [*ukrupnenie*], a part of Zabaikal'skii krai). In Buryatia proper, Ianzhima has become *the* fertility and childbearing site. People communicate with the goddess through prayer, as well as by dropping little handwritten notices with their requests into a special urn. Most important, however, a pilgrimage to see Ianzhima constitutes an act of "darshan," an auspicious sight of the divine, when the

---

22. In the Soviet Union, this title—and all the accompanying social benefits—was granted to mothers with ten or more children. There are now plans to revive this status, reducing the number of children from ten to five.

FIGURES 18, 19. Baby dolls offered to Ianzhima after her reinterpretation as a fertility-granting goddess, Buryatia, 2008. Photos by the author.

visual apprehension of the image is charged with religious meaning (Eck 1998: 3). But what exactly do the worshippers see when they look at this curious stone?

It has been argued that the "act of looking itself contributes to the religious formation and, indeed, constitutes a powerful practice of belief" (Morgan 1999: 3). Vision in general and religious seeing in particular are shaped by various systems of belief (Plate 2002: 11). Self-arisen images are especially interesting in this regard, since they are almost entirely dependent on reception, being more open to interpretation and fantasy than conventional man-made images. Soon wonderfully open-ended images on the stone in Barguzin started multiplying, revealing more than just the goddess. After Ianzhima was initially discovered, people started discerning other smaller mineral deposits by her sides; those were immediately interpreted as two "protector" deities. Different people, however, see different deities; others see animals such as bears and elephants, and some see another dancing woman with a child. "Some people even see entire 'short films' [Rus. *korotkometrazhki*] there while others see nothing at all," a local lama told me. Another Buryat interlocutor, a Russian Orthodox man, reported that he saw nothing, no matter how much he tried, while his wife, a Buddhist, saw many deities there. The same Christian man admitted that he did see Ianzhima quite well on a photo of the rock. A woman who once had difficulties conceiving and then got pregnant after visiting Ianzhima recalls that after her first circumambulation of the site, Ianzhima appeared to her as a dancing woman; after the second one, as a pregnant figure; and after the third circle, holding a child in her arms (Anzhilova 2007). Visuality is thus another way to materialize the past, opening the door to deeper temporalities and visions of the future. In practical terms, the redefinition of this goddess, previously obscure for Buryats, as a fertility-granting deity secured the popular appeal of this newly established pilgrimage site.

As in the other cases I have presented here, this major find spearheaded the appearance of other treasures across the region. In 2008, more than one thousand ritual Buddhist objects, as well Russian imperial coins, musical instruments, and, curiously, a tsarist army sword were unearthed, which had probably been laid as the foundation of a tantric temple of a former monastery. Newspapers reported that the findings were accompanied by "mystical occurrences," such as sudden strong showers and the chimes of bells coming from underground (Makhachkeev 2008a). According to persistent popular rumors, Ianzhima is usually accompanied by her sister Norzhima, the goddess of wealth, who should self-arise (Rus. *proiavit'sia*) any day now. Most important, a new monastery was built near Ianzhima. The Sangha named it the official legal successor to the former Barguzin Monastery, whereas the Kurumkan Monastery (which in fact was built at the exact site of the former monastery) lost its privileges as the representative of the Buryat Buddhist golden age. An official prayer service to Ianzhima marking the day of her manifestation in early May was established and is now held annually by the Khambo Lama and by abbots of all Buryat monasteries, who personally visit Barguzin on this date. By the time of my visit there in 2008, the spot was a well-established pilgrimage site, complete with prodigious local mythology, a new monastery, a pilgrim hotel, and a traditional restaurant. It received thousands of visitors from across Russia and abroad.

The discovery of Ianzhima also casts the perception of the Khambo Lama in an entirely new light. No longer simply a good *khoziaistvennik*, or manager, Aiusheev emerges as a charismatic religious specialist with geomantic powers like those of a Tibetan treasure revealer, a person who is able to read the landscape and make the unseen visible. As in many other cases, the revival of Buddhism in Barguzin was also accompanied by the discovery of a treasure, interpreted as being linked to the dead body of a famous saint believed to be buried somewhere nearby. In turn, this discovery was followed by magical events (the appearance of a self-arisen goddess), giving rise to new sacred geographies, historiographies, and cosmologies of time and space and strengthening the claims to cultural sovereignty.

Recentering

The "treasures" considered in this chapter reveal a particular Buddhist object ideology: the objects are approached as potential expressions of past intentions, of previous lamas. The question of materiality and durability seems significant because the durable qualities of what is left behind or hidden are what make them available. Once discovered, objects—relics, self-arisen images, and ritual implements—become sensible (can be sensed) and visible. In that regard, they are different from the private visions of specialists who see what others cannot, although religious specialists are required to make the initial discovery of an object. It is this materiality that makes them ideal agents for creating new discourses of time and space (because they can move visibly through both), agents that become productive arenas for religio-political struggles.

Treasures reveal an interesting dialectic between continuity and rupture. Analyzing the discourses around treasure discovery in Greece, Charles Stewart notes that while treasures are extremely effective in providing continuity with the past, they themselves are paradoxically products of "rupture": of ethnic cleansings, wars, and invasions (Stewart 2003: 489). Indeed, in Buryatia, there would have been no treasures if not for the violence of the Russian Revolution and subsequent secularization campaigns that forced believers to inter particularly important ritual objects to prevent their being captured by the Militant Godless[23] and either destroyed or placed in the Museum of Atheism.[24] There was another reason, however, to bury the treasures in this particular context that stems specifically from the Buryat Buddhist view of objects' personhood and agency. Buryats believe that Buddhist objects require and even *demand* constant use, but only by qualified specialists. Thus, Buddhist texts must be read—should one have sacred books at home that are not regularly read by a visiting lama, or ritual implements that are not used in ritual, such objects may become dangerous for their keepers. Since most Buddhist books in Buryatia were written in Tibetan, ordinary believers were not usually able to read them. As more lamas were purged and knowledge of the use of the ritual objects was gradually being lost, many believers disposed of their Buddhist objects; they buried them deep in the forest or placed them near the sources of streams, which are locally considered to be places of power. Thus, one was compelled to get rid of sacred objects out of fear of not only the Soviet authorities but also the wrath of the objects themselves.[25] Now, with many qualified religious specialists appearing in Buryatia, it would make sense that the objects are eagerly coming back.

Since it is the powerful dead who are believed to give treasures efficacy, in Buryatia necropolitics has, as in other postsocialist contexts, been crucial in reordering time and space, revising the past, and re-

---

23. The League of the Militant Godless was a mass volunteer antireligious organization started in the Soviet Union in the 1920s.

24. During Soviet times, many objects from destroyed churches, mosques, and Buddhist temples were shown as elements of antireligious exhibitions at the Museum of the History of Religion and Atheism (Muzei istorii religii i ateizma) housed in the Kazan Cathedral in St. Petersburg. In Buryatia, Odigitrievsky Cathedral in Ulan-Ude was used as a museum of atheism.

25. Cf. Lars Højer's observations on avoidance and fear of Buddhist objects and places by postsocialist Mongolians, especially of those religious items and sacred sites that people do not know how to use or how to worship properly (2009).

establishing moral authority. Exemplary dead bodies have reconsecrated the post-Soviet Buryat landscape, setting in motion the appearance of treasure objects, which are believed to have distributed agency and intentionality through their association with past great masters. Other events around dead bodies, such as the miraculous self-arising of images and the discovery of treasure objects at the sites of ruins, have been interpreted as proof of Buryatia's claim to be the up-and-coming center of the Buddhist world. Treasures lengthen Buryat Buddhist history, linking Buryatia to the beginnings of Buddhism in ancient India while giving material support to the local notion that the Buddhist center of gravity has definitively shifted northward. These renovated time-space cosmologies are important not only as ethnographic documentations of changing Buryat universes of meaning, but also as key political claims in their assertions of cultural sovereignty both within the Russian Federation and in the transnational Tibetan Buddhist world. In this context, the treasure objects considered here crucially reconfigure not only Buryat, but also global Buddhist landscape.

FOUR

Disciplining the Monastic Body: Buryat Monks and Nuns

The early Soviet Buryat pilgrims to Lhasa encountered in chapter 2 were among the last to undertake that arduous journey, which had been a regular rite of passage for hundreds since the establishment of Buddhism in Buryat lands in the early eighteenth century. The tightening of borders and the onset of Soviet antireligious campaigns in the late 1920s signaled the end of this long-standing Inner Asian cultural exchange. A few decades later the communist project migrated to Tibet, resulting in the violent curtailment of Tibetan Buddhist culture and the exodus of thousands of Tibetans to India, led by the Dalai Lama himself in 1959. In the next few decades, as thousands of Buryat and Tibetan lamas were sent to labor camps by their socialist governments, it appeared as if these centuries-old religious ties had become an irrevocable thing of the past. The onset of perestroika in the USSR in the 1980s would change that, and Buryat Buddhism would become international once again.

Although Drepung Monastery in Lhasa—a much-sought-after destination for traveling Buryat monks—had slowly started to revive in the early 1980s with the liberalization underway in Beijing since 1978, its spiritual authority for Buryats had been greatly undermined. Drepung, once the world's largest monastery, with more than ten thousand monks at its peak, was now thought of in terms of absence: of learned monks, of religious texts, of some of its religious structures. One absence, however, was decisive for the formation of the postsocialist Buddhist ties: that of the Dalai Lama, whose government-in-exile had now been firmly established in India. The locus of authority for Buryats had now relocated to a new and more prosperous Drepung in the Indian state of Karnataka.[1] Instead of the sight of the legendary golden roofs of Lhasa with which erstwhile Buryat pilgrims were rewarded on first approaching the holy city (Nyima 1996; Tsybikov 1981 [1919]), late socialist pilgrims' first sight would be of the smog-covered contours of the sprawling Indian megalopolis of New Delhi glimpsed through the scratched windows of a Soviet aircraft.

Beginning in 1989, numerous Buryat novices made this journey, pursuing the traditional Geluk curriculum. On entering the monastery, they surrendered many of their possessions, took celibacy vows, and became subject to strict bodily and mental discipline, all with the goal of reviving Buddhist life back home. The task was more complicated than most could imagine.

As the introduction described, having left as young adults and spent most of the turbulent final decade of the twentieth century and the first decade of the twenty-first away from the rapid transformations that shook postsocialist Russia, some have now returned to a country that has, in some ways, become more unreadable to them than the Indian jungle. In the meantime, developments in Siberian Buddhism that led to the production of the new sacred geographies and historiographies described in chapter 3—developments that often placed Buryat Buddhists at odds with their Tibetan coreligionists—have left the Buryat returnees (or, as they have been pointedly nicknamed by the current religious leadership, *indusy*, "Hindus," popularly used in Russian to indicate Indian nationals in general) in a precarious position.

This chapter looks at Buryat life in the Indian Drepung, focusing on the issue of monastic *bodies*. I argue that through travel, pilgrimage, and prolonged sojourns at Tibetan monasteries in India, Buryat monks acquire particular types of bodies, which, while granting them a certain religious status and privilege, sometimes fail to correspond to long-held collective understandings of religious authority, masculinity, and national loyalty.[2]

---

1. For more on the establishment of the Indian Drepung, see Lopez 1995b: 263–264.

2. Besides Drepung, Buryat monks also study at various monastic and lay establishments around Dharamsala in Himachal Pradesh: Gyüto Tantric Monastery, Namgyal Monastery, Tibetan Medical and Astrological College, and the Thangka Painting School.

From Siberia to Tibet and Beyond: Buryat Monastic Communities across Asia

As mentioned in the previous chapter, Tibetan Buddhists base their claims to religious authority largely on lineage, asserting an unbroken line between contemporary Tibetan lamas and the Indian masters from whom Tibetans received their first Buddhist teachings. Ultimately, an authentic lineage should be traceable back to the Buddha himself (Lopez 1997: 24). This lineage is usually represented as essentially oral, with instructions being passed down from master to disciple. Buryats have usually sought direct transmission from Tibetans, whom they have considered legitimate holders of the more ancient Indian tradition, and from Mongolians, who, in turn, received their transmission from Tibetans.

While the first Buryat Buddhist monasteries were nomadic yurt-temples, which moved together with their congregations, in the eighteenth and nineteenth centuries a network of stationary monasteries started to be formed in Buryat territories, many of them defined by what researchers have referred to as the "clan principle" (Rus. *rodovoi printsip*) (Galdanova, Gerasimova, and Dashiev 1983: 34–45). As these scholars point out, the first stationary monastery, Tsongol Datsan, did not become a pan-Buryat monastery: its congregation consisted of several clans who lived nearby and were nominally referred to as the "Tsongol clan," although that larger "clan" included several diverse Buryat and Mongol clans. Soon some of these clans, such as Atagans, Khatagins, Sartuls, and Tabanguts, separated from the Tsongol Monastery and founded their own monasteries based on the clan principle. By the second half of the nineteenth century the clan principle started weakening, as the Russian administration tried to introduce and organize Buryat territories and clans into more stable administrative units. However, as researchers point out, the clan principle remained significant until the first quarter of the twentieth century: often laypeople would come to the monastery, seeking out our "their" lama in a larger monastery; that is, they made their offerings not to the whole monastery but to a particular lama from their specific clan, who would then be in charge of fulfilling their religious needs (Galdanova, Gerasimova, and Dashiev 1983). To some degree, I observed features of this organization even today, especially in large urban monasteries, such as the Ivolginsk Datsan, where lay pilgrims from remote regions would sometimes seek a lama if not from their particular clan, then at least from their village.

Since Buddhism reached Buryat communities in the Transbaikal, some Buryat monks have undertaken arduous journeys abroad to receive classical monastic education in the Geluk tradition. Some have studied in neighboring Urga; others have ventured to the popular monasteries in the province of Amdo, such as Kumbum and Labrang. The most dreamed-of destination, however, was Lhasa, the capital of Tibet and the seat of the Dalai Lama, which only the most dedicated of Buryat pilgrims managed to reach.

Unlike the smaller Buryat "clan" monasteries, across Asia, large monasteries in the Tibetan Geluk tradition constituted multinational centers of learning, with resident monks from many regions, united by the notions of canonical language, lineage, religious authority, and the continuity of the tradition. Monks in the large Tibetan monasteries were divided into the so-called *kantsens* ("regional houses," Tib. *khang tshan*). According to Tibetologist George Dreyfus, monks in Tibetan monasteries were grouped similarly to European medieval universities (by nation, or rather, in the case of Tibetan monasteries, by ethnic group and region) (2003: 50). In Labrang Monastery, for example, which in 1899 counted two thousand five hundred monks, there existed nine kantsens, several of which were Mongol, and one Transbaikal Buryat. The Buryat regional house counted seventy members (Tsybikov 1981 [1919]: 53).[3]

The three major Geluk monasteries in Lhasa—Ganden, Drepung, and Sera—have more complicated structures, each being composed of several monastic colleges (Tib. *grwra tshang*, Bur. *datsan*). For example, Drepung is divided into Gomang, Loseling, Ngakpa, and Deyang Colleges, each with its own grand assembly halls, administrative structures, economic bases, and scholastic curriculum. In fact, as Dreyfus suggests, these colleges should be rightly considered monasteries in their own right and the primary unit of analysis, because monks' first allegiances belong to them, rather than to the larger units, such as Ganden, Drepung, or Sera, which are referred to in Tibetan as "seats" (Tib. *gdan sa*) (Dreyfus 2003: 49). Indeed, when a Buryat is asked which monastery he belongs to, he will most likely reply "Gomang" (or the way Buryats refer to it, *Gomang-datsan*), rather than "Drepung."[4] *Gomang* is literally translated as "Many Doors" (Tib. *sgo mang*), believed to refer

---

3. On the history of the Buryat community in Labrang, see Baradiin 2002: 25–27.

4. When not directly quoting my interlocutors, who always refer to their place of study as "Gomang," I sometimes use "Drepung" interchangeably with "Gomang" throughout this text.

to the advanced monks' abilities to enter through the walls, as if they were doors.

In Lhasa, there were strict rules regarding where Mongolian-related peoples could study. Khalkha Mongols and Buryats, for example, could only enter Drepung and Sera, and within these two seats, they would join a particular college: Gomang in Drepung and Jay in Sera. Most Buryats, however, traditionally studied in the Gomang College. Within a particular college, in turn, Buryats and Khalkha Mongols traditionally joined a specific regional house, Samlo Kantsen, translated as "Concentration and Intelligence Regional House."[5]

Interestingly, despite all the geopolitical transformations under socialism, resulting in the virtual closing of Drepung in Lhasa and the reappearance of an alternative Drepung in South Asia in the mid-1970s, the structure of monastic allegiances after so many decades remained practically untouched. Thus, most Buryat monks with whom I worked in 2008 in Karnataka belonged to Samlo Regional House of Gomang Monastic College, Drepung Monastery.[6] About fifty Buryats of different ages and levels of monastic education lived in Samlo during my stay there (see figs. 20 and 21). What made these young Buryats, most of whom grew up in the Soviet system, abandon the comforts of their well-heated Siberian homes for the ardors of life in monastic cells of tropical India?

"First Contacts": Postsocialist Buryat Pilgrims in the South

Among the first postsocialist pilgrims to visit Drepung were the young Choi-Dorzhi Budaev, whom we met in previous chapters, the late Fedor Samaev, from Tunka, and an *emchi-lama*, Chimit Dorzhe.[7] In 1989, this small group spent about six months in Drepung, studying the Tibetan

5. *Samlo* is an abbreviation of *Bsam gtan blo gros*, which means in Tibetan "Concentration and Intelligence." All presocialist Buryat monasteries followed the curriculum of Drepung Gomang, with the single exception of the Tsongol Monastery, which followed Sera. Lamas from different regions also had different preferences regarding which foreign monastery to study at, probably depending on the links their monasteries had developed over time with the ones abroad. Thus, Aninsk, Atsagat, Tsugol, Zakamensk, and Iangazhinsk lamas usually went to Tibet; Aginsk lamas preferred to study in Labrang; Selenga lamas often chose to study in Urga or larger Buryat monasteries (Galdanova, Gerasimova, and Dashiev 1983: 62).

6. Today's Drepung Gomang College in India counts about one thousand seven hundred monks, divided into sixteen kantsens (interview with a senior Buryat monk studying at Drepung, Karnataka, India, January 2008).

7. *Emchi* signifies a lama specializing in Tibetan medicine.

FIGURE 20. Main assembly hall, Drepung Gomang Monastic College, Karnataka, India, 2008. Photo by the author.

FIGURE 21. Buryat monks with the Dalai Lama, Drepung Monastery, Karnataka, 2008. Photo courtesy of Igor' Iancheglov.

language, basic rituals, and medicine, guided by their famous country-man Agvan Nyima, who, as we saw in chapter 2, had settled there following the 1959 escape to India.[8] This visit was part of the large-scale Buddhist renovation that started in Buryatia in the late 1980s. However, as Buddhist monasteries started to be reconstructed, it became clear that there were no Buddhist masters fully qualified to teach the complex Tibetan curriculum usually studied at Geluk institutions. In 1991, right after the collapse of the Soviet Union, Bakula Rinpoche, a well-known Ladakhi lama from India who entered politics and later served as Indian ambassador to Mongolia, arrived in Buryatia in order to recruit enthusiastic young Buryat novices to study at the Indian Drepung.[9] Bakula had himself studied at Drepung in Tibet during his youth. The candidates were supposed to be selected from the first batch of students who had enrolled in the renewed Ivolginsk Monastery. Chimit, a Buryat monk now in his thirteenth year in India, was one of the students looking to be recruited at the time.

The desire to reach magical distant India obsessed us at the time. When Bakula Rinpoche arrived in 1991 to discuss sending students to Drepung Gomang, a few of us were standing in the hallway near the office while he was talking to our administration. All of us had the jitters: Would they select us? Would they leave us behind? All of a sudden, Bakula Rinpoche rushed out of the office and hurriedly flew by. Later we found out that Rajiv Gandhi had just been killed and Rinpoche had to return urgently to India, where he occupied a major political post. I was sixteen at the time; I had just enrolled at Ivolginsk and was learning the very basics of Buddhism. Two years later, Choi-Dorzhi Budaev, the new Khambo Lama of Buryatia, came to speak to us about his visit to this mysterious land of India. He was saying that there would soon be the Kālacakra initiation given by the Dalai Lama at Drepung and that, in theory, it was possible to just go there, throw away our passports and stay at Drepung. It seemed such a romantic idea at the time.[10]

A few years passed before this dream became reality. In 1995, a first group of Buryat monks and novices who were to begin the full Drepung

---

8. Interview with Damba, Drepung, Karnataka, India, January 2008. I have changed all personal names in this book to protect the identity of my interlocutors. I used real names only for well-known public figures, religious leaders, and intellectuals.

9. Bakula Rinpoche first visited the USSR in 1968, becoming the first foreign lama to visit Soviet Buddhists during the socialist period; many Buryat lamas of the older generation consider him their teacher (Kozhevnikova 2008).

10. Interview with Chimit, a Buryat monk in his thirteenth year in India, Drepung, Karnataka, India, January 2008.

FIGURE 22. A view of the monastery, Karnataka, India, 2008. Photo by the author.

Gomang curriculum was sponsored by Ivolginsk to study at Drepung. They had arrived in Delhi on thirty-day tourist visas and spent the three hottest premonsoon months there, seeking permission to extend their visas and visit the monastery, which is situated in a protected area that requires a special permit.[11] In late May, they finally embarked on a two-day journey by train to Hubli, the closest railway junction, two hours' ride from Drepung. As they were riding in a bus along a dirt road, the first monsoon rain came crashing down. After the initial shock of the scorching heat, chaos, and pollution of Delhi, Drepung, which resembled a miniature, whitewashed, stone city, surrounded by picturesque green fields and tropical trees, seemed like a promised land (see fig. 22). The harsh reality of actual monastic life, however, soon

11. As one of the monks reported, they never received those permits. Instead, they received an extra page with a stamp stapled in their passports, stating that the holder was expecting a decision on a long-term visa. These papers were renewed so many times that the monks dubbed them "rubber visas." As a result, most from the first group stayed in India for five years on these thirty-day permits. By the late 1990s it had become possible to obtain a five-year Indian student visa in Mongolia, allowing subsequent Buryat monks to come on these longer-term documents, going back home (with a brief visit to Mongolia) every five years to renew them. These visa issues influenced the adaptation of the traditional Geluk monastery curriculum to suit Buryat supplicants.

started to settle in, as the mystical otherness of Tibetans soon revealed itself to be a myth:

> After the initial thrill of being in a *real* monastery in India subsided, I could not help but be disappointed. These were real *Tibetan* monks! I naturally expected them to be able to walk through walls, fly, levitate . . . you know, do all these other feats Tibetan monks have been described as doing. However, all they did was chant and memorize their texts, sometimes without even understanding them. They washed dishes, cooked, and went to classes. It turned out they were just regular people with bodies like ours.[12]

Second, the harsh discipline, essential to a monk's progress in a Geluk monastery, turned out to be quite a shock to these young Buryat men (ages fifteen to twenty-one), especially that first group of supplicants, who came of age during the first "wild" and "free" perestroika years.

The typical day of a monk at Drepung Gomang in his first through fourth years of study was highly structured and generally proceeded as shown in box 4.[13]

About once a month, a monk would be required to work in the kitchen, necessitating that he wake up at 3:00 a.m. During the 1990s, all foreign monks, the majority of whom were Khalkha Mongols and Buryats and Kalmyks, were relieved of kitchen duties.[14] However, in recent years, when the number of Mongol monks reached several hundred, they were also required to work kitchen shifts. The only kind of labor from which foreign students were exempt was working in the fields. Monks generally receive one day off per week (Mondays in Gomang),

12. Interview with Oleg, twenty-two, a monk in his third year of study, India, January 2008. Oleg's remark echoed the sentiments expressed some years back in the classic ethnographic film *First Contact* (directed by Bob Connolly and Robin Anderson, 1983).

13. This schedule might change depending on the time of the year, with debates coming in sessions during certain times of the academic year; at other times, there might be no debates, these being replaced instead by philosophy classes or other learning or ritual activities. Sometimes, evening debates become heated and last much longer that their scheduled time. I have witnessed evening debates that ran way until 1 or 2 a.m.

14. Foreign monks were initially exempt from kitchen duties: because they were at a disadvantage compared to Tibetans due to prolonged adjustment periods and difficulties with mastering the Tibetan language, the monastery administration attempted to create optimal learning conditions for them. Since there were very few foreigners, this policy did not provoke any objections. With the sharp increase of foreign students in the late 1990s, some Tibetans objected that they were now doing double shifts, and this rule has been changed. In addition, it has to be pointed out that Buryat monks are generally economically better off than most of their Tibetan counterparts. Some Buryats have laptop computers and expensive cell phones with colored screens (prohibited in the monastery), which have made some Tibetans resent them as rich foreigners with special privileges.

4. A Typical Day at Drepung Gomang for a Buryat Monk in His First through Fourth Years of Study

6:00	Waking time
6:30–8:00	Memorization of texts and preparation for debates
8:00–9:00	Breakfast
9:00–11:00	Morning debate
11:00–12:00	Lunch
12:00–13:00	Break
13:00–16:00	Afternoon philosophy classes
16:00–17:00	Preparation for evening debates, self-study
17:00–18:00	Dinner
18:00–19:00	Evening philosophy classes or homework/recitation
19:00–21:00	Evening prayer assembly
21:00–11:00	Evening debate
11:00–12:00	Memorization and recitation

The schedules of monks of different levels differ, with more flexible schedules as they advance in the curriculum. More advanced monks spend more time in self-study and in private sessions with their masters.

during which they need to do their shopping and laundry, go to the bank and post office, and run other errands. They also have a winter break around the time of the Tibetan New Year (see figs. 23–25).

While this schedule might not seem intense to anyone who might have passed through either intensive academic or military programs, several other factors made monastic life especially demanding for Buryats. First, there were physical considerations, such as the extremely hot climate throughout the year and food which many found difficult. Food in general is very scarce, and an average monastery diet consists of noodles, rice, scant vegetables, and occasional plain curd. Many monks thus returned home before completing their course of study for health reasons. Second, mastering the Tibetan language is a great challenge, since one not only has to read and memorize esoteric texts, but also must be able to participate in daily philosophical debates. However, most challenging of all are the monastic vows, which include the vow of celibacy—something that few Buryat lamas practice at home. Before

FIGURE 23. Buryat monks cooking a vegetarian version of traditional dumplings (*posy*) in their dormitory during "winter break," Karnataka, India, 2008. Photo by the author.

FIGURE 24. Author having a feast with younger monks on the roof of their dormitory, Drepung Monastery, Karnataka, India, 2008. Author's photo.

FIGURE 25. Buryat pilgrims and mothers of monks, at Drepung Monastery, Karnataka, India, 2008. Photo by the author.

I proceed to a more detailed discussion of these rites of restriction, let us review the Geluk curriculum.

The Monastic Curriculum at Drepung Gomang

It typically takes fourteen to fifteen years to complete the entire curriculum and pass examinations for the title of geshe. Some monks then continue their education for a few years at a tantric college. Still others take time off for a prolonged meditation retreat at later stages of their monastic careers. At Gomang, during the first two or three years, students study various aspects of logic and epistemology, partitioned into three major sections: Collected Topics (Tib. *bsdus grwa*), Lorik (Tib. *blo rigs*, types of mind), and Tarik (*rtags rigs*, types of reasoning). During these years, students are also introduced to the art of the Buddhist debate. In the next four or five years, monks study a commentary on the Perfection of Wisdom Sutras, in which the structure and constituents of the Hinayāna and Mahāyāna paths are delineated. This part of the curriculum is known as Parchin (Tib. *phar phyin*, Skt. *Prajñāpāramitā*,

5. Gomang Monastic Curriculum Followed by Buryats

Years 1–2   Collected Topics (Tib. *bsdus grva*) and Knowledge and Awareness (Tib. *blo rig*)

Years 3–4   Logic and Reasoning (Tib. *rtags rig*)

Years 5–9   Perfection of Wisdom (Skt. *Prajñāpāramitā*, Tib. *phar byin*)

Years 10–11 The Middle Way (Skt. *Mādhyamaka*, Tib. *dbu ma*)

Years 12–13 Higher Knowledge (Skt. *Abhidharma*, Tib. *mdzod*)

Years 14–15 Monastic Discipline (Skt. *Vinaya*, Tib. *'dul ba*)[15]

Subsequent years—preparations for the geshe exams of various statutes (about one year of preparation for the simple geshe degree and about six additional years of study and preparations for the Geshe Lharampa degree [the highest degree]).

Perfection of Wisdom). Most Buryats who study in Gomang go only as far as studying the first few years of Parchin, because their visas are given only for five years, and in some cases, renewed for five more. Those who are able to renew their visas sometimes finish Parchin, after which they return home with the degree of *Parchin Rabjampa* (roughly, Master of Parchin). Most Buryat monks who studied at Gomang and returned to teach at Ivolginsk have held this degree.

As of my visit in 2008, there were several Buryat monks who had been in the monastery for more than ten years.[16] These monks were approaching the end of the next major section of the Geluk curriculum, that of Abhidharma, a text on cosmology and doctrine. If they continue their education, they will proceed to study Vinaya, or monastic discipline, for two more years. Should they decide to study for the highest degree of Geshe Lharampa, they will have to spend yet four to six more years preparing for their exam, bringing the full course of monastic education to twenty years. As of 2008, there were no post-socialist Buryat Geshe Lharampas.[17]

15. Tibetan terms in this box are given in the Wylie system.

16. Several Buryat monks from the first 1995 group still remain at Drepung, going into their fourteenth year of study as of 2008. One monk from this group abandoned the monastery but stayed in India, devoting himself to the study and practice of *chöd* (*gcod*) under the auspices of the Ninth Jebdzundamba in Dharamsala (see chap. 5).

17. Since Buryat novices arrive with different levels of knowledge of Tibetan, it can take much longer for some to finish the first major section (Logic). On the other hand, since some

Monks in Gomang are instructed by a variety of teachers, each of whom fulfills a particular function, including "scholastic," "home," and "tantric" teachers (see Dreyfus 2003: 54–75). Monks often develop considerable devotion to their scholastic and tantric teachers (for more on the teacher-disciple relationship, see chap. 2). The first teacher, however, whom a novice encounters in a large monastery like Drepung is the so-called home teacher, who usually lives on the same premises with the novice. On entering the monastery, all Buryat monks are assigned a home teacher; in recent years, older Buryat monks serve as home teachers for younger ones. A home teacher helps the new monk in everyday matters, such as money and health, and serves as the main enforcer of monastic discipline.[18]

While there is no trial period with the boot camp atmosphere known in some of the former Tibetan monasteries, the hardships of monastic discipline still play a central role in the formation of what Foucault might have called "docile" monastic bodies (Dreyfus 2003: 63–65; Foucault 1979 [1975]). Besides the demanding schedule, from the very first days at Drepung, Buryat novices experience significant physical changes, which transform them into full members of the Drepung Gomang monastic community. Chimit remarked:

It is so hot here, seriously, like a sauna. You can combat the heat by trying to take a cold shower many times a day, although usually there is no time for this. The worst is the monsoon season, which starts in mid-May and lasts through August. Sometimes it rains for two weeks straight without stopping. Everything becomes covered with mold: our robes, our sacred books, everything. Almost all of us become sick during this period: flu, painful fever blisters, all kinds of skin rashes and pigmentation problems. . . . Some become bedridden during this period, for others it is the reason to quit the monastery and return home. It usually takes at least two or three years before new Buryat monks can fully function in this climate.[19]

---

sections of this curriculum are already taught at Ivolginsk Monastery in Buryatia, some students arrive with basic knowledge of Logic and fairly good reading skills in Tibetan, which places them approximately in the second or third year of the Gomang curriculum.

18. Besides personal money, supplied by relatives and sponsors, Buryat monks in Gomang have a collective fund, partially sponsored by the Buddhist Traditional Sangha of Russia. According to one of my monk consultants, a significant proportion of funds from this goes for medical expenses that new monks inevitably incur during their acclimatization.

19. Interview, Drepung, 2008. It should be pointed out that Buryatia's climate, despite having the usually long and extremely cold Siberian winters (with temperatures as low as minus fifty degrees Celcius), is extremely dry and sunny throughout the year. Many Buryats are unable to tolerate relatively mild St. Petersburg winters for this reason, due to the higher humidity. The southern Indian monsoon season presents an almost insurmountable challenge. Many Tibetans, especially the ones who arrive in Drepung directly from Tibet, experience similar difficulties.

Most important, however, bodies in Drepung Monastery are formed by the monastic vows that one has to take before embarking on a course of full-time study. Most Buryats arrive already with the so-called five root lay vows, which include the vows not to kill, steal, lie, commit sexual misconduct, or use alcohol or drugs. Shortly after arriving at Drepung, they take the next step by taking the thirty-six *getsul* (novice) vows, after which one is considered to be a novice monk at the first level of the monastic ordination. Later many Buryats take *gelong* (full ordination) vows, a total of 253, after which one is considered to be a fully ordained monk. While some of these numerous rules are considered less important than others, both *getsul* and *gelong* ordination famously include the vow of celibacy, which is considered to be the sine qua non of Buddhist monasticism in Tibet. In Mongolia and Buryatia, however, where married clergy exist alongside celibate monks, many monks insist that issues of celibacy took on an especially crucial significance during the postsocialist period, as Buryat Buddhists struggled to establish their place in the larger Buddhist world.

Celibate Bodies

It were better for you, foolish man, that your male organ enter the mouth of a terrible and poisonous snake, than that it should enter a woman. It were better for you, foolish man, that your male organ should enter a charcoal pit, burning, ablaze, afire, than that it should enter a woman. (Vinaya III.20–23)[20]

This well-known passage comes from the Vinaya, the Buddhist monastic code, which goes to great lengths to delineate the importance of monks' and nuns' abstaining from all sexual activity. While some schools of Tibetan Buddhism allow monks' involvement in sexual yogas at the more advanced stage of their careers, it is generally considered that all four schools of Tibetan Buddhism maintain the rule of celibate monasticism.[21] In the Mongolian cultural area that includes Buryatia, however, the rules of celibacy were never strictly enforced even for or-

20. Quoted from I. B. Horner's translation (1982: 36).
21. In some schools of Tibetan Buddhism, such as Sakya and Nyingma, lamas and other religious practitioners (as opposed to monks) can be married. In Geluk, however, all monks, including those who are incarnate lamas, are required to be celibate. I use the term "monk" here to refer to someone who has taken at least *getsul* (novice) vows, which include the vow of celibacy. Most religious practitioners in Buryatia who wear monastic clothes and often are referred as "monks" should be properly referred to as "lamas" or "teachers."

dained monks (*gelongs*), creating a disjunction with the Geluk school that is dominant in this region. While many both within and outside Mongolia and Buryatia ascribe this fact to the legacy of the Soviet repressions, it appears that in prerevolutionary Buryatia and Mongolia, celibacy in monastic communities was never strictly enforced.[22] Thus, with the renewal of Buddhism in these areas, the practice of celibacy and monasticism (or a lack thereof) became especially controversial.

The practice of celibacy is closely related to particular conceptions of the human body, which, in many religious traditions, is seen as a microcosm of society, thus linking celibacy to the ideas of purity, danger, and boundaries (Olson 2008: 6–7). Bodies are often viewed as bounded systems, with the margins and orifices to be guarded against pollution and transgression. Arguing that danger to bodily boundaries might metaphorically express danger to the community, Mary Douglas famously referred to the view of the body held by one South Asian caste as a "beleaguered town, every ingress and exit guarded for spies and traitors" (2005 [1966]: 152). Similarly, Bernard Faure identifies notions of "open" and "closed" bodies in Buddhist texts, noting that the suspicion with which the female body is viewed might be related to its being more "open," particularly vulnerable to inflows and outflows, such as menstruation and penetration (1998: 58–63). By this logic, it is the community as a whole that is at stake in the maintenance of celibacy by individual monks. According to Janet Gyatso, "sex provides for a community bound by bodily discipline the quintessential test of its very existence." Sex, she writes, threatens the community not only on practical grounds by potentially drawing monks away to family life, and the symbolic significance of abstinence far exceeds the practical one: it is in the domain of sexual desire, which is the most tempting

22. It appears that the standards for monastic discipline in general and requirements regarding celibacy in particular varied widely between different regional Buryat communities. Upon visiting Gusinoozersk Monastery in 1903 (the seat of the Khambo Lamas from 1809 to 1930), Buryat scholar Zhamtsarano was surprised to notice that married lamas showed up for religious services, whereas in Aginsk Monastery and in Khori monasteries in general, it would have been unthinkable (2001: 14). Nineteenth-century researcher V. V. Vashkevich also noted that Buryat lamas often celebrated their own weddings openly. He also mentioned that a girl who got pregnant by a lama actually found a husband faster, since such liaisons had an aura of sacredness. Finally, he reported that although Buryats had strict prohibitions against having sexual relations with close relatives, these restrictions were not followed by lamas. Often lamas had sexual relations with their closest female relatives and kept their illegal sons as nephews (Vashkevich 1885: 17, 63). It has to be pointed out, however, that Vashkevich, a government-employed researcher into Buryat life, might have had a political agenda of "exposing" the decadence of Buryat Buddhists. G. D. Natsov, a former Buryat lama who became a field ethnographer and collected unique oral histories from 1929 to 1941, also mentioned past married lamas in passing (1998: 118, 56).

and difficult to curb, where the "law" (expressed in the Vinaya) can really "plant its flag" and assert its sovereignty over monks' bodies (Gyatso 2005: 287–288). Given that the Buddhist monastic community is often referred to as the "body" of the Sangha, the concern with monastic purity and boundaries assumes primary importance.

If Buddhism generally views the body as something to constantly struggle against in order to maintain purity, it also endorses the special value of the human body as a vehicle to achieve enlightenment. The tantric theory of the body maintains that the human body is a complex system consisting of "channels," "winds," and "drops," that can all be manipulated through elaborate meditation and visualization techniques to achieve buddhahood in this lifetime (Williams 1997). While many of these practices are currently available to any interested layperson, the traditional Geluk view advocates such practices only for advanced individuals, often those who have already mastered the main monastic curriculum (whether they are monks or lay yogins). For novice monks, the practice of celibacy is absolutely required. In fact, it is this possibility of transforming sexual drives into spiritual ones that enables one to acquire special, often supernatural powers. Thus, in Buddhism and Hinduism, it is often the celibacy of the monk or lay ascetic that ensures his ritual efficacy, as such religious figures are widely believed to possess magical powers.

As the ideas of early monastic Buddhism spread from India to East Asia, it is the practice of celibacy that these cultures often found the most difficult to accommodate. In China, for example, the notion of lineage and ancestor worship was so fundamental that the idea of abstinence was at first considered not only eccentric and unhealthy, but also dangerous: since ancestors depended on their descendants who fed them through sacrifice, the decision not to produce any offspring seemed extremely short sighted and unfilial (Kieschnick 2008: 227). Buddhism arrived in China during the first century CE, whereas Buryats were perhaps the last of the "traditional" Asian societies to receive Buddhism, which spread to their communities around Lake Baikal in the early eighteenth century only to be severely suppressed by the new socialist government some two hundred years later. Thus, Buryatia never had the extra centuries it took China to accept this new and seemingly asocial ideal of monastic celibacy. In Buryatia, where the ideas of ancestor worship and lineage remain strong even today, after seventy years of exposure to scientific atheism, monastic celibacy continues to be controversial. Similar to the heated debates related to the transmission of Buddhism to Buryatia (chap. 3), vegetarianism, and the use of particular foods in ritual (chap. 2), the debates centered on the bodies of monks (and sometimes, nuns) express crucial anxieties regarding the very authenticity of the Buryat Buddhist tradition.

Purity and Danger in Buryatia

By and large, the only celibate and fully ordained monks in Buryatia are visiting and émigré Tibetans, the few Buryats who have recently returned from India, and very occasionally individual older Buryat monks.[23] Many Buryats who return from India "give back," that is to say, return their monastic vows and marry, while continuing to work as lamas either privately or for a particular monastery. Some Indian returnees make a point of renouncing their monastic vows preemptively, before they have a chance to violate them, since a deed is considered more grave if one holds a vow to abstain from it. During my research in Buryatia, I discovered another danger related to celibacy, resulting from keeping the vows too long, and for the wrong reasons.

Bair, a monk in his late twenties, spent nine years in Drepung in India, from 2000 to 2009. Having returned to Buryatia, he was appointed Buddhist philosophy instructor at Ivolginsk and rector responsible for education. Three months after his return, he gave back his monastic vows, claiming Buryatia was too "dangerous" a place for people to hold them. He said he had no plans to renounce his celibacy or marry but wanted to give back the vows in order not to accidentally violate them.

AB: If you are not going to marry or have sexual relationships, what is your concern?

Bair: Because it's very dangerous. I decided to be on the safe side. It's dangerous to be a monk here. You can easily lose vows if you don't return them. Very few monks can survive here. Because of the communist mentality, there is no notion that a lama cannot be married. Most people don't know this or don't want to believe it. Girls come to the monastery in skimpy clothes, they approach the monks freely, engage them in conversation. They have seen that all our lamas have wives and children, so they think they can marry a lama, too.[24]

---

23. All Buryat monks in India take celibacy vows, as this is required to study in Drepung.

24. Another interlocutor told me that marrying a lama is considered a good marriage for a girl: lamas do not drink (or drink less than most Buryat men) while having a stable income and high social status.

Bair mentioned that there were more monks with full vows in the early 1990s, inspired by the first Tibetan celibate lamas who arrived there. Since then, many of these Tibetans have returned their vows, some marrying local women. It's been a "really bad example," Bair said. "If Tibetans cannot keep the vows, how can we?"

The Buryat laity is polarized on the issue. Most Buryat monks I interviewed in India said that their parents agreed to have them take a vow of celibacy only if they had other sons in the family. One monk said that, generally, the Buryat laity is unaware of the meaning of celibacy. Another monk said that his parents approved of his going to India, except that his uncle warned him before his departure: "Do not even think about going celibate!" (Rus. *Tol'ko ne vzdumai obet bezbrachiia brat'!*), seemingly unaware that it was a requirement. The same monk mentioned that after he took the vows all the same, he wrote to his girlfriend (who, at the time, was also studying abroad, learning Tibetan medicine in Mongolia) that he was now a monk and might not be able to continue the relationship. She replied, "But you are not going to be a monk forever, right? I will wait."

While most laypeople are unaware of the rules of the Geluk tradition, a handful of advanced lay Buddhist practitioners see this situation as the ultimate degeneration of the dharma. They contemptuously refer to the monastic robes of Buryat lamas as "uniforms" and lamas who wear monastic clothes as *lamy-oborotni* (lama-werewolves), criticizing them for masquerading as monks. They argue that in Tibetan monasticism, maroon robes are supposed to be worn only by "monks with vows" (which is redundant, since, by definition, a monk is someone who has taken the monastic oath), while other religious practitioners, such as noncelibate lamas, should wear other kinds of clothes. Indeed, Tibetan lamas who have disrobed in Russia often continue to be religious teachers but adopt instead traditional Tibetan or Mongolian dress.

Some Buryat Buddhist "opposition" leaders also support this view. Their discourse places particular hope on the Indian returnees, also speaking in terms of "purity" and "danger." Here is what a lama from the religious organization Lamrim, headed by Choi-Dorzhi Budaev (one of the main opponents to the Khambo Lama), said on the issue in 1997, before the first monks returned from India, almost prophetically foreseeing the current situation:

We are collecting money to build a temple [Bur. *dugan*]—not just another building, but a *pure* monastery, where our guys who come back from India with celibacy vows can live. Currently in Russia, we do not have proper conditions for them—they will come back, and all of us are married lamas. A married guy cannot be friends with a bachelor [Rus. *zhenatyi nezhenatomu ne tovarishch*]. They need special life circumstances, a proper base. They should not receive people with mundane questions [Rus. *vesti priem*] to earn their daily bread. They should study, translate, and spread Buddhism. If they come back and disperse to their old monasteries, we will lose them once and for all. They will disappear in Buryatia and get married. Now all the lamas are married, all have their personal interests, all were brought up by Soviet ideology. They are no different from regular people. But these guys should be *carefully protected*: they left for India as very young adults. They did not know anything about this life, and we need to stay away from them in order not to be a bad influence. Let them revive the *real Buddhism*, which used to exist in Buryatia. . . . So for the spread of Buddhism, we must not lump everything together—both *the clean* and *the dirty*. We need to meticulously set aside the most valuable, the most *pure*. That is why we want to build this monastery, not because we want to sit next to *gelongs* and conduct rituals. They have their own karma, and we have our own. Theirs is a little bit higher and ours is a bit lower. (Kozhevnikova 1997)

In this discourse, the celibate lamas trained in India are viewed as a rare endangered species, who should be carefully reintroduced while being guarded against the temptations of everyday life. Ordinary Buryat life is constructed as full of dangers, which await monks at every step. Some monks in India, especially those who have not been back for many years, also express anxiety about going home.

People say that going back seems like going to prison. Everyone is arguing, yelling at each other. Everyone is in a rush. You cannot walk around freely—skinheads can catch you at any moment. Everything is gloomy, it's freezing, and no one smiles.[25]

Another monk who came back to Russia after ten years in India says:

People here are completely different. Every time I ride the bus, I can't help noticing how aggressive everyone is. You won't see this in India: people there are calm, and you rarely see a drunk person. I left for India when I was only fifteen, so I either forgot or perhaps did not even know our people were like this. In India, people are very spiritual: every shop has an altar, and before starting their work, they always pray.[26]

25. Interview with Oleg, India, January 2008. Oleg referred to the growth of the neo-Nazi gangs in Russia, who have been involved in a number of racial killings since the first years of the twenty-first century, including several murders of Buryat nationals.

26. Interview with Tsydyp, twenty-seven, a monk who has returned to Ivolginsk, Buryatia, July, 2008. In an opposing view on the dichotomy between the disciplinary regimes of the mo-

Khambo Lama Aiusheev, however, commented on this in rather different terms:

Those who come back from Drepung have huge problems here. They have forgotten how to deal with Russian reality. Some of them start acting like Tibetans. You know, how Tibetans always smile and say nice, beautiful words? Other returnees develop pride and a huge ego, thinking they are some kind of superhuman. Yet others come back embittered and disillusioned, saying it is because they have seen Tibetan life from the inside. I always tell them to think twice before going: climate conditions are not suitable for Buryats there. I tell them, "In India, everything will be against you. Do you want to have a stomach ulcer by the time you are thirty-five? Wisdom comes after forty, so, what, are you going to give your teachings from a hospital ward?"[27]

Smiling, acting nice, uttering kind words are usually considered "female" qualities in both Russia and Buryatia, and men who act like this, whether monks or not, cannot escape the stigma of being thought of as effeminate. One can identify two conflicting positions regarding what kinds of bodies are acquired by Buryats in Drepung, as well as what kind of bodies are most suitable for the practice of the dharma. According to the pro-Tibetan wing of Buryat Buddhists, the practice of celibacy gives Drepung returnees *pure* bodies, which should be guarded as the most treasured possession. The Khambo Lama, on the other hand, classifies these bodies as *weak* (Rus. *oslablennye*), and thus unsuitable for Buddhist practice. The next section examines the kinds of bodies the Buddhist leader considers best for the practice of the dharma, introducing the question of the female body in relation to the Buddhist practice.

A Body for the Dharma

The Khambo Lama places great significance on monks' being healthy, strong, and masculine. This is the ideal monastic body, representing the body politic of the Sangha. While in Drepung Gomang in India, the monks' only vigorous physical activity is debating and prostrations, the Khambo Lama encourages monks to participate in sports, especially in the three traditional Buryat "manly games" (Bur. *eryn*

nastic and lay life, another monk explained that he dropped out of Drepung because the monks there are always on a hamster wheel (Rus. *kak belka v kolese*).

27. Interview with the Khambo Lama, Ivolginsk, Buryatia, 2008.

gurban naadan): wrestling, horseback riding, and archery.[28] Engagement in these sports, according to the Khambo Lama, himself a former athlete, should compensate for the monks' sedentary lifestyle and "strengthen the spirit of the nation." A journalist recently referred to it as the "Buryat Shaolin" (Beloborodov 2008).[29] In line with his concern for uplifting the nation's "spirit," the Khambo Lama recently revived the tradition of holding lay "manly games" competitions in monasteries, with the winners rewarded with the so-called Sangha prizes (Rus. *na prizy Sangkhi*).[30]

The practice of holding traditional sports competitions at monasteries (usually, during the summer Maidari celebration—the most popular Buryat religious festival, devoted to the celebration of the coming of the future Buddha Maitreya) and rewarding the winners with prizes is a curious mix of pre-Buddhist, prerevolutionary Buddhist, Soviet, and postsocialist Buryat practices. Humphrey writes that these games, originally clan-based ritualized archery competitions, were already heavily buddhicized in prerevolutionary times, being tied to the Buddhist territorial oboo festivals and to the Maidari services at monasteries. One of first Buryat traditions to be secularized in the early 1920s, the games evolved from local events to major national sports competitions, based not on kinship groups but on collective farm units, brigades, and sometimes large administrative districts (Rus. *raiony*), where not only Buryats, but also Russians, Tatars, and other ethnic groups participated. In the early Soviet times, the games were deliberately staged by the Komsomol during monastery services, with loud revolutionary marches played to drown out the sound of monastery drums, thus diverting the public from the monastery to watch the games (Humphrey 1999 [1983]: 378–381, 545).[31] In postsocialist times, the Buddhist clergy

28. Mongolian monks also actively participate in three "manly games" (Hyer and Jagchid 1983: 71; Pedersen 2002: 157–158).

29. Shaolin is the name of a Chinese monastery associated with martial arts.

30. Until recently, the Sangha prize was a Russian-made car, but in 2008 the Khambo Lama announced that the winners would receive a herd of "aboriginal" sheep (Rus. *aborigennaia ovtsa*), to support the revival of traditional herding. The Khambo Lama links the revival of the "Buryat nation" with the revival of traditional "manly" occupations, such as certain sports or herding and related activities, which he sees as essentially male. Among many similar episodes, his remark on visiting an Orongoi farm in the vicinity of Ulan-Ude illustrates this point. It turned out that the only veterinary doctors there were women, who seemed unable to diagnose one of their animals. "'Silly [Rus. *bestolkovye*] Orongoi women! You don't understand anything. Don't you have male veterinarians?' The hierarch gently scolded. The women smiled, all embarrassed. 'No, actually, it's just us'" (Makhachkeev 2009a).

31. The Komsomol also made an attempt to transform the Maidari ritual itself. In the place of the statue of the Buddha Maitreya, usually seated on a chariot pulled by a horse, they set the

again became closely involved in sponsoring and organizing these events (Krist 2004).

In addition to the renewed status of traditional games, "nonethnic" sports such as soccer, which became very popular with Buryats during Soviet times, are also encouraged (or at least not prohibited) among monks in Buryatia. In contrast, Buryat monks living in India expressed frustration that playing soccer had recently been prohibited in Drepung. As I walked into one of the wooden resident monk houses at Ivolginsk, hoping to get an interview with Zhargal, a heavy-set monk in his late twenties who had recently returned from India after six years, he was watching *Evrofutbol*, a European soccer match in which Russia was playing. "Buryats played, play, and will continue to play soccer [Rus. *igrali, igraem i budem igrat'*]. Gomang was like kindergarten in this sense: we ran away to the fields to have secret matches, while disciplinarians were running around, trying to catch us [Rus. *otlavlivali*]. Those who got caught were sent to work in the kitchen."[32] Interestingly, he saw soccer as a mark of modernity, observing that besides Buryats, only those Tibetan monks who grew up in India were able to appreciate this sport. "Others, Tibetans from Tibet, they are just, you know, village guys, yak and sheep herders, they do not appreciate it."

When asked what had changed in Buryatia during his six-year absence, Zhargal touched on two aspects of postsocialist transformations, both in negative terms. First, he said, shaking his head disapprovingly, "everyone became rich and greedy."[33] His second criticism, in particular, struck me as very relevant to how we might understand changing conceptions of the body in this context. "Buryats lost weight!" Zhargal chuckled. "Everyone seems so tall and skinny now [Rus. *dlinnye i khudye*], like in the 'West.' Whatever happened to the *real* stocky [Rus. *korenastye*] Buryats like me?" Whereas the West for Buryats might signify Europe, America, or "European" Russia, the emphasis here is clearly on the distinctiveness of normative Buryat bodies, here conceived as those of the classically trained Mongolian wrestlers: stocky, short, and unambiguously marked as masculine.

The Sangha's general support for sports and especially the revived

---

hammer and sickle and the red star (Humphrey 1999 [1983]: 545). For a renewed version of the Maidari festival, see my documentary ethnographic film *Join Me in Shambhala* (Bernstein 2002b).

32. Many Tibetan monks in India are also very enthusiastic about soccer, with clandestine soccer matches taking place almost weekly (Lempert 2012: 29). Some of these attitudes are also portrayed in the comedy film *The Cup (Phörpa)* (1999) by a Bhutanese filmmaker and lama Khyentse Norbu.

33. For contemporary Buryat discourses on money and wealth, see chapter 6.

tradition of holding "manly games" at monasteries can be interpreted as an attempt to attract more male participation to the Buryat tradition, which is sometimes contemptuously described as "female Buddhism." In an interview with me, the Khambo Lama decried the fact that more women than men are interested in Buddhism today, calling it a "tragedy" (Rus. *beda*). "Today mostly women come here [to Ivolginsk Monastery]. It is because they took too much power lately; consequently they are very busy. They have a lot of problems, both at work and at home, which they are now trying to solve with our help. . . . From the Buddhist point of view, if a woman has five children, she is going to paradise. . . . This has been the great value of women since time immemorial and it is coming back now."[34] As opposed to the discourse of purity of celibate monks, espoused by the Khambo Lama's opposition, the ideal of the body suitable for the practice of the dharma that emerges from the official Sangha discourse is that of a strong monastic male, engaged in competitive "manly" sports, both traditional and modern, in order to summon his individual and the national spirit, while being tough enough to cope with the famously unpredictable "rough" Russian reality.

Women's bodies are conventionally considered poorly suited for the practice of the dharma.[35] While this most generally is applied to laywomen (sometimes to advanced lay female practitioners), a Buryat nun for many people presents a clear aberration.

Currently, there are only two ordained Buryat nuns, one of whom is a high-profile public intellectual and scholar, Dr. Irina Urbanaeva.[36] Both of them were ordained as *getsulmas* (novices) in India by the Dalai Lama. While Urbanaeva returned to Buryatia to resume her work as an academic, the second nun, a thirty-two-year-old Buryat woman, was not able to make a niche for herself back home.[37] The only female tem-

34. Interview with the Khambo Lama, Ivolginsk, August 2008. In a similar manner, a secular official in charge of religious affairs in the president of Buryatia's administration also decried the lack of male participation in Buddhism. "The other day, I went for a Muslim *namaz*: there were all men there! And how they all were praying! But in Buddhism, so far it is just women." For a more detailed and historically grounded discussion of gender issues in Buddhism, see chapter 5, which focuses more on laywomen's religious participation.

35. The debate on whether it is possible to achieve enlightenment in a female body goes back to the times of the Buddha. While the doctrinal responses have been contradictory, the common perception is clear: "No Buddhist in her right mind desires a female body" (Gutschow 2004: 17).

36. There were several more nuns in the first years of the twenty-first century, but recently most of them returned their vows.

37. At the time of my visit, the younger nun was planning to stay indefinitely in India. Unlike Buryat monks, however, her position in India is very uncertain, as she is having difficulties finding a niche in existing female Buddhist institutions.

ple that existed there at the time had lay married women who fulfilled functions similar to those of lamas, conducting rituals and divination and providing Tibetan medical services.

As is so often the case with normative gender restrictions around the world, not only men but also many women appear to be vehemently opposed to female monasticism in Buryatia, which is associated with what they see as dangerous Western-style feminism. While lay female religious practitioners are criticized as "having read too many Western books on Buddhism," a typical discourse chides nuns for having betrayed their duties as Buryat mothers and therefore being selfish and unpatriotic.

Normal women have a maternal instinct and the desire to create a family. When she has already fulfilled her maternal duty by giving birth to another human being . . . when she has become a grandmother, let her take vows to become a *shabgansa*.[38] Even men find it hard to be monks, they are pulled toward the world by the desire to leave descendants. What can we say about women then? I am repelled by these bald girls. . . . It is abnormal when a girl turns into a sexless being [Rus. *bespoloe sushchestvo*]. . . . Numerically small peoples [such as ourselves] do not have and should not have female monasticism.[39]

Although some commentators rightfully observe that celibate male monasticism is just as detrimental to population growth as that of women, clearly, female bodies—as everywhere—are construed as more bound by physiology than men's. However, as anthropologist Charlene Makley observed in her study of nuns in the region of Labrang in China, despite the deliberate gender neutrality of monastic attire for both men and women—identical maroon robes and shaved heads—these attributes were never considered by local laity as "sexless." Instead, they were clearly "gendered masculine," while entering into nunhood in the eyes of the lay community indicated a transgressive "'gender-crossing' that emulated a masculine societal ideal" (Makley 2005: 275). Although, in Buryatia, the term "sexless" is (contemptuously) used to

38. *Shabgansa* is a Buryat term for a very old woman, most often a grandmother, who cuts her hair short and takes five basic lay person's vows (not to kill, steal, intoxicate oneself, tell lies, or commit adultery) in order to spend the remainder of her life in intense prayer and religious service. For a full ceremony of a contemporary shabgansa initiation, see *Join Me in Shambhala* (Bernstein 2002b).

39. Quoted from the discussion thread at the Sait buriatskogo naroda entitled "Zhenskii buddiiskii datsan v Ulan-Ude" [Female Buddhist Monastery in Ulan-Ude], http://www.buryatia .org/modules.php?name=Forums&file=viewtopic&t=3392&postdays=0&postorder=asc&start=0, accessed August 25, 2009.

refer to nuns, the fact of nunhood itself clearly signals intrusion into male territory (see also Makley 2007).

Despite the possibly ambiguous gender status of monks, which Makley calls the "third gender," they are first and foremost *men* (2005: 273). Despite the fact that monastic robes in contemporary Buryatia, where men usually wear trousers,[40] might be more similar to skirts than conventional attributes of manliness, monasticism is so tightly intertwined with masculinity that women donning maroon robes is already considered a violation of conventional gender roles. "Yes, I have talked to one of them," one Buryat woman told me when asked if she had actually seen a Buryat nun. "What a depressing sight. I cannot say she was ugly, she could have attracted young men, but she chose baldness, monastic robes, and prayer beads, instead. Nothing looks stranger on a girl than garb like this."

Unlike some of the Labrang nuns, who seem resentful about such social inequity, Buryat nuns seem to be torn regarding their own monasticism.[41] A young Buryat nun named Nastia related the well-known story that the Buddha agreed to establish a female monastic order but said the dharma would be shortened by five hundred years because of this. Thus, she views her monastic practice as obviously beneficial for herself, praying for a future rebirth in a male body, but not necessarily beneficial for Buddhism in general. "It is much harder to practice the dharma in a female body," says Nastia, who currently lives in India. "Women cannot keep vows. They have too many emotions, too many preconceived ideas." Nastia disapproves of the many Western and some progressive Tibetan nuns who are currently fighting the conservative male monastic establishment to reintroduce the tradition of full female ordination into Tibetan Buddhism.

Full female ordination, which once existed in ancient India, was not preserved (or, according to some sources, ever established) in Tibet, but it has been preserved in China, Korea, Taiwan, and Vietnam (as well as in Chinese and Vietnamese diaspora communities). In recent decades, international Buddhist activists have produced Tibetan translations of

40. Although after the socialist revolution Buryats stopped wearing their traditional Mongol *dels* (a *del* is a long textile gown with sleeves), today *dels* are becoming more popular among both men and women. Their use, however, is so far limited to special occasions, such as rituals and folk festivals.

41. Unlike Tibet, Buryatia never had an institution of female monasticism. In 1921, some efforts to establish it took place under the auspices of the Buddhism reform movement and Agvan Dorzhiev (Natsov 1998: 136). However, due to the subsequent suppression of religion, the plans to open the first female monastery were never realized. Thus, the nuns who appeared in the post-socialist period are the first Buryat nuns.

full female ordination texts from the Chinese Dharmaguptaka Vinaya. During the groundbreaking 2007 International Congress on Buddhist Women at the University of Hamburg, the Dalai Lama announced his endorsement of the use of these texts. Even with the Dalai Lama's support, this issue hinges on the vote of the Tibetan (mostly male) Sangha, which, reportedly, remains staunchly conservative on this issue (for an informative discussion of the current controversy around full female Buddhist ordination, see Mrozik 2009).[42]

Tibetan women at the Hamburg congress did not enthusiastically embrace the push for full female ordination, with one observer calling it the confrontation between West and East, with the West once again attempting to impose its views on others. Susanne Mrozik, who observed that few Tibetan women supported full ordination, nonetheless claims that it should be seen as a conflict between "local" and "international" visions of the Buddhist monastic community, with nuns from Taiwan and South Korea supporting full ordination (2009: 370–371).

One can say that since the very institution of female monasticism is generally viewed as "foreign" in Buryatia, the push for full ordination is far removed from vital Buryat concerns. The nun Nastia claims that Western women who "run to China" to receive full ordination do it "out of pride" and "to show off."[43] Similarly, Dr. Irina Urbanaeva claims that Western nuns who try to receive full ordination are driven by "rather secular motives."

If the lineage was interrupted, why restore it? Yes, there were cases when it did get restored. But these were of a different kind. For example, the transmission of the oral commentaries to the Heart Sutra had been lost, but the Dalai Lama restored it. Why? Because he is an embodiment of Avalokiteshvara. And the teaching of the Heart Sutra had been given by Avalokiteshvara on the Vulture Peak. As far as the line of the *gelongma* [fully ordained nun] goes, who needs it? It is done for self-affirmation by Western nuns who feel they are secondary to monks. But even if they become *gelongmas*, they will still be secondary and subordinate to male *gelongs*. Who prevents them from practicing the Buddha's teaching as *getsulmas* [novices]? So yes, I think this movement for women's equality in Buddhism betrays their completely worldly interests.[44]

42. See also Tsedroen 2006; 2008.
43. Interview, Dharamsala, India, February 2008.
44. Interview, Ulan-Ude, July 2008. Pro-full-ordination Tibetan women argue that their focus is not on abstract "discrimination" and "gender equality" per se, but on practical issue of access to full monastic education. As was described earlier in this chapter, vinaya is studied last in the Geluk monastic curriculum (around Year 14–15), leading to the degree of Geshe. However,

Thus, although the Khambo Lama often reproaches active Buryat Buddhist women for "running after Tibetans," which he sees as unpatriotic, here Buryat nuns, although appearing Western influenced to regular Buryat women, reveal a surprising degree of traditionalism on gender issues.

Religious Bodies Politic

The post-Soviet renovation of Buddhism in Buryatia puts a central focus on the monastic body, understood both as the collective corpus of the Buddhist Sangha and as individual bodies of contemporary monks and nuns. By this logic, these sanctified corporealities always point to something greater than themselves and can be understood as embodied cosmologies, as well as embodied ideas of purity and salvation. For many in Buryatia, the display of maroon-clad monastic bodies—a sight rarely seen on the streets for seventy years—signifies that the clock has been turned back to prerevolutionary times and that the decline of Buddhism has been reversed. Once again, we witness that bodies can create compressions of time: they "reconfigure" time (Verdery 1999: 115). In addition to rewriting temporalities, these bodies become major canvases on which historical, social, and political notions are projected. Just as Itigelov's body became a major site for debates on sovereignty (chap. 2) and *tulkus'* bodies became the focus of expanded geopolitical imaginaries (chap. 3), the bodies of new Buryat monastics have become an arena where competing notions of gender, religious authority, and national loyalty are expressed.

While this attachment to bodies might seem paradoxical in light of the classical Buddhist doctrine of "no-self" and nonattachment to the material body, the next chapter demonstrates that even some of the more radical religious practices for renouncing the body, symbolically cutting it up and offering it as food to a host of nonhuman agents, are thoroughly embedded in the specifically postsocialist processes of exchange, gender formation, and redefining of the place of the dead in one's conceptual universe.

---

only fully ordained monks are allowed to study vinaya, barring women from full monastic education (Mrozik 2009: 371).

FIVE

The Body As Gift: Gender, the Dead, and Exchange in the *Chöd* Ritual Economy

Those of a type who like meat, eat meat!
Those of a type who like blood, drink blood!
Gods and ghosts who like bones, chew on bones!
Enjoy the organs and so on, as you please!

All whatever gathered gods and ghosts here,
Enjoying this deluded flesh-blood body,
Give up evil harmful minds toward all and
Actualize love and compassion!

(ENSA CHÖD, EXCERPT FROM THE "RED FEAST")[1]

As I listened to these verses chanted solemnly one evening by a group of Buryat, Russian, and other Buddhist adepts in upper Dharamsala accompanied by the sound of handheld drums and thighbone trumpets, I, like several generations of bewildered observers before me, experienced a mixture of fascination and nausea with the ritual of *chöd* (Tib. *gcod*). Permission to attend such an event had been difficult, however, so I tried to suppress my puzzlement and listened hard to absorb this somber performance. Chöd, most often translated as "cutting off,"

---

1. I defer here to David Molk's excellent translation of the corresponding verses from *sGyu lus tshogs su sngo ba thabs shes nyams kyi pogs 'don dga' ldan sgrub rgyud spyi nor*, which is also the text used by Buryat adepts (Kyabje Zong Rinpoche 2006: 161).

is a Tibetan meditative technique for cutting attachment to the ego through the central practice of the imaginary offering of one's body as food to various extrahuman agents, including buddhas, bodhisattvas, spirits, gods, and demons. Once widely popular in Buryatia, in the postsocialist period this ritual has become mostly the stuff of legend, related to the subjugation of demons and exorcism.[2] In these stories, chöd (or, as Buryats used to call it, *zhod* or *luizhin*, from Tibetan *lus sbyin*, "to give [one's own] body") often figures as the definitive magical technique used by *zhodchi*-lamas (those who practice chöd) to overcome shamans.[3] Most recently, this practice has once again started to penetrate Buryatia via a curious transnational route, centered on the teachings of the Ninth Jebdzundamba, the recently deceased reincarnation of former Mongolian religious leaders, who resided in the Himalayan foothill town of McLeod Ganj (also known as upper Dharamsala), which became the headquarters of the current Dalai Lama and home to many Tibetan refugees in India.[4]

After a few months of working with Buryat monastics at Drepung

2. G. D. Natsov dates the arrival of chöd in Buryatia to the beginning of the nineteenth century by way of Mongolia and Eastern Tibet (Labrang Monastery). Chöd was most often a specialty of "wandering" lamas (married lamas not affiliated with any monastery), who were always in high demand due to their reputation of being skilled in expelling evil spirits (Natsov 1998: 132). The most representative contemporary collections of folk stories about chöd in Buryatia are found in Mukhanov 2005; Ochirov 2008; and Tenchoy 2004.

3. *Lus sbyin* is the Tibetan translation of Sanskrit *deha-dāna* (gift of the body). For more on the Indian origins of the practice see Ohnuma 2007.

4. A biography of the current Jebdzundamba is available in Sanders 2001. The Ninth Jebdzundamba Jampel Namdrol Chokyi Gyaltsen—or, as Buryats and Russians refer to him, Bogdo Gegen (from Mongolian Bogd Gegen, literally, "holy enlightened one")—first visited Buryatia in 1997. Since then, he has visited Kalmykia, Tuva, and various cities in metropolitan Russia, where he continues to gather large crowds of believers. However, for various political reasons, such as his being ethnic Tibetan and close to the Dalai Lama, which would put a strain on Mongol-Chinese relations, as well as the tension within Mongolia between "Tibetan" and "Mongolian" Buddhisms, he was not welcome in his historical land of leadership throughout the last decade of the twentieth century and the first decade of the twenty-first (Elverskog 2006). More recently, this situation began to change. In 2010, Jebdzundamba received Mongolian citizenship and started visiting Mongolia more often. In November 2011, he was formally enthroned as the head of Gandantegchenlin Monastery (the largest Mongolian monastery), which was reinterpreted in the news as his being proclaimed the head of all Mongolian Buddhists. He also allegedly declared that his next reincarnation was to be found in this country. Some commentators interpret it as the new assertiveness of a democratic Mongolia vis-à-vis its powerful southern neighbor, as, during the same time, Mongolia also issued a visa to the Dalai Lama, who had not been able to visit the country since 2006 due to Chinese protests (Devonshire-Ellis 2011; Dierkes 2011). It is also in line with many Buryat Buddhists' beliefs that the Buddhist center of gravity is moving north, an idea discussed throughout this book. Dierkes also points out that Jebdzundamba's nomination remains controversial, and that heads of other Buddhist monasteries even filed a lawsuit against the former head of the Gandantegchenlin, contesting Jebdzundamba's nomination (Dierkes 2011). As I was putting the finishing touches on this manuscript, I learned that Jebdzundamba had passed away on March 1, 2012, and many of my Buryat informants expressed hope that he

Monastery in southern India (see chap. 4) and being the only woman in the company of more than five thousand resident monks, my new focus on the chöd practice in Dharamsala provided a striking change of landscape. Although there were a few unaffiliated monks and laymen attending the daily practice at the Tak-ten House, the brightly colored Jebdzundamba's residence dramatically perched on a cliff by the road leading from upper to lower Dharamsala, I was surprised to discover a large number of lay female Buddhist pilgrims there. Not all of these women were from the local Tibetan exile community: some were Mongolian while others hailed from various Buddhist regions in Siberia and metropolitan Russia. As I was learning more about chöd, I started to ponder: was there something about this ritual that might account for the greater visibility of women?

Chöd's origins have long been a subject of much scholarly investigation. While most scholars agree that it is ultimately impossible to say how "Indian" or "Tibetan," "Buddhist" or "shamanic" chöd might be, this debate has received an interesting continuation among contemporary practitioners themselves. For Buryat chöd practitioners with whom I have worked in India and Buryatia, the stakes of the debate could hardly be higher: similar to the debates on the authenticity and various lineages of Buryat Buddhism, a thread that runs through the previous chapters, the question of the origin of chöd places it in the position of a signifier for what they imagine "real" Buddhist practice should be. Since chöd has become especially popular with female practitioners (see fig. 26), its practice has acquired particular importance as a means of expressing female religiosity, pointing to the ways in which lay Buryat women are currently creating a space for themselves in the predominantly male Buddhist world. Why, however, did a ritual involving the imaginary dismemberment and offering of one's body as food to the spirits become an arena through which various competing visions are expressed? What specific features of this relatively obscure and esoteric practice might account for the renewed currency it is now gaining among some contemporary Buryats?

One of the earliest travelers who not only observed but also became an apprentice of chöd was the renowned French participant-observer of Tibetan Buddhism Alexandra David-Neel (1868–1969), who first traveled to Tibet in 1924. She referred to chöd as a "drama enacted by a single actor," with its central part being the "dreadful mystic banquet"

---

would be reincarnated very soon. For more on the history of the lineage of the Jebdzundambas, see Bawden 1961.

FIGURE 26. Female chöd practitioner, Ulan-Ude, 2008. Photo by the author.

during which "hungry demons" are invited to feast on the practitioner's body. In her account in her famous work *Magic and Mystery in Tibet*, David-Neel focuses on the psychological effects of chöd, lamenting the fact that many impressionable novice chöd practitioners do damage to their mental health, being driven to madness by the terror of their experiences of being "eaten alive" (David-Neel 1965 [1932]: 148–164). While she does not provide translations of the actual text, around the time of David-Neel's travels in Tibet Theosophist W. Y. Evans-Wentz employed a Sikkimese English teacher and Nyingma practitioner, Kazi Dawa Samdup, to provide an English translation of one chöd text in the Nyingma tradition, the first chöd text to be translated into English.[5]

5. This Nyingma text, "The Laughter of the Dakini," is known to some contemporary Buryats and Mongolian practitioners, although my informants in Dharamsala tended to favor the

If David-Neel only wondered about "the strange mind of the race that has invented chöd and so many other grim practices," Evans-Wentz attempted to provide an anthropological interpretation of the ritual, viewing it as a symbolic form of human sacrifice, similar to transubstantiation (David-Neel 1965 [1932]: 295–297; Evans-Wentz 2000).[6]

Unlike David-Neel and Evans-Wentz, the early academic studies of chöd emphasized its pre-Buddhist and shamanic motifs, such as the dismemberment of the initiate, the use of the drum to enter special meditative states, and the function of *chödpas* (chöd practitioners) as community healers. A celebrated passage in Mircea Eliade canonized this idea:

Tibet has a Tantric rite, named *gchod* [*sic*, for *chöd*], which is clearly shamanic in structure. It consists of offering one's own flesh to be eaten by demons—which is curiously reminiscent of the future shaman's initiatory dismemberment by "demons" and ancestral souls. R. Bleichsteiner describes it as follows: "To the sound of the drum made of human skulls and of the thighbone trumpet, the dance is begun and the spirits are invited to come and feast. The power of meditation evokes a goddess brandishing a naked sword; she springs at the head of the sacrificer, decapitates him, and hacks him to pieces; then the demons and wild beasts rush on the still-quivering fragments, eat the flesh, and drink the blood. The words spoken refer to certain Jātakas, which tell how the Buddha, in the course of his earlier lives, gave his own flesh to starving animals and man-eating demons. But despite this Buddhist coloring," Bleichsteiner concludes, the rite is but "a sinister mystery going back to the most primitive times." (Eliade 1964 [1951]: 436)[7]

While the approach of the Viennese ethnographer Robert Bleichsteiner, upon whose observations Eliade seems to have based his analysis, expresses an emotionally colored primitivizing "othering" typical of ethnographers of his time, Eliade proposes a more detached view of

---

ritual text in the Geluk tradition, "The Offering of the Illusionary Body," quoted throughout this chapter.

6. Like David-Neel, Evans-Wentz refers to chöd as a "mystery drama" with a single actor, although the "mystery play" upon which he bases his comparison is unrelated to chöd (Evans-Wentz 2000: 284–285). He, however, correctly makes the connection between the sacrifice of the body performed by the bodhisattva and chöd; many contemporary practitioners also make this link. Namobuddha, one of the sacred Tibetan Buddhist sites located in Nepal, celebrates the place where the bodhisattva Mahāsattva is believed to have given his body to a starving tigress. The site features the "original" tigress's cave, multiple statues of tigers, and a stupa called Takmo Lujin (Tib. *stag mo lus sbyin*, Tigress Body Gift). It is frequently visited by Buryat and Mongolian chödpa pilgrims.

7. Eliade quotes Robert Bleichsteiner, *L'Eglise jaune* (Paris, 1937), pp. 194–195; originally published as *Die gelbe Kirche* (Vienna, 1937).

chöd, albeit fitting it into his characteristically evolutionary paradigm. He compares chöd to other tantric meditations, such as contemplating one's body as a skeleton, and asserts that chöd presents an example of the transformation of the shamanic schema, when the latter becomes incorporated into a complex philosophical system (Eliade 1964 [1951]: 437). Similarly, chöd's dismemberment element had been compared to that in the Eskimo shamanic initiation rites (Van Tuyl 1979).

The chöd practitioners themselves, however, have always had a clear genealogy of the development of their tradition. They claim it was transmitted to Tibet by the prominent Indian yogin Padampa Sangyé (Tib. Pha dam pa sangs ryas), who incorporated various teachings from tantric Indian Buddhism to develop his own technique of Zhiché (Tib. *zhi byed*), the "pacification" (of suffering). He later passed it to his Tibetan female student, Machik Lapdrön (Ma gcig lab sgron, 1055–1149), who further developed it into a distinctive technique of chöd (Davidson 2005: 247, 291).[8] Machik Lapdrön lived during the time of the so-called Tibetan renaissance, a time of intellectual and religious uplift, when Tibetans were actively importing new teachings from India, indigenizing them, and developing their own. This "Tibetan renaissance" was also characterized by the appearance of many nonclerical, mystical, and visionary movements and personalities, who functioned outside established institutional monastic frameworks. Yogins, such as Milarepa with his disciples and Machik Lapdrön, are some of the most influential representatives of this tradition (Edou 1996: 2). It is also during this period that the position of Buddhist women in Tibet, unlike that of the women in India, whose religious aspirations had already been suppressed, became solidified, only to be suppressed by the end of the twelfth century with the emergence of a strong neoconservative movement (Davidson 2005: 293).

Tibetan religious scholars and practitioners link chöd specifically to the teachings of Prajñāpāramitā, or the Perfection of Wisdom, a class of Mahāyāna Buddhist scriptures that focus on the achievement of buddhahood through the cultivation of six perfections (Skt. *pāramitās*): giving (Skt. *dāna*), ethical conduct, effort, patience, concentration, and wisdom. The gift of the body in chöd is viewed as the ultimate act of giving, a practice of the *dāna-pāramitā*, the perfection of giving. Some Tibetologists argue that there is legitimate evidence for an ancient In-

---

8. Davidson writes that, most likely, the actual practice of chöd came from the conversation between Padampa and Machik (2005: 291).

dian Buddhist source for chöd, such that it should not be viewed as an attempt to embellish a "shamanic" rite with trappings of classical Buddhism (Edou 1996; Gyatso 1985). Others assert that chöd's Indian roots are somewhat dubious (Davidson 2005). The doctrine of emptiness set forth in Prajñāpāramitā scriptures is central to chöd, as chöd is seen as means of overcoming attachment to the self. Besides the Prajñāpāramitā connection, there is also a parallel with the Jātakas—a corpus of canonical stories related to the previous lives of the Buddha. In the Jātakas, the bodhisattva repeatedly sacrifices his body or body parts as food: to feed a hungry tigress, to provide blood for a mosquito, or to offer his meat to a holy man (this time taking the form of a hare) (Ohnuma 2007). Davidson, on the other hand, claims that chöd's fundamental visualization was influenced by what has been called "sky burial" in Western literature: the Tibetan postmortem ritual of offering the dismembered body to vultures (2005: 291).

As mentioned above, some of these long-standing scholarly debates are mirrored among the contemporary practitioners themselves. Many today ask: Is chöd a kind of shamanism or is it authentic Buddhist practice with roots in ancient India? Is it too dangerous for beginning practitioners? Can laypeople practice it along with monastics? Women along with men? And finally, what exactly is being given away in chöd, to whom, and for what purpose? In a broader sense, the ability of chöd practitioners to manipulate their own mortality, albeit virtually, places them among other key bodies discussed here, which become sites for the competing ideas of sovereignty and belonging. Death, sacrifice, and in particular, self-sacrifice have long been linked to agency and struggles for sovereignty, as bodies of modern martyrs—whether they be hunger strikers, jihadists, or self-immolating Buddhist monks—have been used as powerful weapons (and in some cases, literal weapons) in contemporary necropolitics (Mbembe 2003; Bataille 1991; Hansen and Stepputat 2004). What can chöd, as a ritual technique involving voluntary body dismemberment and sacrifice, tell us about the ways in which bodies become sites where broader sociopolitical processes are being inscribed?

There are three possible reasons that chöd recently became such a contested practice in the Buryat Buddhist self-fashioning. First, it provides an outlet for lay Buddhists, particularly women, to engage in meaningful Buddhist practice, both indigenous and cosmopolitan, traditional and modernist, from which they had been excluded by the monastic establishment. Second, similar to the relic "treasures" discussed in chapter 3, chöd has a certain kind of dead body politics, as the dead are being retheorized. Through entering into a ritual economy with the deceased, Buryat adepts reconfigure entire universes of meaning, as the living and the dead are linked into one interrelated chain of causality. And finally, considered through the lens of a gift exchange, chöd reflects changing notions of reciprocity, morality, and the market, characteristic of postsocialist societies. In other words, the prominence of this particular ritual is related to the three broad shifts essential to postsocialism: the transformations of the ideas of gender, the dead, and exchange.

With these questions in mind, in March 2008, I joined a group of Buryat monks from Drepung Monastery on their journey north for the annual spring teachings of the Dalai Lama, hoping to use their extensive networks to locate Buryat chöd masters. Finding these practitioners, however, turned out to be a greater challenge than I had thought.

Tracking Buryat *Chödpas* in India: The Torment of Secrecy

As a student of shamanism I have long heard about chöd, often in the terms used by Eliade.[9] Later I studied Tibetological works on the issue. Recent ethnographic descriptions of chöd have been relatively scarce, with notable exceptions being a review of chöd lineages in contemporary Mongolia (Havnevik, Byambaa, and Bareja-Starzynska 2007) and a study of rural Buddhism in Nepal, where chöd is often practiced in the context of funeral rites (Mumford 1989: 205–209). I least expected to hear about it at the most scholarly of all Tibetan monasteries, the Drepung Gomang Monastic College in southern India. In fact, while the "specter" of chöd had accompanied me from the first day of my fieldwork, I understood that it was by no means open to all interested parties, however practiced or curious. As in all tantric practices, a special initiation is required for those who would like to be admitted to a

---

9. The phrase "torment of secrecy" comes from Hugh B. Urban's article on secrecy (1998); Urban, in turn, borrowed the title from Edward Shils's study of governmental secrecy in the United States (Shils 1956). Urban, however, formulated quite a different meaning of "torment" in this context. As applied to a researcher of esoteric traditions, the "torment of secrecy" refers to the following dilemma: in order to learn anything about an esoteric tradition, one requires initiation. However, once the initiation into the secret teachings had been obtained, how can one speak about this tradition to an audience of uninitiated outsiders? As Urban succinctly phrased it, "In short, if one 'knows,' one cannot speak; and if one speaks, one must not really 'know'" (1998: 210).

chöd ritual. In southern India, the monk who picked me up at the Karnataka train junction of Hubli to give me a ride to the monastery mentioned a certain female Buryat friend of a friend who did a four-month wandering chöd retreat in the Himalayas. A few weeks later, during an interview with Chimit, a Buryat monk in his thirties whom we met in the previous chapter, as he was describing his difficult passage to India, I heard about chöd once again. This time, it turned out that this monk, who spent six years studying at Drepung, later dropped out because he became fascinated with the practice of chöd.[10] Due to his excellent command of Tibetan, he became the main assistant and translator to the Jebdzundamba, helping him to restore lost manuscripts of chöd in the Geluk tradition. According to Chimit, until recently many Buddhists generally associated chöd with the schools of Nyingma and Kagyu, although it exists in virtually all Tibetan schools. Geluk chöd, he asserts, is underrepresented and misunderstood: "Some Buddhists think that there is no chöd in Geluk. But all of this is a slander coming from the Karma Kagyu. To think that Ole Nydahl claims there is no Tantra in Geluk! They think we are just these dry intellectuals who can't do Tantra."[11]

Hence, the goal of his work with the Jebdzundamba is to restore chöd as a legitimate part of the Geluk tradition. While the view of Geluk as somehow less "tantric" resonates interestingly with the conclusions of some Tibetologists that Geluk is the most "clerical" and least "shamanic" of all Tibetan Buddhist schools (Samuel 1993), I was particularly intrigued by the fact that the claim that Geluk might somehow be less tantric than other schools upset this Buryat monk. When asked specifically to talk about the practice of chöd, however, Chimit quickly clammed up, restricting himself to general phrases, such as that it both promotes the cultivation of wisdom and cuts the attachment to ego, mentioning the connection to Prajñāpāramitā teachings. He still could not resist showing me an unfinished movie he had created himself,

10. Chöd is usually not allowed at large Geluk scholastic monasteries like Drepung. Chimit told me, however, that while he was still a Drepung monk, they practiced "bed chöd," a semi-silent recitation while lying in bed (Tib. *nyal gcod*). Although chöd is extremely widespread in contemporary Mongolia, it is associated mostly with the "red tradition," which in this context refers to Nyingma. Thus, in Gandantegchenlin, the main Geluk monastery in Mongolia, chöd is not allowed, although individual monks practice it outside the monastery (Havnevik, Byambaa, and Bareja-Starzynska 2007: 234–235).

11. Ole Nydahl is a world-renowned Danish Buddhist teacher in the Karma Kagyu tradition, founder of Diamond Way Buddhism, a transnational lay Buddhist organization with about six hundred centers in more than forty-four countries.

consisting of still shots with a soundtrack of Russian rock, of what is referred to as a chöd retreat of one hundred springs.[12]

While at Drepung, I understood that I was facing a problem encountered by many anthropologists studying esoteric religious traditions: secrecy. Most Buddhist tantric practices—including chöd—require special initiations not only to participate in the rite, but even to be allowed to peruse the texts. In order to engage in a particular tantric teaching, one needs to receive not only an initiation (Tib. *dbang*) but also a so-called oral transmission (Tib. *rlung*) from an authorized lama, who, in turn, has received it from previous eminent teachers, thus creating lineages believed to go back to the Buddha. These initiatory practices, which constitute one of the most important modes of authority in Tibetan Buddhism (Dreyfus 2003: 149–164), are usually surrounded with this aura of protection.

Secrecy has been identified as a "discursive strategy that transforms a given piece of knowledge into a scarce and precious resource, a valuable commodity, the possession of which in turn bestows status, prestige, or symbolic capital on its owner" (Urban 1998: 210). The strategy of secrecy used by Chimit employed common techniques of the "back-and-forth movement between concealment and revelation" (Taussig 1998: 355), which elevate the value of the information being concealed while giving power to the secret holder.

Having arrived in McLeod Ganj, home to Tibetans in exile and many Buryat pilgrims and long-term residents, just at the time when the Dalai Lama was giving his annual spring public teachings, I again made an attempt to find out more about chöd. Coincidentally, the subject of the teachings this time was the Jātakas, the tales of the previous lives of the Buddha, in which he often sacrificed his body. The Dalai Lama's semiannual teachings are an impressively organized event, truly cosmopolitan in scale. After a brief ritual, the Dalai Lama proceeds to his throne, installed in a cramped courtyard of his Namgyal Monastery while thousands of local Tibetans, Europeans, Americans, Russians, Taiwanese, and representatives of other nations kneel down at his feet. Although the translations in foreign languages are transmitted on a specific wavelength for each language and are listened to through handheld radio receivers, compatriots usually sit together around the

---

12. During this retreat, which lasts for 128 days, practitioners spend most of the day performing various chöd meditations while every night they are supposed to move their tents and belongings to a new place (usually, near a spring or water source), symbolizing nonattachment to comfort, place, and all earthly desires.

live translator. Thus, I easily located the Russian (Rus. *rossiiskaia*) group, composed of Buryats, Tuvans, Kalmyks, Russians, and a mix of other nationalities of the Russian Federation. Besides the monks, most were women, especially apparent in the gender-separated queues to enter the monastery premises.

In a few weeks, short-term pilgrims, who were here just for the teachings, left, and I was finally able to identify a dozen Buryats who live in Dharamsala permanently or who had come for an extended period of time. Most of them came to study chöd. I scheduled a few interviews, but as soon as I mentioned the subject of chöd, the conversation quickly died out. Unlike my fieldwork in Drepung a few weeks prior, where my days were jam-packed with participation in monastery life, here, for the first few weeks, my research consisted of wandering the two steep streets of McLeod Ganj, enjoying the gorgeous views of the peaks and precipitous valley below. My real goal, however, was to "accidentally" bump into an acquaintance, strike up a casual conversation, and if I got lucky, be invited for a bite to eat in one of the many cheap Tibetan eateries and tea shops around. While this strategy paid off to some degree, I soon understood that the only person who could override the vow of secrecy was the person who bestowed it, namely, the Jebdzundamba himself.

I scheduled an audience with him, in the course of which I clearly presented myself as a scholar as opposed to a religious seeker. We discussed a number of subjects, from the origins of chöd to the status of Tibetan refugees to my life in the United States as a Russian Jewish émigré to different kinds of exile. As he warmed up to me, he declared that in order to understand and write about chöd, I definitely needed to study the main ritual text and observe the ritual often. He granted me permission to do research on chöd without having to undergo formal initiation.[13]

As I exited his residence at the Tak-ten House (see fig. 27), where some of his Buryat and Russian followers also live, the rumors of my visit started to spread. What most impressed his devotees was the fact that Rinpoche (as the Jebdzundamba is most commonly called by his students) had spent more than one hour talking to me. Rinpoche's health has been deteriorating, and the longest audience anyone could remember was about thirty minutes, while regular devotee audiences usually last five to ten minutes. Through this seemingly mundane visit to the

---

13. During the visit, the Jebdzundamba and I also agreed that there were certain aspects of chöd that I would not write about.

FIGURE 27. Tak-ten House, residence of the late Ninth Jebdzundamba, Dharamsala, India, 2008. Photo by the author.

hierarch, I accumulated so much "symbolic capital" that my status and prestige somehow increased enormously in a matter of hours. On the same day, I was able to drop casually by the devotee's quarters, borrow the coveted texts, and take them to the copiers, as well as receive an invitation to attend the daily evening ritual.[14] I wanted to know: what exactly was taking place in the altar room at Tak-ten House?

Double Giving: The Body and the Dharma

My mind exits from the heart of the main deity
In the form of the dakini, holding a curved knife,
Like a vulture circling over a corpse, I swoop down,
Slit the body with my knife from crown to crotch.

From heart to tips of right and left hands, I cut
From crotch to tips of right and left feet, I cut.

14. In a more cynical manner, my Russian Buddhist friend noted, "Ia zhe govoril, nuzhno vsegda snachala k nachal'stvu obrashchat'sia!" (See, I told you, speak to the boss first!).

I spread out the red peeled skin
Above it is the three-human-head tripod

Over it is placed the severed skull and into it are poured
Brains, juice, marrow, and all refined body parts.
With curved knife I stir it around three times to the right,
I turn it into the ocean of healing wisdom nectar.
(ENSA CHÖD, EXCERPT FROM THE "WHITE FEAST")[15]

Traditionally chöd is supposed to be practiced in the so-called places of power: cemeteries, cremation grounds, crossroads, and lone trees, as well as other places considered "frightening." Such places are believed to attract spirits and challenge the practitioner to face his or her deepest fears. In general, both in Tibet and Buryatia, chödpas are notorious for their unconventional behavior. Today, rumors about fellow practitioners going to the cemetery "unprepared" only to go insane for the rest of their life have become Buddhist urban legends. According to the contemporary practitioners themselves, not many people these days are sufficiently spiritually prepared to practice chöd safely. Thus, as beginning chödpas, they perform a daily collective practice in the altar room of the Tak-ten House. Once one is comfortable enough with this practice (usually after a few years), he or she might seek the Jebdzundamba's permission to undertake a four-month wandering retreat, after which one is considered suitable to practice independently. As I was trying to follow the Tibetan chanting with my text, I discovered that while the content of the ritual was structurally similar to what Bleichsteiner described, there were some crucial differences.

After the initial prayers, the meditator transfers his or her consciousness outside the body in the form of Vajravārāhī, a wrathful form of the goddess Vajrayoginī holding a cleaver. Consciousness transfer (Tib. 'pho ba) is a Tibetan tantric technique which involves ejecting consciousness from the body. While there exist many kinds of 'pho ba, most famously those employed at the moment of dying, chöd has a number of its own distinctive methods (Edou 1996: 133n33). A common technique is to visualize one's consciousness in one's heart in the form of Vajravārāhī and then make it fly up one's central channel and

15. I modified Molk's translation of corresponding verses (Kyabje Zong Rinpoche 2006: 159–161) in order to make it as close as possible to the particular version of the chöd ritual text used by the Buryat adepts. The text used by my Buryat consultants, which includes both original Tibetan and Russian translation printed side by side, is slightly different from the one provided by Molk: it includes specific verses devoted to the Jebdzundamba's lineage, some verses do not correspond, and their order varies.

shoot up through the so-called Brahma aperture on the top of one's head. As soon as consciousness exits the body, the body becomes a corpse and collapses in a heap (Patrul 1998: 298). As the practitioner, now in the form of Vajravārāhī, sees the lifeless corpse lying on the ground, he or she starts to dismember it with the cleaver, separating different body parts, according to specific instructions given in the ritual text.

The offering occurs through the three successive "feasts" (sometimes also glossed in English as "banquets" or "distributions"). The "white feast" is construed as an offering of body parts that are considered refined: brains, juice, and marrow, which the practitioners visualize turning into the divine nectar. Contrary to the impressions of early researchers, "white" and "red" feasts do not signify a distinction between benevolent and harmful deities. The white feast is offered not only to tutelary deities (Tib. *yi dam*), dakinis (Tib. *mkha' 'gro*), and protectors (Tib. *mgon po*), but also to "karmic creditors" (Tib. *lan chags mgron*) and obstructing spirits (Tib. *gdon bgegs*) (Ensa Chöd, verses 40–41). The red feast, which consists of the offering of meat, blood, and bones, generally addresses "all gods and demons" (Tib. *lha 'dre*) but focuses more expressly on harmful spirits and "masters of the land" spirits (Tib. *gnod byed, gdon bgegs, gzhi bdag*) (Ensa Chöd, verse 44). In fact, Bleichsteiner's description seems to correspond specifically to the red feast part of the chöd ritual, as the femur trumpet is blown mostly during the red feast, as a way to attract the most dangerous spirits. The only other time it is blown thrice is during the Guru Yoga prayer in the beginning of the ritual, when the Guru, in this case joined with Machik Lapdrön, is visualized as Vajravārāhī. The evil spirits and demons are then called for the first time (Ensa Chöd, verses 11–14).

During the last feast, the "manifold feast," one's skin is transformed into a variety of objects to satisfy desires of different beings: among them are silver, gold, bedding, cloth, medicines, and jewelry (Ensa Chöd, verse 48). It is what happens after the last feast that is most often omitted in the treatment of chöd as a kind of shamanism. The "manifold" offering is followed by the giving of the Buddhist teaching to the visitors. The spirit guests, whose desires for food have already been satisfied, are now urged to seek liberation by accepting the dharma. They are also urged to stop committing evil deeds and embark on the path of the Buddha (Ensa Chöd, verses 49–53). At the end, the spirits and gods are declared to be liberated through this double giving—of the material body and of the dharma—and are asked to leave:

Return to your homes in earth, sky, mountain, valley,
Water, rocks, and become altruistic!
(ENSA CHÖD, VERSE 54, MOLK'S TRANSLATION P. 162)

Before I discuss the significance of this symbolism for the notions of
gift exchange and relations with the dead, let us meet the actual people
who practice this rite today.

Female Chöd Practitioners

Recent decades have seen some radical changes in the position of
women in Tibetan Buddhism in exile. As more progressive figures
among Tibetans in exile and especially their Western female disciples
pushed for the greater engagement of women in Buddhism, certain
transformations, such as opening the philosophical curriculum at female monasteries, educating laywomen, and campaigning for full
female ordination have taken place. None of these movements, however, have influenced Buryatia in any significant way. First, because
the original transmission of Buddhism into Mongolia did not include
the Buddhist institution of nuns, it was never established among Buryats. Hence in both Mongolia and Buryatia, Buddhist women occupied
rather subordinate positions. Second, despite the fairly high status of
women in the former USSR, Buryats have undergone a retraditionaliza-
tion of gender, which has resulted in an increasingly "masculine" interpretation of Buddhism and the exclusion of women from the religious
public sphere. As discussed in the previous chapter, the male clergy
laments that "Buryat Buddhism is too female," referring to the fact that
the majority of temple visitors are women. A common explanation I
heard was, "Don't you know how it is in Russia? Men just drink and
women get into religion." Trying to counteract this trend and increase
male participation, the Khambo Lama has linked religion to "masculine" national sports, such as wrestling, archery, and horseback riding,
at monasteries during major Buddhist holidays. Thus, Buryat Buddhist
gender dynamics are a curious combination of Tibetan Buddhist per-
ceptions of gender and postsocialist ideas of masculinity and femininity common throughout Russia.

Denied official roles in the Buddhist establishment, Buryat women
remain prevalent in lay transnational religious movements. Interestingly, in cultural politics, women's religious movements are more often

in line with the Tibetan model, which has come increasingly under attack from the Buddhist establishment (see chap. 3). Considering "women's Buddhism" as being not only unworthy but also antinational, the Buddhist leadership often decries Buryat women's "blind worship" of Tibetan lamas. Since the early 1990s, many Buryat women have become engaged in lay tantric practices, becoming disciples of specific Tibetan lamas. Many who come to India have Dharamsala as their main destination, with the goal of mastering the chöd tradition and choosing the Ninth Jebdzundamba (an ethnic Tibetan) as their root teacher.

As demonstrated in previous chapters, the position of ethnic Buddhists from the former USSR (Buryats, Kalmyks, and Tuvans) vis-à-vis the rest of the Asian Buddhist world is extremely ambiguous. When abroad, Buryats appear to wear the indelible imprint of their country, as their fellow Asian coreligionists persist in calling them *urusu* (Tibetan for "Russians"). Despite this marginality, by entering a monastery and demonstrating scholarly aptitude, Buryat men have a chance of securing a place in the transnational Buddhist institutional structures. Although in the past, certain Buryats managed to achieve prestigious spiritual status and even found new transnational incarnation lineages—as described in chapter 2—this remains for the most part an exception. Although marginal and alienated in India, Buryat monks enjoy great success when they return home. Their perilous long-term relocation to study at a Tibetan monastery in India is considered a highly revered vocation as well as a respected (and potentially lucrative) career path. Sending Buryat novices to India mobilizes entire villages and clans to pool resources to sponsor these young men, and their return is eagerly awaited.

None of this is possible for Buryat Buddhist women. Yet from the very first weeks of research in India, which coincided with a huge influx of Buryat pilgrims to Drepung to see the Dalai Lama there, it became clear to me that there were almost as many Buryat women as men there, although, given the lack of institutional structures, the female population appeared to be more mobile and less visible. Drifting between Siberia and India several times per year, usually timing their stints in India with major ritual events, Buryat women constitute a major part of the transnational pilgrim circuits. In fact, I have rarely seen a male Buryat pilgrim in India, apart from the occasional husband, accompanying his wife. The other nonmonastic male Buryats in India are journalists, businessmen, and academics on short-term visits.

It took me some time, however, to notice the differences in status between the genders. While Buryat monks might experience some discrimination at Tibetan monasteries as a minority, Buryat women find themselves in a position of extreme marginality on both fronts. Despised at home for having failed to fulfill their traditional gender roles of domesticity and motherhood, in India they are subject to the same discrimination by their monastic compatriots.[16] The derogatory terms applied to these pilgrims by Buryat monks are *uletevshie* (Rus. for "flipped out"; literally, "those who flew away") and *kosmonavty* (Rus. for "cosmonauts"). These terms refer to the esoteric practices in which the women engage, allegedly without the approval of monks. Without institutional structures for female Buddhist education (such as Buddhist nunneries in Buryatia),[17] women have become involved in nonclerical tantric practices such as chöd.

There are many reasons why chöd appears particularly attractive to Buryat Buddhist women. First, it is a rare practice founded by a female saint, Machik Lapdrön, with whom many Buryat women identify. A standard reference to Machik's life is her sacred biography, which turns on its head many of the accepted conventions of Tibetan religious life (translations of her biography are available in Allione 1984; Edou 1996; and Machik Labdrön 2003). Like all sacred biographies, it begins with description of her previous lives. However, here without precedent, the consciousness of an Indian yogin transfers to the body of a young Tibetan girl. A rare reincarnation lineage, although with an original male at the apex, the chöd lineage starting from Machik later had mostly female reincarnations, although the current reincarnation is a man who renounced religious life (Edou 1996: 5). Scholars have noted that the institution of reincarnation and some tantric rituals, particularly those of initiation, served to exclude women from reproduction, establishing male-only lineages (Faure 2003: 145; Mills 2000). Chöd constitutes one

---

16. Here I refer more to long-term female pilgrims, who are either childless and unmarried or separated or divorced with children at home with their grandparents. Both situations are regarded with great disapproval by most Buryats. I know of only one long-term pilgrim who managed to bring her son with her and place him in a local monastery.

17. One female religious institution known in Russian as *Zhenskii datsan* (Rus. for "Female Temple") was established in Ulan-Ude in the midnineties. However, it lacks ordained nuns and is run by two laywoman religious specialists who perform some of the same rituals performed in other Buryat *datsans*, such as private divination, astrology, and public services, including chöd. The chöd they recite is not of the Geluk Ganden lineage but that of the Jonang school also taught by the Ninth Jebdzundamba. Similar to other women described in this chapter, these two women received chöd initiation from the Ninth Jebdzundamba. However, they draw their legitimacy as institutionalized but nonmonastic female religious specialists from having studied in Mongolia, where similar religious establishments are widespread (interview with Sesegma, a female "lama" at the temple, Ulan-Ude, 2008). Havnevik, Byambaa, and Bareja-Starzynska describe such Mongolian temples, where lay religious female specialists regularly perform chöd (2007).

such lineage, in which females have also managed to find a form of nonsexual reproduction, similar to that used by male lineages.[18]

Many of my Buryat female interlocutors mentioned that chöd suits women better, because one visualizes oneself as a female deity, Vajrayoginī, which is "difficult for men."[19] Some said the chöd melody is naturally attractive to women, while others stressed that women, by nature, are "more giving." However, what I found particularly striking is how Buryat women have found a way to use chöd to combine shamanic patterns of thinking with their Buddhist aspirations. Similar to the Buddhist Sangha monks who renounce shamanism as a "primitive" religion, women chöd practitioners, especially those on long-term apprenticeships in India, also overtly condemn *shamano-buddizm* (Rus. for "shamanic Buddhism"), which they think is practiced by the majority in their homelands. Nonetheless, most of my chödpa interlocutors revealed an understanding of the spirit world that was more in line with broader Buryat beliefs about spirits than the beliefs of the Buddhist orthodoxy. I suggest that chöd, in turn, enabled them to find a radically different way to define their relationship with traditional spirits, inserting them into a legitimate Buddhist framework and thus reasserting their roles as Buddhist women.

The ways in which Buryat women come to chöd are very telling about gender dynamics in the republic. Usually, people discover chöd through a string of coincidences, encounters, and dreams, which are interpreted as meaningful signs. Buddhists, however, believe that there are no coincidences, and that if someone is drawn to chöd, it means that he or she has already encountered it in a previous life; they refer to these latent memories as "imprints" (Rus. *otpechatki*). Chöd adepts usually describe an irrational pull toward this practice, while having to overcome many obstacles before they are finally able to practice. One practitioner, Marianna, a Buryat woman in her early thirties now living in Dharamsala, said that when she first saw the Jebdzundamba during his visit to Russia in 1997, she knew almost nothing about chöd. During a brief audience to receive a head blessing from him, Marianna, then a young girl in her late teens, jumped across the room to his throne, almost screaming, "Give me chöd!" (Rus. *Daite mne chod!*). (In Russian Buddhist parlance, to "give" a particular teaching means to

---

18. Despite that, the last incarnation of Machik, a prominent nun, Jetsun Rigdzin Chonyi Zangmo (1852–1953), expressed a wish to be reborn in a male body (Edou 1996: 5).

19. Although there exist other tantric visualization in Geluk and elsewhere, which include visualization of female deities, my informants appear to be unaware of them.

conduct an appropriate initiation ceremony.) The Jebdzundamba, quite surprised at such earnestness, laughed and said, semijokingly, that she should come to India and study with him. "After this, I was obsessed with chöd," she later admitted to me. Marianna started preparing to go to India, but her parents, themselves practicing Buddhists, decided to seek the advice of the Khambo Lama. The Khambo Lama, already dubious about the legitimacy of some Tibetan teachers at the time, said it was a particularly bad idea for Marianna to go to India now. "Until she gets married and gives birth, she is not to go anywhere," he said then, to her great disappointment. "So that is exactly what I did," Marianna laughs. "I got married, had a kid, got divorced, and here I am, living in India for five years already." Marianna's son remains with her parents.[20]

Another Buryat female chödpa, a thirty-five-year-old woman named Sveta living in Dharamsala, told me that everything in her life was leading her to become a shaman. Her family had shamanic ancestors, she was often sick as a child, and she was born with special marks on her body. "When I was born, they said, 'The child is marked' [Rus. *rebenok mechenyi*]," she said. Later she survived three clinical deaths, the experiences of which led her to become interested in Buddhism. This is how Sveta describes her relationship with spirits as a child:

When I was little, I saw things and I heard things. But I was afraid, I was always terrified. . . . Darkness . . . fear of darkness . . . someone was always following me. I would wake up at night and see how everything around me was moving. There were many spirits. I feel them sometimes. I hear their voices. Nagas, for example. When you are at the river bank. When the water is prattling. Or in the presence of the masters of the water, masters of the earth, masters of the trees. . . . There are many spirits everywhere.

Sveta comes from a picturesque mountainous region of Buryatia, which some Tibetans liked to visit in the mid-1990s because it was a perfect environment for Buddhist retreats. Through these visits, Sveta became seriously interested in Buddhism, and by the first years of the twenty-first century, permanently moved to Dharamsala to become a chöd

---

20. When I asked Marianna why she thought the Khambo Lama was so opposed to her going to India, she said he did not want her to date Tibetans (Rus. *chtob ne begala s tibettsami*). "He already knew that not all Tibetans were good. You know how we Buryats, when we saw a Tibetan before, it was like, wow, a guru! Actually, I am kind of glad I listened to him then," she said. "Now I understand: all these loser Tibetan young guys who scream 'I love you, beautiful!' when you pass by on the street, all they want is just to get you in bed with them."

apprentice with the Jebdzundamba. She also brought her fourteen-year-old son and younger brother with her, both of whom became successfully incorporated into Tibetan exile structures: the brother attends the Tibetan Medical and Astrological Institute, while the son, after a brief stint as a novice at Gyüto Monastery, now studies *thangka* painting at the local iconography school. She describes her current relationship with spirits as being radically different from that of her childhood:

It's very good for chödpas to have shamanic roots. We have a special relationship with spirits. We talk to the spirits and make offerings to them. One should not be afraid of them, but be compassionate. They come here for help. They suffer a lot. And the practice of chöd helps them really well, at their level. We love them and express compassion. We do not take refuge in them, not at all—and this is very important to remember—on the contrary, *we* help *them*. Like in shamanism, we communicate with them, but through compassion.

Another young Buryat woman in her early thirties described the difference between shamanism and chöd as follows:

In shamanism, only one deity is being called upon. This deity is above the shaman, it dictates to him, while the shaman asks him for help and protection. Here we invite many deities, and we do not ask anything of them. On the contrary, it is *us* who give to them. Women, as mothers, have a much more organic tendency to give and to share. That is why, in some ways, chöd is easier for us than for men.[21]

Thus, without giving up shamanic beliefs, Buryat Buddhist women develop a particular relationship with spirits through chöd, which is different from that of shamans and Buddhist men. While shamans, in their eyes, supplicate them, and male Buddhist saints, such as Padmasambhava in Tibet or Namanei Lama[22] in Buryatia, famously "tame" indigenous spirits, forcefully turning them into "protectors" of Buddhism, chöd practitioners, both female and male, interact with them through compassion. The "conversion" of spirits also takes place at the end of the chöd ritual, but is treated as another kind of a gift. Chöd,

21. The statement that there is a single deity above the shaman and the shaman asks the deity for help does not necessarily comply with ethnographic evidence. From my own work with Buryat shamans, I learned that shamans might have multiple spirit helpers while the relationships between shamans and their spirits are not limited to the simple offering/protection exchange.
22. Namanei Lama is a popular saint in the Aga region, well known for his activities of "converting" shamanic spirits and binding them by oath.

thus, according to adepts, constitutes a double giving—of the body and of the dharma. In fact, the idea of giving and of the "free gift" is central to the discourses of chöd. But are these gifts truly free?

The "Pure" Gift?

The gift has been a crucial topic since the beginnings of anthropology, usually related to the role of exchange in human societies. One of the most influential works, Marcel Mauss's *The Gift*, broke new ground in a number of ways. First, he blurred the lines between "gift" and "commodity" societies, showing that all societies have elements of both, although to varying degrees. He focused, however, on the theme of how gifts (and exchange in general) serve to build social relationships through giving, receiving, and reciprocating. Second, he described the gift as a "total social phenomenon," in which "all kinds of institutions are given expression at one and the same time—religious, judicial, and moral . . . likewise economic" (Mauss 2000 [1925]: 3). Finally, Mauss questioned Malinowski's notion of the "pure gift," suggesting that no gift is ever really free.[23] Since the notion of the pure gift is quintessential for Buddhists in general and chöd practitioners in particular, let us revisit the debate over the free or pure gift.

A pure gift is an act of giving for which nothing is given in return. In *Argonauts of the Western Pacific*, Malinowski argued that such gifts occur between husbands and wives and parents and children (Malinowski 1961 [1922]: 177). Mauss doubts that this gift is either disinterested or free, seeing the gifts of husbands to the wives as reciprocating for sexual services (Mauss 2000 [1925]: 73). Similarly, Derrida argued that a free gift was impossible, a kind of misrecognition:

For there to be a gift, *it is necessary* that the donee not give back, amortize, reimburse, acquit himself, enter into a contract and that he never have contracted a debt. . . . It is thus necessary, at the limit, that he not *recognize* the gift as gift. If he recognizes it *as* gift, if the gift *appears to him as such*, if the present is present to him *as present*, this simple recognition suffices to annul the gift. Why? Because it gives back, in the place, let us say, of the thing itself, a symbolic equivalent. (Derrida 1992: 13, original emphasis)

---

23. Malinowski later revised his position in *Crime and Custom in Savage Society*, denying his earlier idea that transactions between Trobriand spouses are "pure gifts" (1926: 41).

According to Derrida, if a free gift were to exist, not only would there have to be no debt contracted, but the gift could not be recognized as such by either the donor or the recipient. Mauss's and Derrida's insights have set the terms for subsequent debates. Mauss's singling out of "reciprocity" as the defining feature of the gift has provoked criticism by Indologists, who all pointed out that Mauss purposefully omitted the discussion of unreciprocated gifts in the Indic religions, relegating it to a footnote (2000 [1925]: 146–147n61). In Hinduism, Buddhism, and Jainism *dāna* is the special category of the gift which *must not* be reciprocated (Laidlaw 2000; Ohnuma 2007; Parry 1986; Raheja 1988; Trautmann 1981). Analyzing Jain rituals of almsgiving to renouncers, James Laidlaw suggests that Jain laypeople's gifts to renouncers come close to fulfilling Derrida's requirements: these gifts are not reciprocated or recognized as gifts in the classic sense by either donors or recipients. By donating food, the laypeople do not expect any immediate benefits from the renouncers. These gifts, however, are not completely selfless, because such gifts generate karmic merit (Laidlaw 2000). Related to this is that Jainism, like Buddhism, features a doctrine of the "worthy recipient"—the higher the recipient, the more merit such a gift will generate.[24] Food donations to renouncers are motivated by the desire to accumulate as much good karma as possible. On the other hand, the renouncers are not expected to give teachings in return for these gifts. Thus, "Jain society," Laidlaw suggests, rests on a system of unreciprocated gifts. Giving to a worthy recipient is an example of the so-called free gift denied by Mauss and Derrida (Laidlaw 2000: 626). But can the gift given with a certain purpose, albeit nonreciprocal, be considered free?

To organize the many varieties of *dāna* in Indian Buddhism, Reiko Ohnuma proposes the threefold typology of *giving up*, *giving down*, and another meaning of *giving up*, which involves giving up the world, renunciation. Ohnuma suggests that most religious gifts in Buddhism are those that flow "upward," that is, from a regular practitioner to individual virtuous monks, the entire Sangha, and the Buddha. Contrary to Laidlaw, however, she does not consider such offerings pure gifts, but simply a kind of exchange, in which offerings are given in order to accumulate karmic merit. The higher the recipient, the more merit

---

24. The notion of a worthy recipient has direct socioeconomic implications for contemporary Himalayan Buddhist monasticism. Since Buddhist notions of women discussed in the previous chapter mark nuns as less worthy recipients, most lay donors prefer to give to monks, as it accumulates more merit. As a result, monks who are viewed as more virtuous are also richer, while nuns always remain poor (Gutschow 2004: 17).

one earns by giving, since the Buddha himself is said to have advocated choosing one's recipients "with discrimination." Giving down, on the other hand, produces very little merit, either worldly or transcendent. Some examples of giving down are giving to wicked people, animals, and beggars. The motivations for giving up and giving down are also entirely different: giving upward is done out of respect and worship with the goal of earning merit; giving downward is done out of compassion with no expectation of reward (Ohnuma 2007: 152–153).[25] Would giving down then be a free gift, an act of pure generosity, when no reciprocity is expected either from the immediate recipient or from impersonal forces like karma? Ohnuma appears to believe that indeed, it would be, suggesting the kind of giving down done by exceptional beings, such as the bodhisattva's gift of his body or the Buddha's gift of the dharma, constitute an example of such a pure gift (2007: 167).

To summarize, we have two competing candidates for the status of the free gift in Indic religions—one is the Jain (and Buddhist) giving up to superior beings and the other is giving down to inferior beings when performed by enlightened beings, such as buddhas and bodhisattvas. But what about giving down performed by nonexceptional beings, such as humans, to beings that are most definitely not "worthy recipients"? While chöd involves both giving up (to superior deities during the "white feast" part) and giving down (during all three feasts), its emphasis is dramatically on inferior beings, who are first given the body parts and then the dharma. The entire symbolic universe of chöd, from its taking place on the cremation ground to using the thighbone trumpet to summon harmful spirits, is organized around gifts to recipients who are usually not considered "worthy." This giving is said to be done exclusively out of compassion and, at least according to the practitioners, does not require anything in return.

Chöd is, of course, not the only Buddhist ritual that involves giving down. One instance of giving down in common Buryat rituals would be the Buddhist version of the oboo rituals discussed in chapter 2, which involve offerings to *savdaks* (Buryat from Tibetan *sa bdag*), the "land master" spirits, who, while being important to the laity, come at the bottom of the official Buddhist hierarchy. Lamas recognize that

25. The consideration of who is a worthy recipient is, however, not quite consistent in Buddhist thinking. Some schools, for example, advocate giving to the sick, regardless of their actual spiritual worthiness, as it brings merit. Other schools actively oppose the whole hierarchy of worthiness, stating that it is unacceptable that "one person's merit is dependent upon the moral qualities of another (the recipient), thus violating a strict understanding of karma" (Ohnuma 2007: 154).

savdaks, who have a fickle and unreliable nature, can cause real harm and thus must be occasionally appeased with presents in exchange for their good behavior. As one monk put it, "Shamans pray to savdaks, but we just give orders to them." While the oboo ritual is a kind of giving down, it is different from those described by Ohnuma and Laidlaw in that it is not done with compassion but with the expectation of direct reciprocity. Chöd, on the other hand, involves *unreciprocated* giving down, or so it is said.

Unreciprocated free gifts are also those that are entirely disinterested or desireless. Buddhism, however, involves a "hierarchy of desires," in which higher and more subtle desires (as Ohnuma calls them, "approved" desires) approach the status of being "desireless." Such desires include the desire to attain nirvāṇa or Buddhahood, to become an arhat or a bodhisattva, or a desire for desirelessness itself (Ohnuma 2007: 150–152). While the gift of the body in chöd is not entirely desireless, it involves approved desires, such as to abandon the sense of self, necessary for achieving enlightenment. In terms of the pureness of the gift, chöd is thus more similar to the alms given by Laidlaw's Jains, which engage laypeople and renouncers in a system of unreciprocated gifts. The spirits receive both the body and the dharma, yet the practitioner expects nothing from the spirits themselves. The only thing that is asked from the harmful spirits is to "become altruistic" (Ensa Chöd, verse 54, Molk's translation p. 162). The practitioner's benefits will come later in the form of impersonal karmic merit.

A significant contrast between a Jain's unreciprocated gifts and chöd is the object of the offering. Offering one's body, essentially self-sacrifice, has a strikingly different ontological status from offering any other kind of sacrifice.[26] Death, according to Georges Bataille, cannot be an example of meaningful exchange; it is instead an instance of what he calls "excess" and "absolute expenditure" (which for him is the ultimate characteristic of sovereignty) (Bataille 1991). By Buddhist logic, controlling one's own death, as it happens in chöd, is the ultimate domain of sovereignty. Buddhist sovereignty also requires the realization of selflessness, completely abandoning the notion of an independently existing "self" achieved through both intellectual deconstruction of this concept and by engaging in actions and desires that are classified

---

26. Most recently, self-sacrifice among Tibetan Buddhists has been discussed in relation to the proliferation of acts of self-immolation among Tibetans. See a special online forum by the journal *Cultural Anthropology* devoted to this issue, especially da Col 2012a, Makley 2012, and Gyatso 2012. See Willerslev 2009 for theorization of self-sacrifice based on Siberian field materials.

as selfless. In this context, by committing self-sacrifice as a selfless act (or at least construed as selfless by most practitioners), chödpas attempt to constitute themselves as sovereign subjects. In this way, it appears as if death were the ultimate free gift, an *anti-economy*, as Bataille would have it.[27] Should we then consider the gift of one's own body pure and free, since it is excessive to the point of being wasteful and most likely never reciprocal?

Yet self-sacrifice and death are only "wasteful" (in Bataille's sense) if we have a closed system where there is no rebirth or links between beings from different lifetimes.[28] If for a moment we put aside Mauss's and Derrida's skepticism of the very possibility of the free gift, doctrinally, chöd appears to comply with the idea of the unreciprocated gift or at least the gift that is not directly reciprocated (having the benefit of return in form of impersonal karmic merit). During my ethnographic research, however, I came to observe certain aspects of the ritual, quite meaningful to practitioners but not necessarily emphasized in the devotional text (although not absent from it, either), which suggest that the gift of the body might in fact bring some returns. One such aspect is the prominence in Buryat discourse of so-called karmic creditors (Tib. *lan chags mgron*) as recipients of the gift in chöd.

"Karmic creditors" are beings to whom one "owes" something from previous lifetimes. These could be one's parents, ancestors, or people from important past relationships, but also animals that have been eaten or used for other purposes, such as transportation or medical experiments. The notion of a creditor, a person or an entity to whom something is owed, immediately cancels out the idea not only of the *free* gift, but of the gift per se, since, as Derrida noted, in order for there to be a gift, one must never have contracted a debt (1992: 13). For an average Buddhist, however, the list of creditors is so long that repayment of debts often becomes central to the very practice. I suggest that if Buryat chöd does not quite involve a free gift, it is precisely because practitioners are bound by reciprocal obligations to these particular recipients of the gift. Although karmic creditors can include various beings, many Buryats mentioned their ancestors when asked about karmic creditors. Indeed, the relationship with the dead always involves a system of reciprocal obligations, an economy, where, as the anthropologist Alan Klima has argued in a rather different Buddhist setting, "it is possibly the case that in general everyone owes something to the

---

27. For an incisive analysis of the notion of death in Bataille, see Baudrillard 1998.
28. I thank Gray Tuttle for this observation.

dead whether they realize it or not, which is to say, whether or not they are mindful that there is 'economy' in a possible, true sense of the term between the living and the dead. A life-and-death obligation, you might say" (2002: 239). By this logic, chöd no longer qualifies as an antieconomy defined by excess and useless expenditure, but is a quite real exchange economy. As I argued earlier, establishing relationships with the dead is crucial for many postsocialist societies, since it constitutes a productive way to restructure meaningful universes and establish continuity of time and space in the wake of the political and social collapse. How does chöd contribute to this emerging necroeconomics?

Karmic Creditors

According to chödpas, karmic creditors are beings to which one owes something from previous lives, and until a practitioner pays his or her "debt" to them, he or she will encounter various obstacles in this life. This model is referred to as "karmic retribution," a distinctively Buddhist explanation of misfortune (Mumford 1989: 161). Most famously, in chöd, the creditors from various temporal planes arrive as hungry ghosts, to whom their share is given. Many chödpa women told me that children were among our main karmic creditors; they are born so that we can pay them back. They, in turn, most likely will be paying us in their next lives. In the same way, we need to pay back those ancestors who remained behind, as they have all been our parents in one of the lifetimes. Related to this, women claim themselves to be more suitable as chöd practitioners, since they are naturally more "giving." How does the discourse of the gift in chöd coexist with one of karmic retribution? What exactly is being paid back to the creditors?

The question of what exactly is being given in chöd provokes lively discussions among practitioners themselves. While I was in India, I observed the following debate, which took place both among Buryats and Russians in Dharamsala and virtually, through Internet Russian-language Buddhist forums. One chöd practitioner, a Russian, criticized the notion allegedly expressed by the Jebdzundamba in one of his lectures that "it is better to feed one bodiless spirit than one hundred monks."[29] The critic,

29. Many Russian Buddhists who practice chöd do not belong to the Gelukpa school and thus do not consider the Jebdzundamba an unquestionable authority. Many practice chöd in other Tibetan traditions, such as Kagyu or Nyingma. Most Buryats, who are Gelukpas, practice chöd under the Jebdzundamba's auspices and are very sensitive to such criticisms.

visibly scandalized by such an unexpected reversal of traditionally worthy (monks) and unworthy (hungry ghosts) recipients of the gifts, provoked the audience further by stating that true *dāna* would be a real gift
of blood. He continued his point by ridiculing the chödpas, these "self-
proclaimed bodhisattvas, who sit around imagining their bodies being
devoured by demons" while the world is being plagued by real problems,
such as poverty and disease. The Buryat chödpas, who initially were at a
loss as to how to react to such a serious accusation, eventually addressed
Chimit, the Buryat monk working closely with the Jebdzundamba.
Chimit argued back (and later his statement was recorded, transcribed,
and copied to multiple Internet forums) that the critic misunderstood,
first, the real meaning of *dāna-pāramitā* (Skt. for "the perfection of giving") and, second, what is being given in chöd.[30] Referring to Tsongkhapa's Lamrim, he said: "The perfection of giving does not depend on
whether we deliver living beings from poverty or other problems. If this
were the case, enlightened beings of the ages past must not have practiced it well, as otherwise we would not have any poor today. . . . The
perfection of giving is when we give away even the fruits of our giving
[meaning earned karmic merit]."[31] Stressing the intention of giving away
the results of giving as superior to regular material gifts, he referred to
the Buddhist traditional distinction between two types of giving: "outer"
giving (giving of material objects, such as money and food) and "inner"
giving, such as the offering of one's own body, but, most important, the
dharma. The dharma is what is really being given in chöd, he emphasized. Who are the main recipients of this dharma?

Although karmic creditors are usually conceptualized in Buddhism
as various human and nonhuman beings, including animals, when
asked about the recipients in chöd, many Buryat practitioners whom I
interviewed emphasized the importance of the ritual for their departed
ancestors. Buddhism abounds in stories of non-Buddhist ancestors who
have become hungry ghosts and need to be rescued from various hells.
In China, Buddhism succeeded only by recuperating Chinese family
values: as filial piety penetrated into Buddhism, parents were included
in prayers, resulting in the institutionalization of the Ghost Festival,
uniquely devoted to the salvation of ancestors. During this festival, laypeople present offerings to Buddhist monks to gain salvation for their

30. For example, at http://chodru.livejournal.com/6576.html.
31. Lamrim, "The Stages of the Path," the magnum opus of the founder of the Gelukpa school
Tsong kha pa (1357–1419), is the quintessential text studied by all serious Buryat Buddhists, both
lay and monastic.

ancestors because the Buddha states in a famous story that it is impossible for family members to provide gifts directly to their departed ancestors (Faure 2003: 146; Teiser 1988). Buryat chöd practitioners, I suggest, have found a way to save their own ancestors by giving them the most precious gift—that of the dharma. As they articulated, the creditors appear to come from various temporalities: from the distant shamanic ancestors to the most immediate atheist socialist ancestors. What unites them is that not having been properly exposed to Buddhism, the karmic creditors might be languishing in one of the Buddhist hells and must be saved as a return for their kindness in one's previous lives. While all harmful spirits are offered salvation,[32] it appears that the karmic creditors are the only ones involved in the relations of reciprocity, because by saving the creditors, one's own debt is also being paid.

The Poison of the Free Gift: On Religion and Postsocialist Economy

From samsara's peak down to the hells,
Gathered gods and ghosts, whatever appear and exist
'Specially harmers, demons, obstructers and
Local spirits, have loving mind and come here!
(ENSA CHÖD, EXCERPT FROM THE "RED FEAST")

All these beings have been my parents
To return their beginningless kind care
Having pleased them giving my material form
Also, giving Dharma, I shall free them.
(ENSA CHÖD, EXCERPT FROM "TONGLEN MEDITATION").[33]

Many a time, during the performance of chöd at Tak-ten House, I marveled at how the chöd ritual integrated the central Tibetan Buddhist practice of *tonglen* (literally translated from Tibetan as "give-take"). Tonglen, a meditation practice of taking others' sufferings and giving one's happiness to others, usually followed the white, red, and manifold feasts. While tonglen does not necessarily presuppose exchange only with those whom we earlier identified as karmic creditors, many

32. While it might appear that these "other" harmful spirits might take part in an exceptional case of a free gift, the earning of merit and their "conversion" to Buddhism still seem like an adequate return.

33. Molk's translation (Kyabje Zong Rinpoche 2006: 161–162).

chöd practitioners, when asked to whom specifically they are giving their bodies and the dharma, refer to this class of beings. I have also noticed that most do not perceive tonglen or the feast practices as free gifts, but rather as the return of payment. Curious about what may lie behind this insistence on repaying one's debts, I conducted further investigation of the term "karmic creditors" as used in the postsocialist Buryat and wider Russian context.

Interestingly, it turned out that the notion of karmic creditors (Rus. *karmicheskie kreditory*) was no longer unique to Buryat Buddhists. It has become incorporated into the generic spiritualist Russian New Age–like discourse, as well as those of major religions. The notion of karma has become so dissociated from its Indic religious connotations that even Orthodox Christians today can be heard speaking about one's karma and even "karma of the nation." In the initial postperestroika years of the 1990s, the imagination of ex-Soviet citizens of all backgrounds was captured by the series Diagnostics of Karma, written by S. N. Lazarev, the Russian researcher in the field of "bioenergetics" and healing. After the phenomenal success of this book series, which, taking the most general notion of karma as the cumulative effect of one's actions in this and all previous lives, offered specific methods of "diagnosing" and "correcting" it in order to influence the course of events in one's life, "karmic" discourse in Russia became part of the mainstream. Cleaning one's aura, fixing one's karma, and opening one's chakras (Rus. *pochistit' auru, podpravit' karmu, otkryt' chakry*) became common services offered by practitioners of all stripes, with most Russians unaware of its origin in Indic thought. While advanced Buddhist believers obviously discredit these attempts as a misunderstanding of the idea of karma, New Age ideas of "balance" in all spheres of life, including one's checkbook, and Buddhist notions of karmic credit and debt became mutually constitutive. Perhaps tellingly, many of my Buryat interlocutors admitted going through a phase of being exposed to New Age ideas in the early nineties—such as being fascinated by H. P. Blavatsky's writings or attending lectures of the Roerich Society—before "discovering" their "traditional" religion.[34]

Anthropologists have long noticed the relationship between postsocialist economic transformation and religious beliefs, especially in

34. H. P. Blavatsky (1831–1891) was a popular Russian mystic philosopher, founder of the Theosophy movement. Nicolas Roerich (1874–1947), also a Theosophist, was a Russian painter, spiritual philosopher, and explorer of Central Asia, Tibet, and India. These two authors have been extremely influential not only in the Russian New Age movement, but in indigenous religious revivals of non-Russian minorities within the Russian Federation.

relation to notions of morality (Lindquist 2000; Rogers 2005b; Verdery 1996a). If the economic transition from socialism—which depended greatly on personal links—consisted in transformations of this communal sociality into the more impersonal relations of the market, how might it manifest itself in the religious sphere? On the one hand, one can always discern new "market relations" in the sphere of quasi-religious services, such as shamanic healing, divination, and magic. Indeed, New Age ideas have been shown to agree remarkably well with the spirit of capitalism and personal entrepreneurship (see, for example, Heelas 1996: 95–96). Whatever its origins might be, the deployment of the ideology of balance as expressed in the notion of the karmic creditors and debtors in traditional Slavic-style magic, Siberian shamanism, and Buddhist traditions strikes one as a curious combination of karmic and capitalist discourse. Asked whether it is morally appropriate to ask for payment for her services, one Russian magic practitioner replied: "I always require payment. Partially, it helps to get rid of those who want to get the divination for free [Rus. *prosto tak*] or those who are used to free stuff [Rus. *khaliava*] and think everyone owes something to them. But there are energy laws. If you gave something away, you should receive something back. Otherwise, you create karmic debtors."

In a similar way, another one said, "Any work should be compensated. This is the law of the conservation of energy." Yet another practitioner opined that if a diviner is not able to fix a price for her services, she must subconsciously have a low opinion of herself—not a good thing for a "white" magic specialist focused on fixing others' problems! Most practitioners agreed that services and favors, as opposed to strictly cash, should also be considered adequate payment.

Although controversial, *khaliava*, "free stuff," has often been locally construed as appealing to the "Russian soul" in its potentially subversive and anticapitalist implications. The rejection of khaliava has often been related to the rejection of old socialist values both by Russians themselves and by scholars (Borenstein 1999). It has to be pointed out, however, that khaliava in socialist times most commonly implied getting something for free from the state while maintaining social reciprocity, such as described in the quotation above, and was quintessential for the functioning of the system. While it is tempting to oppose a socialist "economy of favors" to the logic of the market and qualify this "give-and-take" discourse as characteristic of postsocialist market relations, it has been noted by many anthropologists that the idea of reciprocity of services was crucial to all precapitalist societies. In many Siberian societies, for example, it is widely believed that the shaman must not cure for free—at least a symbolic payment must be given, or the ritual will not be effective (Potanin 1883: 61).[35]

Hence, the free gift is not only anathema to capitalism. Jonathan Parry describes an instance when an unreciprocated gift can be "poisonous"—the case of Benares priests whose position obliges them to receive gifts, although with these gifts they also absorb the sins and pollution of the givers (Parry 1989: 66–77). Similarly, Gloria Goodwin Raheja demonstrates how certain free gifts can transfer evil, sin, and affliction to the recipient (1988). Parry and Raheja choose to focus on the role of the free gift in removing inauspiciousness, as well as on the fact that there exist certain categories of people who cannot reject the gift. They demonstrate that what appears to be a free gift can be greatly harmful to the recipient while the giver, by contrast, gets rid of his sins.

I have observed in the Russian and Buryat contexts that the free gift might also be harmful to the giver (albeit for very different reasons than in the Indian context). There is a persistent belief among religious specialists in Russia that one cannot perform services for free, for when nothing is being transacted between the healer and the client, the practitioner might lose his or her "gift" of healing (Rus. *dar*).[36] Instead of being poisonous for the receiver, the free gift here acts as poison for the giver, threatening to destroy his or her most precious possession, the ability to heal. The fact that free gifts can be damaging for both the giver and receiver confirms Mauss's intuition of the centrality of social reciprocity.

At first sight, the chöd practice, with which this chapter has been concerned, appears somewhat removed from both the real-world exchange of favors and market transactions, since for a non-Buddhist the give-and-take remains imaginary. Whether or not the particular situation of postsocialism might have informed the understandings of the transactions in the symbolic universe of chöd, the lofty idea of the free

35. Potanin writes that, according to the rule, the shaman's drum cannot be removed from its place without putting a gift on the place from where it was removed (1883: 61). In contemporary Tuva, there exist many expressions to signify payments for shamanic services: *dat' pod buben* (Rus. for "give something in exchange for the drum," for example, *dat' pod buben loshad'*, "to give a horse for the drum") or *polozhit' vmesto bubna* (Rus. for "to put instead of the drum," for example, *polozhit' chai ili sakhar vmesto bubna*, "to put sugar or tea instead of the drum") signifies payment for shamanic services. I thank Ksenia Pimenova for this information.

36. Charging too much money, however, may also result in the punishment of the practitioner by taking away his or her *dar*. The gift of healing must not be abused, which signifies that magical services are still construed as separate from the rest of the market, subject to the ideas of morality and partially resisting commodification.

gift manages to coexist with market-like relations between "creditors" and "debtors." Chöd, however, has another, more practical dimension, which goes beyond the scope of this chapter, since it is only beginning to take root among contemporary Buryats (despite its widespread popularity in prerevolutionary times).

On their return to Buryatia, some Dharamsala adepts perform chöd not as a private meditational practice, but as a magical service for clients pursuing particular goals, mostly healing of illnesses believed to be of nonbiological origin (those caused by harmful spirits).[37] Chöd has also begun to be established as a regular religious service in some temples, which everyone can attend for a donation. In order to unravel the implications of such developments, it is necessary to consider the functioning of everyday Buddhism in Buryatia, which is built around temple and private rituals attended by believers with specific practical goals. Most often, these goals include prosperity, health, and obtaining luck in various tasks, for which specialized daily services devoted to particular Buddhist deities responsible for these domains have been institutionalized. If prosperity is in question, one is advised to attend a temple service for Namsarai (Skt. Vaishravana), the god of wealth, or, if one needs to improve his or her health, a service for the Medicine Buddha needs to be requested. Individual monks are also available to perform these services privately for a donation. Lamas routinely serve as family counselors, psychotherapists, diviners, and shamans, with their "symbolic capital" coming directly from being effective in such practices. While, in many other Buddhist countries, the performance of these rituals also constitutes the major activity and income of monasteries and individual incomes of religious specialists, in contemporary Buryatia such ritual exchanges might also tell us a great deal about the relationship between the specifically postsocialist economic shifts and emerging political imaginaries. The next chapter will examine these processes while considering the story of another key Buryat religious personality, whose body and mind became emblematic of a desired modernity and religious reform, allowing for alternative sources of sovereignty within larger transnational religious and economic orders.

37. In contemporary Mongolia, chöd is sometimes also recited for the sick and dying. Bawden also notes, quoting contemporary Mongolian reference books on local customs, that chöd formed part of certain burial rites (1997: 40).

SIX

Buddhism after Socialism: Money and Morality in the World of *Saṃsāra*

"Oh, I've always wanted to meet someone from America. I plan to get there soon . . . on a business trip [Rus. *po biznesu*]." The lama pointed to the kitchen corner, where heaps of empty boxes displaying the Amway logo were stacked. He proudly informed us about his recent involvement with the US multilevel marketing company Amway, distributing its "environmentally friendly" products, which included a host of personal care and domestic items, from laundry detergents to toothpaste and breath fresheners to multivitamins.

I had just arrived in one of the most beautiful regions in Buryatia, with snowy peaks, blue lakes, and pine forests interspersed with picturesquely grouped white boulders, resembling miniature Zen gardens. In order to get there, I pooled my financial and logistical resources with a Buryat colleague, a scholar of Buddhist philosophy, who had won a grant to catalog surviving Buddhist book culture, finding himself in the unfamiliar role of fieldworker. Darima, my landlady in Ulan-Ude, referred us to her distant cousin Timofei, a well-known and respected local lama, who agreed to be our host and guide for the next few weeks. We had just set up camp in one of the spare bedrooms in the lama's spacious wooden village house and were enjoying tea in his sun-lit summer kitchen while making our introductions.

As our conversation progressed, the lama proclaimed that the "old" theory of prescribed poverty for the Buddhist monk had become completely unsustainable in modern times. In general, he said, the negative view of wealth, which, according to him, was still prevalent in contemporary Russia, should be considered a shameful legacy of the Soviet period. "Thanks to the possibility of becoming Amway distributors," he continued, "our villagers finally started to lift themselves out of poverty without the help of the state, which, anyway, is not doing much for us these days." Saṃsāra (the endless cycle of death and rebirth), he declared, was having to work nine to five for a meager state salary, whereas individual entrepreneurship provided a true way to Buddhist liberation. This last statement turned out to be too much to stomach for a classically trained Buddhologist. Raising his eyebrows, my colleague politely asked if the lama had ever opened the Vinaya, the code of monastic discipline. Wanting to remain proper guests, I kicked my friend under the table. But it was too late. Our host clammed up, bringing our chat to an end.

Ironically, it was the proper, St. Petersburg–educated Orientalist who may have been in the wrong, for, as the recent Buddhological research has demonstrated, a careful study of Vinaya reveals complex and contradictory attitudes toward private property and wealth in early monastic communities, not simple asceticism, which itself might be a product of the Western colonial imagination (Schopen 2004a). For more modern times, we need to ask about the peculiar relationship among postsocialist economic transformations, contemporary religious practice, and "classical" Buddhist doctrine, or rather, what is generally *perceived* as classical Buddhist doctrine. The question of "markets and moralities" in recent postsocialist life has been well studied (Humphrey 2002b; Lemon 1998; Mandel and Humprey 2002; Grant 1999), yet the religious dimension awaits fuller treatment (Rogers 2005a; Lindquist 2000; Verdery 1996a).

After the awkwardness of our first conversation subsided, and the lama accompanied us in our research in the surrounding communities, I repeatedly found our triangular relationship—of the entrepreneurial lama, the classical Buddhologist, and the anthropologist—to raise questions about the many forms of religious life under postsocialism. In this chapter, I continue to explore changing discourses about money, religion, and morality in the new Russia. My aim is to demonstrate how Buryats combine particular interpretations of Buddhist doctrine with enduring socialist and newer postsocialist values to navigate broader economic realms.

Buddhism, Ethics, and Political Economy

One famous strand of thought in the scholarship on religion, ethics, and political economy is Max Weber's thesis on the relationship between the rise of bourgeois capitalism and Protestant ethics. In *The Protestant Ethic*, Weber identified a particular disposition characteristic of sixteenth-century Protestants that he described as "inner-worldly asceticism," which, he argued, contributed to the rise of capitalism (1958 [1930]). Less cited is Weber's work on Asian religions, such as his sociology of Buddhism and Hinduism, where he continued these themes, examining these religions from the standpoint of their attitudes toward political economies (1958).

Buddhism, according to Weber, was the ultimate world-rejecting religion, preoccupied with mystical illumination rather than the control of economic affairs within the world. Buddhism's most important characteristic was "world flight," which precluded the development of any rational economic ethic. For Weber, Buddhism was a religion of pure salvation; it did not concern itself with exerting methodical control over everyday life, as did the ascetic forms of Protestantism. The "acquisitive drive" of capitalism, Weber says, existed among Asian religions, including Buddhist traders, artisans, and peasants: it was no weaker among Buddhists than Protestants. What was lacking, however, was a distinctive capitalist "spirit" that Weber argued was characteristic of ascetic Puritanism, whose "ethical and rational limitation of the quest for profit" enabled capital accumulation. Like many scholars, including Buddhologists of his age, Weber believed there was an "authentic" Buddhism, practiced in ancient India. However, the drive for mystical illumination was not prevalent among the "completely altered manifestations Buddhism assumed in Tibetan, Chinese, and Japanese popular religions." Still, popular magical religiosity did not lead to a rational, methodical, and "disenchanted" control of life, relying instead on rituals and sacramental procedures (1993 [1922]: 266–269).

While he made accommodations for the "popular" Buddhisms elsewhere in Asia, Indian Buddhist monasticism for Weber remained the "ideal type." Buddhism was a "specifically unpolitical and anti-political status religion, more precisely, a religious 'technology' of wandering and of intellectually-schooled mendicant monks." Since monks were not allowed to deal with money, have private property, or work, he concludes that no rational economic ethic could have developed (Weber 1958: 206, 216). Such a view of Buddhist asceticism, advanced by European sociologists and philosophers on the basis of their reading of secondary sources, was so prevalent that even the polymath sociologist Georg Simmel used Buddhist monks to illuminate his argument in his pioneering work *The Philosophy of Money*. Buddhist monks, according to Simmel, are an example of how poverty, functioning as a positive value, can elevate money to absolute importance. Buddhist monks, he writes, are prohibited from owning anything but the "little things of daily use."

This prohibition is most severe with regard to gold and silver. The benefactor who has intended to give money to the monks cannot do so and has to give it to an artisan or trader instead, who thereupon hands over to the monks the value of the money in kind. If a monk does accept gold or silver, he has to do penance before the community and the money is given to a friendly layman to purchase basic necessities, since the monk himself is not allowed to provide them. . . . Poverty has become a jealously guarded possession, a precious part of the inventory of value in an existence estranged from the diversity and the interests of the world. (Simmel 2004 [1900]: 251–254)

While what Simmel writes is true in Theravada traditions, in which monks do not touch money and often have attendants who carry their money ("not touching gold and silver" is one of the novice vows in the Vinaya), this is not the whole story, as the Vinaya also has ways of getting around such rules.[1] As demonstrated by recent research in Buddhist studies, one of the early Indian Vinayas, the Mulasarvastivada, redacted in the fifth and sixth centuries CE (this Vinaya is also held by all monks of all sects in Tibet), included all sorts of provisions for monks to have property and wealth.

In his article "The Good Monk and His Money in a Buddhist Monasticism of 'the Mahāyāna Period,'" Gregory Schopen decries the fact that "neither Indian Buddhist monasticism nor the Buddhist monastery in India has been allowed to have anything like a real history." Using original textual and archaeological sources, he demonstrates that monks had personal property and private wealth, left wills, engaged in trade, inherited property, took interest-bearing loans, hired and over-

---

1. The handling of gold and silver by monks was controversial from very early in the tradition. According to a Theravada account, some one hundred years after the passing of the Buddha, a council was held in Vaisali to consider ten practices of certain monks that were seen by other monks as violations of the monastic code. One of these practices was touching gold and silver. The council ruled that this constituted a violation of the code, but some monks refused to accept the ruling, leading to a schism in the sangha (Lamotte 1988: 126–140).

saw laborers, and accepted money, emphasizing that these were not violations or exceptions, but normative rules recorded in the Mulasarvastivada Vinaya. This Vinaya included a range of economic instruments from written wills to permanent endowments, monetary deposits, securities, and even health insurance. An important source of revenue for an Indian Buddhist monastery was providing facilities for the sick—not the poor, but the rich laity, with the expectation that when they died, their estates would go to the monastery (Schopen 2004a: 1, 6–10). Although Schopen deals with a slightly later period in Indian Buddhism than Weber's ambiguous ancient tradition, he doubts that Buddhist monks were ever required to renounce private property, arguing that European scholars' assumptions about Buddhist monasticism's requirements for the renunciation of private wealth and property are derived from St. Benedict (Schopen 2004a: 14).

It appears, however, that St. Benedict's version of monasticism influenced not only Western scholars of Buddhism, but many present-day Asian Buddhists as well. Given Buryats' Eurasian history and orientation, it is perhaps less surprising that they would hold Buddhist monks to the Benedictine standard, believing that the Buddhist Vinaya proscribes wealth. The scene of my Buryat Buddhologist colleague shaming the lama for not properly reading the Vinaya and engaging in practices supposedly incompatible with it is only one ironic testament to these permutations. Another was the pervasiveness of specifically Weberian themes among contemporary Buryats.

The Buddha and the Spirit of Postsocialism: Buryats Read Weber

Some Buryats I have talked to about the current economic situation have complained that it is their religion, Buddhism, that may prevent them from becoming financially successful by placing negative values on wealth. The perceived incompatibility between two postsocialist transformations in Buryatia—the renewal of Buddhist practice and the advent of the free market—makes some Buryat Buddhists anxious. Some educated Buryats cite Weber, saying that their nation and other Asian Buddhist nations are forever behind Europe and America, due to Buddhism's inherent lack of the Protestant-like qualities necessary for the development of capitalism. I have been surprised, in contrast, to discover that some Buryat public intellectuals are attempting to put Weber's ideas into practice by arguing that Buddhism does not lack any of the qualities highlighted in Weber's description of Protestantism. They argue that what needs to be done is first to rectify and clarify to the public what "real" Buddhism used to be and then attempt to change certain attitudes toward money in contemporary Buryatia.

Recently, something akin to a manifesto on money and morality in Buddhism has been posted at Sait buriatskogo naroda (Site of the Buryat Nation)—an increasingly important Buryat Internet portal which includes a discussion forum. Since its creation in the first years of the twenty-first century, the forum has played a key role in bringing together many well-known young Buryat intellectuals and activists in Buryatia, European Russia, and abroad, turning it into a main hub for the Buryat diasporic blogosphere and a vital alternative to the official media. For some of my Buryat interlocutors, this forum was the only way to make their ideas public. As they explained to me, they saw their mission on the forum as "educational," since the forum is read daily by hundreds of Buryats who seek answers to pressing cultural and historical questions. A thread typically starts with a question from a reader, which one of the intellectuals constantly monitoring the forum attempts to answer, often sparking agitated debates. Some of these debates last for years: One thread, running from 2004 to 2008, was entitled "Buddhism and Private Property/State Power." It began with the following query posted in 2004: "It seems to me that Buddhism does not really like money or business. I think it says that since there is nothing eternal, it is not worthwhile to accumulate money and aspire to be rich. Please share your thoughts or references regarding this."[2]

The first reply stated that all religions preach complete asceticism in everything, because what is important for a religion is to work on the spiritual, not the material. The next contributor objected that this is not quite so. For example, Protestantism perceives one's success as an indication of a person's hardworking nature, which, in turn, pleases God. "I have heard somewhere," he continued, that "American Protestantism was a religion of businessmen." The long reply by a well-known Buryat intellectual started by saying that

Protestantism did not appear out of nowhere. It was part of Christianity, an ideology of the poor. However, the Reformation created a true revolution in people's minds. Buddhism also needs reform, which has been started but not finished by the

---

2. This and all the subsequent quotes in this section come from Sait buriatskogo naroda, http://www.buryatia.org/modules.php?name=Forums&file=viewtopic&t=3450&postdays=0&postorder=asc&start=0, accessed July 16, 2009.

Buryat reform movement [Rus. *obnovlentsy*] and which, it appears to me, has been completely forgotten by the contemporary clergy. Just think, if these reforms had been successful, Buryatia would have played the role of Calvinist Switzerland for the Buddhist world, because while in the early twentieth century in other Buddhist countries Buddhist reforms were just in the incipient stage, Buryatia had already started to implement real change.

Contradicting Weber's idea of Buddhism as a "flight from the world," he argued that, like Protestantism, Buddhism emphasizes the importance of social responsibility and acting in this world: "The notion of karma itself is built upon the idea of the responsibility of a person for his or her actions or words. The same idea is shared by the ideology of civilized business." The contributor continued by appealing to early Buddhist history, arguing that Buddhism has a full range of potential to cultivate successful entrepreneurship, citing the case of Anathapindada, the chief lay disciple of the Buddha, an extremely wealthy man and a patron of Buddhism, who became the model for a lay, wealthy saintlike character.

Buryats should institutionalize and popularize the cult of Anathapindada. Through this, we will be able to promote a positive image of a prosperous hardworking person, worthy of respect. Since a great part of Buryatia is under the enormous influence of Buddhism, let religion give us the moral right to be rich. . . . Ancient Buddhists encouraged entrepreneurship as a socially responsible business. These people were venerated at monasteries, receiving honorable titles of Protectors of the Teaching and Supporters of the Dharma. Buddhists understood perfectly well that a society of beggars would not be able to properly support the Dharma. . . . The Buddhist church of Buryatia absolutely must—moreover, this is in its own interests—support these tendencies in our society. Successful businessmen who participate in charity should be rewarded with the most flattering and honorable titles. The figure of the responsible businessman should be elevated. . . . Unfortunately, the *obnovlentsy* were not able to include this in their program, because they lived during the times of the Soviet cult of poverty. But what prevents us from doing it today?

Interestingly, he believes that had the *obnovlentsy*—such as Baradiin, Zhamtsarano, and other early twentieth-century native intellectuals introduced in chapter 1—not lived under the newly established socialism, they would have included in their project the reformation of Buddhist morality by encouraging private entrepreneurship as beneficial for the development of the dharma. It appears that nothing of the kind was included in their program, for officially, they were trying to reconcile Buddhism with communism, and not with private enterprise. Whether there are real historical grounds for this statement—for it is clear that the position of the *obnovlentsy* was a carefully calculated one aimed to protect their national and cultural autonomy—this projection of capitalist values by contemporary reformers onto their cherished predecessors indicates a major shift of values regarding money and private enterprise that has occurred in Buryatia, as well as in Russia in general, in the postsocialist period.

The Diamond Cutter

Another example of Weberian thinking among Buryats is the current controversy around Geshe Michael Roach, American Buddhist monk and diamond dealer, one of the handful of Westerners to obtain a geshe degree from a southern Indian Tibetan monastery. His immensely popular books, such as *The Diamond Cutter: The Buddha on Managing Your Business and Your Life*, recently translated into Russian as *Almaznyi ogranshchik: Budda o tom kak upravliat' biznesom i lichnoi zhizn'iu*, convinced some Buryat intellectuals not only that Buddhist spirituality was perfectly compatible with striving for material prosperity and personal enrichment, but also that the most ancient Buddhist texts actually include coded messages indicating the latter (Roach 2008, 2000). The following Russian editorial description of *Almaznyi ogranshchik* was posted in the same discussion thread:

Can a Buddhist monk do business? Can he be successful in business? Is there really a contradiction between the spiritual practice and material enrichment? The practical response to these questions is the life story of the author of this book, Geshe Michael Roach. Twenty years of persistent study of Buddhism got him a degree of the doctor of Buddhist philosophy. Seventeen years in the diamond business allowed him to transform a small firm with starter capital of fifty thousand dollars into a multinational company with annual sales in excess of one hundred million dollars. The author believes that the goal of both business and the ancient Tibetan wisdom, as well as of all human aspirations is one and the same: to become rich and to attain both outer and inner prosperity.[3]

---

3. The book includes parts of the canonical Buddhist text the Diamond Sutra, consisting of conversations between the Buddha and his disciple Subhuti, in which Roach integrates Tibetan commentaries and his own experiences as both a Buddhist and a businessman. He bases his

The legitimacy that Roach acquired in Russia originally stemmed from his involvement in 1992 with the Institut vostochnykh rukopisei (Institute of Oriental Manuscripts) (formerly Institut vostokovedenia [Institute of Orientalism]), the premier academic institution devoted to the study of the "East" at the Russian Academy of Sciences in St. Petersburg. Roach, whom some of my Buryat colleagues personally met as students in St. Petersburg in the early nineties, approached the Institute of Oriental Manuscripts, offering to sponsor the creation of a computer catalog of Tibetan manuscripts. This innovative proposal came from his Asian Classics Input Project (ACIP), a well-respected organization devoted to the preservation of Buddhist scriptures, of which Roach was a founding director. Roach trained Tibetan exiles to enter manuscripts into a computer and brought several Tibetan refugee monks from southern India to St. Petersburg, where they spent several years cataloging the scriptures.[4]

The fact that Roach was a founding director of such a major Tibetological project in the early 1990s means that he is often more generously regarded by his Buryat readers than by their Russian and American coreligionists.[5] His supporters try to stress the links between his writings and Buryat Buddhist culture. They argue that the Diamond Sutra is a text intimately familiar to prerevolutionary Buryats and Mongols, who kept it on their altars and invited lamas to their homes to

---

analysis on the commentary entitled *Sunlight on the Path to Freedom*, which he found in St. Petersburg's former Institute of Orientalism, where it had allegedly been brought from Tibet by an early Russian explorer. Roach states that the text was written by the Tibetan lama Choney Drakpa Shedrup (1675–1748) of Sera Mey Monastery. The Tibetan title of the text is *Thar par bgrod pa'i lam bzang zab don gsal ba'i nyi ma*, translated as *Sunlight to See the Profound, the Excellent Path to Travel to Freedom*, quoted from http://www.asianclassics.org/chone_lama/index_roman.html, accessed March 1, 2010.

4. See the ACIP website, http://www.asianclassics.org/. For more information on the St. Petersburg catalog, http://www.asianclassics.org/projects/st-petersburg and http://tibetica.oriental studies.ru/rus/index.php?option=content&task=view&id=2322. Some monks who have been involved in this catalog project have been among the first Tibetan refugees in postsocialist Russia who eventually became naturalized. Upon the completion of the project, some disrobed while others moved to Buryatia to become lamas there, adding to the transnational links I have described in earlier chapters.

5. See, for example, an American site denouncing Roach, http://diamond-cutter.org/index .html, as well as the discussion of Roach on Buddiiskii forum, a pan-Russian Buddhist discussion board, http://board.buddhist.ru/showthread.php?t=8272&highlight=%CC%E0%E9%EA%EB+% D0%EE%F3%F7, accessed July 22, 2009. A recent *New York Times* article questioned whether he is keeping his celibacy vows, given the fact that he lives in a yurt in the Arizona desert with "Lama Christie," a young woman whom he calls his "spiritual partner"; they have taken vows to never be more than fifteen feet apart from one another. The article quotes the Dalai Lama and Robert Thurman, who openly condemn Roach's behavior, urging him to disrobe. Roach, on the other hand, sees himself as a radical reformer, pushing the boundaries to adapt Buddhism for Western publics (Kaufman 2008).

recite it for them at least once a year. The recitation of the sutra was believed to bring good luck. The Roach enthusiasts on the Internet forum mentioned above even recommend that the readers go and look at their grandmothers' home altars: the sutra might still be there. They recommend reading it very carefully first and then seeing how Roach applied key principles from the sutra to build his multi-million-dollar diamond business while delineating a particularly Buddhist business ethic.

The so-called Diamond Cutter Sutra (Skt. *Vajracchedikā-prajñāpāramitā-sūtra*), a short and highly cryptic Sanskrit text written around the fourth century CE and translated into Chinese, Tibetan, and Mongolian, has challenged scholars and translators for centuries.[6] Composed in the form of a dialogue between the Buddha and his disciple Subhuti, the Diamond Cutter Sutra is regarded by commentators as setting forth the doctrine of emptiness and "no-self" (although the term *śūnyatā* [Skt. for "emptiness"] does not appear in the text) (Schopen 2004b). The sutra is purported to reorient the mind, upon repeated readings, in a radical way.[7] Roach, translating it stanza by stanza, applies basic concepts of what might be called "Buddhist pop psychology," to business. For example, using the doctrine of emptiness as signifying a socially and psychologically constructed nature of reality, he argues that all problems are "empty" and really just depend on our perspective, that what is a problem for one person is an opportunity for another, that nothing that happens is inherently "good" or "bad," and that we should welcome all problems as opportunities to learn something important about the nature of reality and its causes (Roach 2000: 187). He also cleverly plays on the central metaphor of a "diamond" as something "cutting through the nature of reality," discerning some mystical link between its centrality in the sutra and in his career as a diamond dealer.[8]

After having read Roach's *Diamond Cutter*, many were convinced by his arguments. According to one contribution to the Sait buryiatskogo naroda,

6. The title of the sutra might more accurately be translated as "The Perfection of Wisdom That Cuts like a Thunderbolt" (Schopen 2004b).

7. The Diamond Sutra was the first sutra translated into a European language by I. Ia. Schmidt, an Orientalist specializing in Tibetan and Mongolian and a Moravian missionary to the Kalmyks. It is considered to be the first book ever to be printed (in Chinese).

8. Ironically, *vajra* most likely does not mean "diamond" in the original sutra. A *vajra* is a Sanskrit term for a mythical weapon in the form of thunderbolt wielded by the god Indra and capable of cutting through anything. A diamond is called a vajra because it is said to be made from a thunderbolt.

The book is undoubtedly very interesting, which confirms the fact that in a religious teaching, a lot depends on the Teacher's interpretation. I really liked Roach's interpretation of *The Diamond Cutter*. That said, of course, I do not know the original, so I cannot compare. I am now obsessed with this thought about the power of interpretation, as I keep thinking: If *The Diamond Cutter* is present at every Mongol's house and they must read this book every year, why does not it influence the mind of the Mongols? They remain just as they have always been: one of the poorest peoples on earth.[9]

Ironically, this contributor appears to confuse Roach's *Diamond Cutter* with the original Diamond Cutter Sutra. Although subsequent commentators quickly pointed out that Buryats and Mongols did not keep Michael Roach's *Diamond Cutter* on their altars, the question, with its Weberian overtones, still hovered: why, despite a key text allegedly encouraging us to be both Buddhist and rich, are we still poor? Roach, who always gave his diamond money "back to the dharma," on the other hand, is viewed as an example of the "socially responsible" businessman, a model for emergent Buryat entrepreneurs.

In view of the elevation of the figure of the businessman-cum-Buddhist-patron, what do we make of Timofei, the multilevel marketing lama? Is he a visionary and a reformer or a confused individual compromising basic Buddhist tenets? In some ways, his views and activities are particularly reflective of postsocialist transformations of the notions of money and wealth. Before I discuss Timofei's case in greater detail, however, let us briefly consider what exactly these transformations have entailed for former Soviet citizens.

Between God and Mammon

Scholars have long observed how the Marxist idea of the "true value" created by labor led to the negative view of traders in the Soviet Union. Any income that did not come from production was considered immoral.[10] Buying something in one city or village and reselling it in another was considered a serious crime and punished with a prison

---

9. Quoted from Sait buriatskogo naroda, http://www.buryatia.org/modules.php?name=Forums&file=viewtopic&t=3450&postdays=0&postorder=asc&start=105, accessed July 22, 2009.

10. The attitude that trade and lending at interest are immoral, of course, existed long before Marx. Possibly taking its origin from Aristotle, this idea then resurfaced in the writings of Thomas Aquinas (Parry and Bloch 1989: 2–3).

sentence. People who engaged in such activities were referred to by the derogatory term "speculators" (Rus. *spekulianty*) and were almost universally condemned. The labor of speculators was not considered worthy of being remunerated, since they themselves did not produce anything. The central reason for this particular ideology was that the state held a monopoly on the distribution of goods, which were perpetually scarce (Humphrey 2002b: 59–60). Katherine Verdery has demonstrated that most socialist systems relied not on capital accumulation but on accumulation of the means of production. In contrast to capitalism, whose driving force is to maximize surplus value, socialism's "motor" was to maximize redistributive power, which Verdery called "allocative power." Thus, profit was somewhat irrelevant to socialist systems, in which one's ability to procure and redistribute goods counted much more than cash (1996b: 25–26; 1991: 420–421).

Humphrey notes that in both socialist and postsocialist Russia, an "economy" is impossible to separate from a "political economy," for all economic activities are laden with political-ideological values (Humphrey 2002b: 43). Money in Russia—as perhaps everywhere—has always been morally assessed, and a remarkable continuity might be observed from the Russian Orthodox theological opposition of God versus Mammon, with money held in deep contempt (Dinello 1998: 45–48), to the Soviet ideology, which appropriated village values of generosity and mutual aid (Pesmen 2000: 127). These older values conveniently merged with both the Marxist ideological opposition to the free market and the actual weakness of money under socialism, where no amount of money could buy the desired goods without proper social connections (Rus. *blat*) (Ledeneva 1998).

Out of all major transformations of postsocialism, it is the new importance of money that arguably became the most crucial. Starting with the "shock therapy" of the early 1990s, money "suddenly emerged as an independent social institution, almost totally disconnected from previous habitual practices and assumptions" (Oushakine 2009: 24–25). The strong moral resistance with which the general population continued to view trade and *biznes* (business) throughout the nineties was reflected in the contempt for the "New Russians" (the nouveaux riches of the nineties) and the persistence of the idea that all trade involved profiteering and even theft and thus was morally shameful and bad for the "Russian soul" (Pesmen 2000: 129). Drawing on Jonathan Parry and Maurice Bloch's classic investigation of money and morality, which makes a distinction between a sphere of short-term cash exchanges concerned with individual competition and transactions concerned with the reproduction of long-term cosmic and social order (Parry and Bloch 1989: 24), Serguei Oushakine applies their insights to theorize the post-Soviet situation.

Discussing the outburst of protest to the 2005 state finance reforms, when long-held social benefits, such as free transportation and medicine for pensioners and war veterans, were replaced with fixed cash allowances, he argues that it was not money's newly acquired importance per se that was offensive to former Soviet citizens, but the fact that social achievements had now been directly assigned monetary equivalences (instead of nonmonetary benefits associated with it in the past), breaking the link between short- and long-term transactions (Oushakine 2009: 26). As Parry and Bloch state, it is when the short-term cycle threatens to replace the long-term cycle that money, a "morally indeterminate instrument," becomes something "morally opprobrious" (1989: 28). Thus, the Russian long-standing moral ambivalence toward money exacerbated by the specifically socialist ideology, together with the disruptions of links with the past social order, all contributed to money being viewed with ambivalence in postsocialist Russia.

These existential anxieties had been aggravated, at least throughout the nineties, by more mundane reasons to view money with suspicion, as the embattled state failed on multiple occasions to maintain sovereignty over its own currency. As someone whose youth coincided with this turbulent period, I can attest that my own generation's awareness of money's transience sprang from reasons less metaphysical than practical. I remember my exhilaration when in 1993, during yet another currency recall caused by a massive inflation, an entrepreneur friend handed me, a newly unemployed high school graduate, and my equally poor bohemian friend a thick stack of rubles, some still with a Lenin portrait. "If you manage to exchange this wooden money [Rus. *dereviannye*, a common derogatory epithet for rubles at the time], it's yours," he said with a sigh.[11] "As for me, I have an important meeting to go to."

After spending a good part of the day happily queuing with panicked pensioners at a local Sberbank (the main state bank), we emerged with a much smaller stack of freshly printed bills without Soviet leaders' faces on them—bills so tiny that many people saw a "visual joke on devaluation" (Lemon 1998: 31). A few hours later, we happily converted

11. The joke of the time went: "U Vas den'gi est'? Deneg net, tol'ko rubli." ("Do you have money?" "No, no money, only rubles.")

the sum that just a few days ago had been a small fortune into a few bottles of imported liqueurs and Snickers bars, the ultimate objects of desire at the time.[12] Most, however, were not so lucky or carefree. With other obligations that left them no time to stand in endless Sberbank lines, they lost their life savings.[13]

Given this long-standing suspicion of money, did a new logic of the market finally become internalized? The fact that the Russian deep-seated distrust of money had slowly started to change became apparent during my subsequent research in Putin's Russia from 2001 to 2008—years that were characterized by a surge of general wealth, generated by Russia's energy resources. As I have witnessed many of my friends, acquaintances, and interlocutors—both in Moscow and in Buryatia—stocking up on imported cars, renovating their apartments, buying land for dachas in the countryside, and going on vacations to exotic spots all over the world, praising their newfound ability to "live as humans" (Rus. *zhit' po-chelovecheski*), I have wondered if the perceived contradictions, such as those between a long-lionized Russian "soul" and money's dubious moral status that so prominently figured in the researchers' accounts of Russia in the the 1990s, have become obsolete.[14]

12. Humphrey notes that the historical appearance of those luxury goods, which flooded the market in 1992–1993, is explained by the fact the first entrepreneurs in Russia started by importing the most profitable goods (2002b: 48). The "Karl Mars" and "Friedrich Snickers" bars, which were not luxury items, became such in Russia, because they were not affordable to most people in 1992–1993.

13. The traumatic memories of financial instability are still strongest among the oldest generation. In July of 2009, Russian television reported how a band of young female swindlers in Moscow had found out that a certain retired couple had a significant sum of cash (equivalent to thirty thousand dollars) sitting in their cupboard. The retirees were hoarding this money to contribute to purchasing an apartment for their daughter and to finish the renovation of their own apartment. Having introduced themselves as social workers, the swindlers came by their apartment, informing the couple about the upcoming money reform, in which current money would need to be exchanged for new bills within a very short period. Claiming that the social service specifically assigned them to make sure the pensioners would be the first to change their money, they convinced the couple to hand over all their cash, promising to bring back the new money shortly. They also warned the couple not to share this information with anyone, in order to make sure their money was changed before the reform was announced on television and everyone rushed to the banks. The couple never saw the con artists after this and only later called the police. As *Vremia* showed the desperate old couple huddling in their dilapidated apartment in the middle of unfinished *remont* (renovations) for which they no longer had the cash, it warned its viewers that these crimes were fairly common and instructed citizens that no real employee of a social service would ever show up at their apartment uninvited.

14. By the end of my fieldwork in November 2008, as the reality of the global economic crisis had started settling in people's minds, many of my friends, especially those working in the creative fields, had started recalling the nineties with great nostalgia as the time of no money but great cultural grassroots creativity, which had all but disappeared in the affluent early years of the twenty-first century. As budgets for cultural production were cut and the first layoffs took

Indeed, scholars working in post-1998 financial crisis Russia have observed radically changed attitudes regarding money, which is now viewed as a positive reflection of a person's hard work and merit. Analyzing the case of schoolteachers in St. Petersburg who have become direct sellers of Tupperware, Jennifer Patico demonstrates how they try to find meaningful ways to engage with transnational capital, refashioning trade from a shameful activity to a means of self-development and self-transformation (2009). Certain kinds of commerce in Russia can be very well integrated with religion and spirituality. Moreover, under certain conditions, trade itself becomes a *spiritual* pursuit.

Paths to Liberation: From Tantra to Grassroots Capitalism

When the lama mentioned at the outset of this chapter first brought up Amway, I recalled seeing Amway products in the bathroom of my landlady Darima (Timofei's distant cousin) in Ulan-Ude. "Yes, Darima works under me," the lama said, referring to the recruitment system characteristic of multilevel marketing strategies, in which each direct seller is encouraged to create his or her own distribution networks. The individual sellers, referred to as Amway Independent Entrepreneurs (AIEs), get products at discounted rates and make profits not only from their own sales and commissions but also from those they have recruited to work under them, who, in turn, may also attempt to recruit others, thus creating a pyramid distribution system. AIEs are rewarded with performances bonuses, as well as promoted to various levels (silver, gold, platinum, emerald, and diamond), according to the amount of their sales, which, in turn, depends on the number of people recruited as sellers. What originally sparked our conversation about Amway was Timofei's aspirations to become an emerald member (Rus. *kogda ia stanu izumrudnym*), which would win him a free trip to the United States.

Multilevel marketing is a form of direct sale, a billion-dollar industry created in the 1940s in the United States with roots in colonial-era peddlers who served as distribution channels in the absence of a reliable rail system. While this system is considered somewhat obsolete in the United States, sales in developing countries constitute nearly half of Amway's revenues (Cahn 2006: 126–127). Scholars who have studied direct marketing in Thailand and postsocialist China and Russia con-

---

place, some started looking toward the uncertain future with dark exhilaration, saying the end of the first decade of the twenty-first century might well be "the new nineties."

clude that its popularity in these countries derives from their serving as training grounds for new capitalist subjects, promoting their self-fashioning into entrepreneurs who take control of their own life and money (Patico 2009; Jeffrey 2001; Wilson 1999). Multilevel marketing (MLM) in this case becomes a symbol of desired modernity: "Whereas Maoism equated capitalism with immorality, today we find a discourse (both official and popular) of the market as a civilizing place that implies and confers the proximity to the modern. Despite widespread anti-MLM sentiment, chuanxiao [MLM] made sense to millions of people within the context of this larger progressive narrative" (Jeffrey 2001: 25).

Peter Cahn, studying multilevel marketing in Mexico, takes a different approach by arguing that, rather than understanding the explosion of direct selling around the world in terms of creating new modern economic subjects, one needs to look at how distributors rebuild and fortify the foundations of their faith through buying, selling, and consuming. Examining the strategies adopted by the direct-selling company Omnilife in Mexico, he demonstrates how the work of a direct marketer, which could otherwise be viewed as alienated, is imbued with spiritual significance. He also points out that many companies—in particular, Amway—were originally created with an explicit evangelical bent, which, despite being Protestant, appeals to Catholic religious sensibilities as well, defining marketing work as a "charitable mission" expressed in the slogan "people helping people" (Cahn 2006: 127, 133). Below, I suggest that Lama Timofei embodies and reconciles both of these conclusions: while serving as a case study of a new economic subject in a newly legitimated market economy, he clearly sees his distribution work as a mission, harmonious with and complementary to his religious vocation. In addition, like Chinese direct marketers who redraw and subvert established social geographies of both marginality and centrality by participating in multilevel marketing (Jeffrey 2001), Timofei redefines his position in global transnational networks while expressing resistance vis-à-vis the state.

A few days after our initial conversation, I discovered that Amway was in fact a "total institution," whose presence penetrated all nooks and crannies of Timofei's house, overtaking the entire sphere of domestic and personal care consumption. In addition to laundry detergents, kitchen and bathroom cleaners, vitamins, and nutritional supplements, there were also toothpaste, shampoos, body lotions, and makeup. Despite the costliness of these products—almost double what comparable common Russian and imported brands cost in shops at the time—the superiority of Amway products was regularly affirmed with unshakable faith. The toothpaste is expensive, but it "lasts much longer than a regular one—you just need to squeeze out a tiny bit"; the mascara and hydrating creams are "safe for your skin and eyes while regular ones are full of chemicals"; "children don't get enough vitamins," Timofei and his wife explained to me. However, using and distributing Amway products was not so much a matter of personal interest and health care as a social and religious calling. Timofei explained to us that he saw his mission as twofold: first, he supported the environmentally friendly products he distributed, and second, he saw multilevel marketing as an activity leading to a self-transformation that advanced the properly Buddhist path to liberation.

A self-proclaimed environmentalist, Timofei championed the cause of saving the environment, which is related to the maintenance of peaceful relationships with local land master spirits—one of his premier tasks as a Buddhist leader and practitioner. The importance of land master spirits and oboo rituals devoted to them, analyzed in chapter 2, is indeed the cornerstone of Buryat shamanic and Buddhist environmental ethics. Both shamans and lamas in Buryatia see themselves as key actors in mediating nature, and stories about wrathful acts of spirits as a reaction to the polluted environment abound. In the first years of the twenty-first century, shamans and Buddhist lamas joined forces with environmentalists in protesting against the Yukos oil company's proposed pipeline passing through Tunka National Park.[15] Local lore has it that shamans conducted a secret ritual to put a curse on Yukos's president, Mikhail Khodorkovsky, a persistent rumor that became especially poignant when he was imprisoned in 2003. Other popular stories include a helicopter crash with key European investors of a gold mining company, flooding of the Irkutsk region due to the construction of the Angara power plants, and individual acts of disrespect such as spilling a barrel of diesel oil in the forest, all ending in the tragic demise of the perpetrators (see Bernstein 2008). Describing how his village had become hopelessly polluted before he introduced Amway, Timofei showed me a patch in his garden where potatoes did not grow well—"because we used to pour soapy water from a regular laundry detergent." After switching to the "ecologically clean" Amway detergent, which can be poured into the ground

---

15. For an analysis of local environmental politics in Tunka National Park, see Metzo 2009.

with no consequences, potatoes had started to thrive in this long-bald patch.[16]

The second goal achieved by engaging in business is self-transformation, which involves organizing one's labor as meaningful and nonalienated. In his initial comparison of salaried nine-to-five work with saṃsāra, the Buddhist term for cyclic existence through endless rebirths and suffering, the lama attempts to transform the mundane into the existential. He sees his multilevel marketing work as a continuation of his religious work, which involves the practice of compassion. Indeed, the daily work of the Buryat lama consists of seeing people and solving their problems through ritual, advice, and sometimes just listening, thus combining the work of a religious specialist with that of a psychotherapist and counselor. By far the three most common problems that Buryats bring to lamas and shamans concern health, family, and finances.

The typical structure of these visits is as follows: first, the client states the problem; the lama then uses astrological calendars to determine the underlying cause. If the problem is assessed to be spiritual, divination might be used to determine what specific rituals and prayers are needed. Some are conducted on the spot while for others more elaborate religious services might be recommended. Often, the lama instructs his clients on what the Buddhist view of a particular problem should be, suggesting how to change one's outlook and train the mind to avoid these issues in the future. Sometimes, simple practical advice is given, such as leaving an abusive husband or changing one's job. Timofei does not usually recruit people during such work, but if a person confides financial difficulty, he might offer them an Amway brochure, just as he might recommend a particular doctor in case of a health problem. Interestingly, Timofei de-emphasized his magical propensities, suggesting that his work is essentially to "encourage" people (Rus. *podbodrit'*, *voodushevit'*). The following excerpt from my interview with the lama illustrates the significance of this power of positive thinking:

AB—What kind of problems do people bring to you?
LT (Lama Timofei)—Usually, it is the ignorance of the laws of nature. A person thinks that some problem is unsolvable. We encourage him and channel his efforts

---

16. The lama also told us that Amway cleaning liquids are so purifying that the locals have found a new use for them—they drink them as a remedy for hangovers. They are believed to be efficient in cleansing the body of the noxious effects of alcohol.

[Rus. *napravit' v pravil'noe ruslo*]. In fact, I think that things don't depend on me that much, I think our congregation members achieve everything themselves, we just help to channel these efforts a bit.

AB—Could you give some examples of common problems?

LT—For example, a person's son is leaving for some business. The parents worry, they want their son to be well received in whatever place he is going. In this case, we do some offerings to the spirits with tea and milk, we make this person confident in his actions. Before coming to us, the person was walking with shaky steps, but we tell him that everything will be fine, and he starts walking firmly. You saw how today this woman came, she was unsure when and whether she should have her surgery. I did all the necessary rituals and told her that everything would be all right. And now she is going to her surgery with confidence. They solve everything themselves, we just direct and encourage them [Rus. *napravliaem i podbadrivaem*].

I was particularly struck by a rhetoric that was strongly reminiscent of the New Age and self-help discourse of "positive thinking." In the previous chapter, I pointed out how religious discourse in Russia, whether Buddhist, Muslim, shamanic, or Orthodox, had become intertwined with New Age discourse, which, in turn, has become ubiquitous in the postsocialist period. Multilevel marketing appears to utilize this same rhetoric, which could be characterized as "quasi-religious."[17] This may explain the easy adoption of multilevel marketing by both religious specialists and their lay followers, as well as the integration of this business with religious worldviews. For his devotees, Timofei embodies not only a new subject of global capitalism, but also a person refashioning himself through spiritual labor. By engaging in private entrepreneurship, the lama expresses a profound distrust of the state as an institution, consciously choosing to join grassroots and transnational networks to bypass the state. Timofei's deep suspicion of the state, in turn, defines his position in the crucial local debate, addressed throughout this book, that still divides Buddhists in Buryatia: the debate over the place and the future of Buryat Buddhism within the larger transnational Tibetan world and within the Russian Federation.

For his followers, Timofei's practice of multilevel marketing as a joint religious and business vocation becomes a site for various types

---

17. Cahn argues in his article that companies like Amway should be considered "quasi-religious" organizations, defining the latter as institutions that do not "encourage devotion to a specific supreme being, yet still induce radical transformation in their participants' worldview" (2006: 134).

of mobility and positioning. First, by joining what he sees as a global grassroots capitalist network, the lama incorporates himself and like-minded Buryat adepts into yet another transnational order, the others being various international Buddhist networks discussed earlier in this study. Second, he represents upward social mobility, as he is seeking not to replicate the lives of his impoverished ancestors. While retelling his biography to me, Timofei emphasized the culture of poverty during his childhood, with his parents working as herders at a remote *zaimka* (farmstead) as part of a sheepherding brigade. Most of the year Timofei lived with his grandmother in the village while helping his parents to herd during the summer. Describing these overcrowded and unsanitary conditions, Timofei said he spent his whole childhood trying to figure out what career to choose to better his life. After a stint as a driver and in the military, he finally settled on that of a lama. Having studied for a few years at the Ivolginsk Monastery, he learned Tibetan and eventually took a job teaching at the Asian Languages Department of the Buryat State University in Ulan-Ude. The university teacher's salary, however, he stresses, was ludicrous, complicated by the economic crisis of the late nineties. In 2000, he moved back to his native town, started practicing as a Buddhist lama, and, joining forces with other young lamas, eventually raised the money for his own monastery.

The monastery in fact became his first independent enterprise. They built it from scratch, mostly by their own efforts, by converting a decrepit village house into a modern-style Buddhist *datsan*. The construction has taken many years and, although by the time of my visit, the main building already looked complete, work was still going on: as more money was arriving, stupas and gates were being added in the courtyard and a new lighting system was planned. Timofei stressed the importance of lighting, because, among other things, he sees his mission as educational, aimed to divert village youth from *gribki* (literally meaning "small mushrooms," but used to describe kiosks selling alcohol at night) and make the monastery courtyard a beautiful public space, where the young could meet at night for non-alcohol-induced activities.

The *datsan* proved very successful. This area already had an older monastery, restored from its prerevolutionary ruins, but in keeping with tradition, it was located outside of town, requiring a drive or a long walk. Timofei, on the other hand, built his temple right in the middle of town, so people often drop by for a quick prayer and ritual. The *datsan* is different from other monasteries described earlier mostly due to its small size—it qualifies as an example of an emergent phenomenon, the "private" family temple; besides Timofei, currently there is only one part-time lama permanently "employed" there. Timofei took two young apprentices from needy local families, whom he taught basic Tibetan in exchange for various services they performed for the maintenance of the temple. The income from visitors' donations was used for maintenance of the monastery and partially distributed among the part-time lamas, while the income from private sessions and rituals constituted the bulk of Timofei's income. In the early stages, when the monastery was still under construction, to supplement his income, Timofei spent a couple of years working as a teacher and class supervisor in a local middle school, a job he left after discovering multilevel marketing in 2007.

Talking about multilevel marketing, Timofei often expressed his admiration for a certain motivational speaker, author, and producer of *How to Get Rich in 60 Minutes* videos, Robert T. Kiyosaki, whose books in PDF files (translated into Russian) the lama keeps on his desktop computer. According to Timofei, Kiyosaki "writes like the Dalai Lama, because he encourages people. That is what lamas do too. Then people solve their problems themselves." Before I left, Timofei suggested that he copy the Amway reading materials he has been studying onto my flash drive. I agreed, thinking that I might later benefit from a discourse analysis of Amway's Russian localization strategies. Instead, he copied a large PDF file with Kiyosaki's 1992 book *If You Want to Be Rich and Happy: Don't Go to School?*, which in Russian translation, for some reason, lacked a question mark. That Timofei chose as his favorite book one that presents the failures of the educational system to make everyone rich reflects his suspicion of state-sponsored ways of learning. It might also be a part of a much larger skepticism and bitterness, derived from Timofei's generation's profound distrust of the Russian state as an institution.

Indeed, a recurrent theme in Timofei's personal narrative is a sense of betrayal by the state that "no longer cares"—a refrain widespread among people of the "transition" generation (Timofei was born in 1975), whose coming of age had been split between the last years of late socialism and the first postsocialist years.[18] Having been instructed

18. Those born from around 1972 to 1978 are notoriously difficult to classify in terms of the dichotomy between the "last Soviet" and the "first post-Soviet" generations. While Yurchak refers to people who were born between the 1950s and early 1970s and came of age between the 1970s and the mid-1980s as the "last Soviet generation" (2006: 31), many people born in the mid- and late 1970s, myself included, share much of the habitus of the properly "last Soviet" generation, while experiencing a distinct sense of rupture and alienation from the next, truly

in socialist values throughout most of his compulsory secondary education, Timofei then experienced the full spectrum of postsocialist transformations from hyperinflation and currency recalls to the near-complete erosion of the socialist welfare state. At the time of my visit, he talked with bitterness about his stints as a state employee. When he worked as a teacher for the Buryat State University and for a local middle school, the salary was humiliating and not conducive to his spiritual development. The state, in his worldview, was something that exploits or cheats you, and not to be trusted. Multilevel marketing, on the other hand, he asserted, was more like Buddhist Tantra—a secret knowledge passed through oral transmission based on direct personal experience. Both were conceived as grassroots initiatives existing outside state institutions, where horizontal, intimate, face-to-face connections were perceived as naturally more trustworthy than the impersonality of the vertical structures of power. Although Amway is not unlike the notorious Romanian pyramid schemes described by Verdery, teaching people not "market rationality but its mystification," with the market economy appearing as an "abstraction not governed by human agents" (1996a: 192–193, 202, cf. also Comaroff and Comaroff 2000), it presents itself as a platform for human action and self-realization.

Struck by this image of the venerable Buddhist method of oral transmission of knowledge from the teacher to the disciple applied to the capitalist business model, I wondered if Timofei's worldview signified a shift to an indigenously constructed version of postsocialist-influenced "Protestant Buddhism"—not in the sense of a middle-class Buddhism with distinct bourgeois values described by Richard Gombrich and Gananath Obeyesekere (1988: 202–241), but in the sense of emphasizing particular types of work as a vocation in this life, de-emphasizing magical practices, and highlighting its scientific, rational, and spiritual principles. This Buddhism stands in stark contrast to what is known in Buryatia as "traditional" Buddhism, "traditional" in this case signifying desired links with the pre-Soviet, nineteenth-century Buryat Buddhism in its alleged golden age. Timofei was extremely skeptical of the activities of "traditional" Buddhists headed by the Khambo Lama, expressing disbelief at what he called their "production of miracles," such as treasures found in the ground and goddesses self-arising on stones.

Politically, Timofei did not support the Khambo Lama's "Buryat

---

"postsocialist," generation. The rapid transformations in the country radically sped up time in the formation of a generation: from the late 1970s, every five or six years could be considered a new generation.

Buddhism," and thus his monastery did not belong to the Traditional Sangha of Russia. Instead, he and his followers viewed themselves as disciples of émigré Tibetan teachers, with Timofei's congregation being a member of the Board of Buddhists, an alternative umbrella organization uniting various Buddhist lay and monastic communities that attempted to go beyond the nationalist rhetoric by allying themselves with what they perceived as a more universalist form of Tibetan Buddhism led by the Dalai Lama. Timofei saw himself belonging to this larger imaginary religious community, which he viewed as a modern and reformed version of Buddhism. Likewise, for him, multilevel marketing presented a certain version of this desired modernity, one which included reformed and rational Buddhism. Ultimately, Timofei believed, these transnational networks of spiritualized commerce could put an end to Buryat poverty, which he attributed to Russian colonialism, Soviet collectivization, and finally to the marginalization of Buryats in the postsocialist economy, and could transform Buryatia from a humble *dotatsionnaia* (subsidized) republic to a more sovereign political body. If assertions of sovereignty in the Russian republics correspond directly to the level of indigenous economic competence (Bahry 2005), Buryat economic ideas discussed here clearly perform important political and cultural work.[19]

From Buryat Buddhist intellectuals seeking to revive an ancient Indian cult of Anathapindada, Buddha's favorite "socially responsible businessman," to suggesting that with the modernization of Buddhism through capitalism, Buryatia would become a "Calvinist Switzerland," to regarding certain kinds of commerce as a specifically *spiritual* vocation—in all of these one can discern a profound quest for a different kind of modernity. Socialism was also a modernist project, yet these new aspirations have forced people to remoralize money, disengaging it from the traditional negativity of Russian Orthodoxy, socialism, and Buddhism. In the process, they have come to visualize themselves as part of a different transnational order.

19. In connection with the financial crisis in Russia, in 2009 the central government issued a decree that all republics and autonomous regions whose debt exceeded 10% of their budget would lose their economic independence and would be governed directly from Moscow. In local parlance, the list of the regions lined up to lose their financial self-governance was quickly dubbed "the black list," estimated to include more than half of the Russian Federation's territorial subjects. Buryatia, whose debt is just under 10%, narrowly escaped being "blacklisted." Before 2009, a debt of 30% and higher would constitute the grounds for repealing economic self-government. Local politicians view the lowering of this number as part of the Russian government's strategy to impose centralized control on its regions and curtail their sovereignty (Zolotarev 2009).

Bodies, Gifts, and Sovereignty

A monastery is just like an airport, where the temples, stupas, and other religious structures serve as the signal towers. During the service, lamas invite gods to descend to earth in their airliners and help each believer participating in the service as much as they are able. And here the lamas play the role of the control tower officers. When the service ends, all the celestial visitors get back on their airliners and fly home. The believers in this case are sponsors who pay for gas. KHAMBO LAMA AIUSHEEV[1]

In the first years of the twenty-first century, Buryatia slowly started to recover from the instability and turmoil of the 1990s, entering a period of relative prosperity. It was around this time that Khambo Lama Aiusheev attempted to delineate, with characteristic humor and candor, the specific ways in which religion has come to be mediated in postsocialist life. In comparing a monastery to an airport and lamas to the control tower officers and identifying congregation members as responsible for the fuel charges, the controversial leader of Buryat Buddhism inadvertently touched upon some of the central themes that have long animated debates among both practitioners and scholars of religion: the role of priests and religious virtuosi in the maintenance of the cosmic order, the ritual economy required to support it, and the responsibilities of the faithful in this exchange.

1. This quote comes from a collection of contemporary stories about lamas and shamans collected and published by the folklore enthusiast Igor' Mukhanov (2005: 26).

This provocative statement immediately struck home, although interpretations differed. While some perceived it as an example of the "blatant commercialization" of post-Soviet Buryat Buddhism, others saw in it a positive validation of a religion in touch with the times. What "the times" entail is anyone's guess, but almost all readily discern signs of "modernity" in the circulation of money in the religious field, whether in the form of cash donations, monks with expensive cars and cell phones, or direct phone lines to the Ivolginsk Monastery, where one can order a specific prayer service through the operator, who enters one's astrological information into a computerized database accessible to lamas (Amogolonova 2008: 163). Whether this ritual economy is fervently disparaged, cheerfully embraced, or grudgingly tolerated, it is almost universally viewed as a sign of rupture with a purported originary form of Buddhism, almost invariably located elsewhere, be it ancient India, pre-Chinese Tibet, prerevolutionary Buryatia, or mythical Shambhala, all long-distance authorizations of a different kind.

Yet Buddhist monasteries have long served as "spaces for giving and receiving": it is precisely ritual exchanges involving giving and merit making that have always held and continue to hold Buddhist communities together (Benavides 2005: 86). What is striking, however, is that money, understood as a "condensation of deferred satisfaction," has much in common with both sacrifice and asceticism: all require postponements of immediate desires for the sake of a greater fulfillment at a later time. By this logic, Gustavo Benavides writes, "to solve the mystery of giving and receiving, of sacrifice and asceticism, of work, leisure, and agency, would be to solve the mystery of religion" (2005: 81–86). While that mystery must be left for another time, this study has sought to identify some of the complex connections among materiality, mediation, and technologies of transmission between northern and southern Asia, which together enable a renovation and transformation of Buryat Buddhist practice in the postsocialist period.

Consider some of the mediations which constitute contemporary Buddhism in Buryatia. Many of its narratives of origin and present identity hinge on the materiality of bodies, and hence, bodies have become quintessential technologies of transmission that can simultaneously make the past present and reveal the future. Exemplary bodies have paraded through this book—dead bodies, famous bodies, reincarnated bodies, celibate and ascetic bodies, and virtually dismembered bodies. From undead lamas to those haunted by their previous incarnations to those assembling and reassembling their own bodies, I have described how a characteristic mix of the Buddhist, Russian Orthodox,

Soviet, and postsocialist body politics, developed by Buryats over the centuries of borderland existence both within the Russian state and across the larger Tibeto-Mongolian world, have enabled extraordinary mobility across space, time, and even across life and death.

As in many other postsocialist contexts, necropolitics has been crucial in reordering cosmologies of time and space, revising the past, and reestablishing moral authority. Dead bodies have reconsecrated the post-Soviet Buryat landscape, setting in motion the appearance of treasure objects, which themselves acquire agency and intentionality by becoming enmeshed in social relationships. As we saw earlier, other events around dead bodies, including miraculous self-arisen images and treasure objects at the sites of ruins, have been interpreted as proof of Buryatia's move from quintessential periphery and extreme marginality in the Buddhist world right onto center stage, just as its religious history is being lengthened and authenticated. The Buddhist dead have literally come back to haunt the living.

Such empirical flows across areas that are not normally considered central to most historiographies, religious histories, and ethnographies offer a great deal to the explanation of broader issues of religion and postsocialism, offering a perspective on how our own knowledge about such regions is construed. By subverting established hierarchies of centers and peripheries, Buryat Buddhists are rebuilding their own legitimacy, staking out a place for themselves in the global religious marketplace. As I observed Buryats laboring to assert themselves as an alternative center of gravity for contemporary Buddhism, I could not help but ask: What would Buryat life look like if it were not located at someone else's periphery—whether Mongolian, Tibetan, Russian, or Inner Asian? What would the world look like if it were really at the center? Without fetishizing such centrality, I believe these questions help us rethink the ways in which academic knowledge has been configured through conventional area studies. They also help us reassess the larger impacts of these Cold War closures, new nationalisms, and postsocialist mobilities.

On a broader scale, such processes contribute to the ongoing reorganization of world religions caused by the end of socialism, in effect by *recentering* world Buddhism.[2] The end of socialism introduced new players on the stage of world religions, as faiths that had been suppressed for most of the twentieth century entered the now-global spiritual mar-

---

2. I thank Katherine Verdery for this observation.

ketplace. At the same time, formerly socialist territories attracted the attention of other religions, previously excluded from proselytizing there.[3] In her examination of the "restless bones" of the Transylvanian bishop Inochentie Micu, Katherine Verdery demonstrates the manifold ways in which these mobile religious relics contributed to shifting the power balance between Catholic and Eastern Christian churches in Europe (1999: 55–95). The Buddhist dead bodies considered here have played their own part in reconfiguring not only Buryatia, but the global Buddhist landscape as well.

Buryat body politics, however, are not exclusively necropolitics. The prominence of recent debates on issues of purity, masculinity, femininity, and national loyalties centered on religiously "redesigned" bodies, such as those of monastics and lay tantric practitioners, have turned these bodies into sites where competing understandings of the most pressing concerns of contemporary Buryat Buddhists are centered. The reappearance on Buryatia's streets of maroon- and yellow-clad bodies, also understood as a collective corpus of the Buddhist Sangha, points to "turning back the clock," marking Buryatia's self-display as a Buddhist nation and embodying economies of purity clad in soteriological anxieties. In this context, even the corpses voluntarily dismembered and renounced by their very owners, such as those of the chöd practitioners, cannot avoid being politicized, as notions of religious giving and taking clash, and sometimes seamlessly mesh with, postsocialist economic discourses and practices.

Powerful in their concreteness and immediacy, these bodies come face to face with another, albeit more abstract medium of potent postsocialist religious revival: money, required, in accordance with the Khambo Lama's quote above, to provide fuel for the celestial visitors' airliners. The newly monetized post-Soviet economy today is still a political economy, imbued with ideological values and linked to issues of power, nation building, and self-determination. It is in this context that the idioms of bodies, giving and taking, and sovereignty come together.

Using a striking corporeal metaphor of "dismemberment" (Rus. *ra-*

---

3. In Russia, the application of the 1997 Federal Law on Freedom of Conscience and Religious Associations resulted in difficulties with registration for "foreign" churches and reinforced the perception of Russia's four "traditional" religions—Russian Orthodoxy, Islam, Judaism, and Buddhism—as having more rights. While the federal authorities are not very knowledgeable about different Buddhist denominations, the Buryat Buddhist leadership attempts to interpret this law so as to restrict the rights of non-Geluk schools, at least in Buryatia. The Khambo Lama famously compares his "problems" with the Karma Kagyu school to those the Russian Orthodox Church faces with Protestants.

schlenenie) to refer to the Stalin-era separation of their ancestral territories, one of the early calls advanced by indigenous activists after the declaration of the Republic of Buryatia's sovereignty in 1990 was to join these parts back to the main body.[4] Almost twenty years later, the reverse has taken place: instead of being joined back to Buryatia, the two alienated territories have lost their autonomous status and became incorporated into larger territorial units: Irkutsk Oblast' and Zabaikal'skii Krai. It is worth pausing a moment to contemplate the language used by the Russian government, which calls these mergings of Soviet-era smaller units *ukrupnenie* (literally, enlargement) usually glossed in English as "amalgamation." The verb *ukrupnit'* (to enlarge), however, came to have a double meaning depending on the size of the referent. Thus, saying that Buryat autonomous okrugs of Aga and Ust'-Orda have been *ukrupneny* (enlarged) effectively signifies the opposite: that they have been eliminated and lost the status of "Federation subjects".[5]

This shifting of givers and takers is endemic to histories of sovereignties, as is well documented in another post-Soviet context (Grant 2009). Unlike the more porous discourses of sovereign rule in the Caucasus, however, Buryatia appears to have been forever branded a "taker." The Republic of Buryatia, like nearly all the twenty-one current republics within the Russian Federation, is referred to as a *dotatsionnyi* region. The regular English translation of *dotatsionnyi* as "subsidized," however, does not capture the etymology of the Russian term from the Latin *dotare* (to give, to endow), which correlates with the Russian *davat'* (give, bestow).[6] Regions that are not subsidized are called "donor regions" (Rus. *regiony-donory*). Tellingly, as of late 2009, the "donor" republics, such as Yakutia (Sakha) and Tatarstan, have been among the most reluctant to drop references to sovereignty from their constitutions (Goble 2009).

---

4. The Buryat-Mongol Autonomous Soviet Socialist Republic was established in 1923 and lost Aga and Ust'-Orda regions in 1937.

5. It is only when applied to the larger regions, which became receivers of extra territories, that *ukrupnenie* refers to the actual enlargement. As of January 2010, the Russian Federation consists of eighty-three territorial units (referred to as "Federation subjects" or just "subjects"), twenty-one of which are republics. Others include provinces (*oblasti*), territories (*kraia*), autonomous provinces (*avtononomnye oblasti*), and autonomous districts (*avtonomnye okruga*). Much of this is part of the early Soviet legacy, and the current politics of the federal center is to centralize by reducing the number of subjects. Subjects differ in the degree of autonomy they enjoy, with a republic, considered an "ethnic homeland" for an indigenous minority, having a nominal autonomy and its own parliament, president, and constitution.

6. A territorial unit of the Russian Federation is considered *dotatsionnyi* (subsidized) if most of its budget is coming from the federal budget. Currently seventy-one of eighty-three territorial units are considered subsidized (Anonymous 2010b).

Although seemingly grounded in solid economic statistics, the donor-donee relationship in the context of the new Russian federalism is as slippery and contingent as that of the givers and receivers in the chöd ritual, with its ever-shifting and constantly renegotiated give-and-take between karmic creditors and debtors. Even at the peak of regional assertiveness in the early 1990s, the central government put heavy restrictions on regional economic autonomy by imposing excessive taxation, quotas, and licensing on the overseas sale of critical resources, making it impossible for the so-called sovereign regions to develop any kind of independent economic life bypassing Moscow (Bahry 2005: 131–135). In this context, even "donor" republics rich in oil and diamonds can quickly become "donees," and thus candidates for losing much of their autonomy.[7]

As the Russian state "giveth and taketh" sovereignties, Buryatia now faces even greater challenges. A mere taker from the Russian point of view, unlike other more prosperous republics, it could not afford the luxury of resistance when it was designated to lose its sovereignty, however nominal it might have been. A few years ago anxieties about the elimination of the Buryat Republic itself seemed an exaggeration voiced only by "ethnonationalists." Yet, as of early 2010, Russian politics have realized the worst fears of many Buryats. In February 2010, a few months after the last references to sovereignty were dropped from Buryatia's constitution, the speaker of the State Duma, Boris Gryzlov, made national news that scandalized Buryat—as well as most other regional—publics by suggesting that *dotatsionnye* regions do not deserve to be considered "Federation subjects."[8] If pursued, this policy will make Buryatia, a 60% subsidized region, a prime candidate for a

---

7. Commenting on the fact that Mongolia is now economically ahead of Buryatia, the vice minister of Buryatia's economic development and foreign relations, Sergei Meshcheriakov, directly linked economic growth to regional sovereignty: "For a long time, our relationship with Mongolia was defined by the formula 'big brother—little brother.' . . . But now we are behind Mongolia. If you go to Mongolia, you can see the advertisements of Korean and Japanese firms everywhere. The cars on the streets are mostly Korean. . . . Unlike the leaders of Russian territorial units of the Federation, Mongolian governors have more opportunities to establish direct relations with foreign partners and attract investors. By contrast, we cannot influence the decisions of our federal central government. I think the solution would be to give more freedom to the Russian regions" (Volkhonskii 2007: 3).

8. Literally, Gryzlov announced that "a 'territorial unit' [Rus. *sub"ekt Federatsii*] is a high title, to which one should correspond. In my opinion, there should not be any federation units that are not self-sufficient. If only ten, twelve, or fifteen of our territorial units are 'donors' and the rest of them are subsidized (*dotatsionnye*) and live at the expense of the donor regions, I think that such regions should not have the right to be called 'sub"ekty'" (Sas 2010).

radical demotion of its status.[9] While the actual sovereignty of Buryat national units, both the republic and former autonomous districts, is clearly nominal, some Buryat intellectuals claim that their function is primarily *therapeutic*, arguing that history has shown that Buryats assimilate faster when they live outside these ethnic administrative units.[10] "The Republic of Buryatia," Nikolai Tsyrempilov said in an interview with me, "is the last bastion of our statehood. Buryats do not have any statehood anywhere—not in Mongolia, not in China. . . . Of course this statehood was created by the Bolsheviks, who handed out [Rus. *razdali*] these sovereignties and quasi statehoods right and left. It's like they have let the genie of national consciousness out of the bottle—it is no longer possible to squeeze it back in."[11]

It is not surprising that, caught in uneasy games of giving and taking, the Buddhist politics considered here have much at stake. In a way, by making direct alliances with the president's administration by claiming Dmitrii Medvedev's body as the goddess White Tārā, the Buryat Buddhist church is unlinking itself from territorial issues: should the Republic of Buryatia cease to exist, the position of Buddhism is expected to remain unchanged.[12] On the other hand, the stakes for Buryats here are not limited to the relationship with the Russian state. They include the contested issues of where Buryatia belongs within the larger Asian Buddhist world. Take, for example, the recent statement of the current Khambo Lama that minimized the role of Tibet in the transmission of Buddhism to Buryatia—a statement that scandalized many intellectuals and Buddhist adepts, making some seriously ques-

9. The recent proliferation of the idioms of *dotatsionnost'* in Russian politics deserves critical attention for its repercussions for the discourse of radical Russian nationalism. Increasingly, nationalists invoke this notion to argue that all ethnic entities within the Russian Federation are essentially *nakhlebniki* (freeloaders) feeding off Russia. A familiar refrain of "my ikh kormim, a oni eshche nedovol'ny" (we feed them, and they are still not happy) circulates widely in these circles. For more examples of the "we gave them so much" discourse, see Grant 2009.

10. The assimilation of "Western" or Irkutsk Buryats who are predominantly Russian Orthodox and rarely speak Buryat is sometimes quoted to support this argument. It has to be pointed out, however, that the assimilation of Irkutsk Buryats started with tsarist policies before the creation of socialist autonomous regions (see the introduction).

11. Interview, Ulan-Ude, September 2008.

12. One can even say that such alliances are a continuation of the early Buryat history in the Russian empire, when the Buryat Buddhist church was relatively independent of the local Siberian administration, governed directly from the capital. Indeed, the unshaken belief in the "good tsar" displayed by many ordinary Russians and non-Russian minorities has been well-documented (Trepavlov 2007). In a similar manner, Buryats have often believed that the source of their oppression was the tyranny and abuse of the local administration (Rus. *proizvol chinovnikov*) and sent countless delegations and petitions to the tsars, from Peter the Great to Nicolas the II, trying to rectify the situation, sometimes successfully.

tion not only his political inclinations but also his personal integrity. While the Khambo Lama is well aware of the standard narrative of the Buddhist transmission accepted in religious and scholarly circles (India-Tibet-Mongolia-Buryatia), when one considers the impact that idioms of the gift have for issues of self-determination, his cheerful denial of history might have deeper roots than a shallow nationalism. As he remarked in an interview with me, "Remember, what is different about Buryat Buddhism is that we did not *receive* it from Tibet or India like other nations, we just went there and *took* the parts we liked." A vast potpourri of historical facts and semifacts is being deployed in similar ways and has taken root in the popular imaginary: from the Mongols' political role in the development of Buddhism in Tibet, to the founder of the Gelukpa's school being "ours,"[13] to the early twentieth-century Buryat lamas who headed Tibetan monasteries and wrote "the best" Tibetan dictionaries, to the recent "arrival" of Itigelov—allegedly unprecedented in the Buddhist world. [14]

In the meantime, Buryat Buddhism is anything but homogenous, with many aspects of its history and present state open to wide interpretation. Many openly contest the position of the Buddhist Traditional Sangha of Russia, while some especially pious dissenters express their disagreement by voting with their feet and calling Dharamsala rather than Buryatia their spiritual homeland. "Opposition" Buddhist leaders dispute the legitimacy of terms such as "Buryat Buddhism," arguing that "even Mongols" do not exhibit such delusions of grandeur regarding their own more ancient Buddhist culture. Some Buddhist women, going against all odds of cultural stigma, don the robes of nuns, while others bemoan this as a threat to the survival of Buryats as a nation. Tibetan lamas who built their temples and congregations in Buryatia continue to enjoy great success and veneration, often blissfully unaware of the poignancies of local religious politics. The openness of the borders that enabled these unprecedented transnational flows has led to a never-ending influx of fresh ideas from many directions at once: from India through Buryat monks who study in Tibetan monasteries,

13. Some Buryats, including the Khambo Lama, believe that Tsong kha pa was a "Mongol." It is not quite clear on what they are basing this claim.

14. The dictionary was compiled by Geshe Chödrak (Chos grags, 1898–1972), a Buryat who escaped to Lhasa in 1923 to join the Sera Jey Monastery. He was later accused of being a "Soviet revisionist spy" by the Chinese during the Cultural Revolution and placed under house arrest (Horkhang 2005). His dictionary was published in China as *Dge bshes Chos kyi grags pas btsams pa'i brda dag ming tshig gsal ba (Gexi Quzha Zangwen cidian: Zang, Han duizhao)* (Beijing: Mi rigs dpe skrun khang/Minzu chubanshe, 1995 [1949]).

from Tibetan lamas who frequently visit or even permanently settle in Buryatia, from all parts of Buddhist Asia through modern-day cosmopolitan Buryat pilgrims, and from the "West" (which, in Buryats' view, includes European Russia, Europe, and North America) in the form of Buddhist teachers, as well as tourists, academics, and globetrotters.

While Gelukpa remains the predominant sect, practically all other forms of Tibetan Buddhism are now represented in Buryatia. Furthermore, non-Tibetan denominations have also been established, including certain Theravada currents from Southeast Asia. The shamanic community is as vibrant as ever, as are Buryat converts to a host of other religions, from Russian Orthodoxy to Islam to Hinduism to Evangelical Christianity, as well as those who creatively combine all the above to suit their needs. While many have gained their faith during the postsocialist period, others have turned decisively atheist or agnostic. It is these translations, appropriations, imitations, and repossessions, so fragmentary in nature, that are currently transforming Buryat society and religion.

Bibliography

Abaeva, L. L. 1991. *Kul't gor i buddizm v Buriatii* [Cult of the Mountains and Buddhism in Buryatia]. Moscow: Nauka.

Agamben, Giorgio. 1998 [1995]. *Homo Sacer: Sovereign Power and Bare Life*. Translated by Daniel Heller-Roazen. Stanford: Stanford University Press.

Aggarwal, Ravina. 2001. "At the Margins of Death: Ritual Space and the Politics of Location in an Indo-Himalayan Border Village." *American Ethnologist* 28 (3): 549–573.

Allione, Tsultrim. 1984. *Women of Wisdom*. London: Routledge and Kegan Paul.

Amogolonova, D. D. 2008. *Sovremennaia buriatskaia etnosfera: Diskursy, paradigmy, sotsiokul'turnye praktiki*. [Contemporary Buryat Ethnosphere: Discourses, Paradigms, Sociocultural Practices]. Ulan-Ude: Buriatskii gosudarstvennyi universitet.

Andreyev, Alexandre. 2001. "Russian Buddhists in Tibet, from the End of the Nineteenth Century–1930." *Journal of the Royal Asiatic Society* 11 (3): 349–362.

———. 2003. *Soviet Russia and Tibet: The Debacle of Soviet Secret Diplomacy, 1918–1930s*. Leiden: Brill.

———. 2006. *Tibet v politike tsarskoi, sovetskoi i postsovetskoi Rossii*. [Tibet in the Politics of Tsarist, Soviet, and Post-Soviet Russia] St. Petersburg: St. Petersburg University Press—Nartang.

Anonymous. 2004a. "Russkie buriaty v Kitae" [Russian Buryats in China]. *Inform-Polis*, July 7. Accessed March 1, 2011. http://www.infpol.ru/news/457/3123.php.

———. 2004b. "Otreksia ot sana: Sopernichestvo sredi tibetskikh lam v Rossii vylilos' v aktsiiu protesta" [Disrobed: Rivalry between Tibetan Lamas in Russia Ended Up in a Protest Action]. *Inform-Polis*, December 15, 4.

———. 2005. "Buriatskii Lenin: Interesnye i neob"iasnimye fakty" [Buryat Lenin: Interesting and Unexplained Facts]. Accessed August 8, 2009. http://www.koicombat.org/forum/viewtopic.php?f=7&t=8709.

———. 2006. "Na sto grammov tiazheleet khambo lama Itigelov posle vstrech s veruiushchimi" [Khambo Lama Itigelov Gains 100 Grams in Weight after Meetings with Believers]. *Inform-Polis*, May 17. Accessed October 8, 2009. http://www.infpol.ru/news/576/4638.php.

———. 2007. "Lenin, Mao i drugie mumii: Kak khraniat znamenitye tela" [Lenin, Mao and Other Mummies: How Famous Bodies Are Being Kept]. Accessed October 8, 2009. http://www.topnews.ru/photo_id_891_1.html.

———. 2009. "Konstitutsionnyi sud predlozhil respublikam zabyt' o suverenitete" [The Constitutional Court Proposed That Republics Forget about Sovereignty]. *Izvestiia*, June 8. Accessed August 5, 2009. http://www.izvestia.ru/news/news206618.

———. 2010a. *National Geographic Milestones*. Accessed December 2, 2009. http://press.nationalgeographic.com/about-national-geographic/milestones.

———. 2010b. "Regional'nye politiki prizyvaiut k vzveshennomu podkhodu pri ukrupnenii sub"ektov RF" [Regional Politicians Call for a Balanced Approach for the Amalgamation of the Subjects of RF]. *Izvestiia*, January 22. Accessed February 8, 2010. http://www.izvestia.ru/news/news229305?print.

———. 2012. "Buriat men'she, chem iakutov, no bol'she, chem sibiriakov" [Buryats Number Less Than Yakuts, but More Than Sibiriaki]. *Novaia Buriatiia*, January 16. Accessed September 2012. www.newbur.ru/articles/5911.

Anzhilova, Dara. 2007. "Chtoby rodit'—vniz golovoi!" [To Give Birth Take a Header!]. *Argumenty i fakty v Buriatii*, no. 40.

Appadurai, Arjun. 1981. "Gastro-Politics in Hindu South Asia." *American Ethnologist* 8 (3): 494–511.

Attwood, Lynne. 1990. *The New Soviet Man and Woman: Sex-Role Socialization in the USSR*. Bloomington: Indiana University Press.

Atwood, Christopher P. 1996. "Buddhism and the Popular Ritual in Mongolian Religion: A Re-examination of the Fire Cult." *History of Religions* 36:112–139.

———. 2002. *Young Mongols and Vigilantes in Inner Mongolia's Interregnum Decades, 1911–1931*. Leiden: Brill.

Aziz, Barbara. 1976. "Reincarnation Reconsidered; or, The Reincarnate Lama as Shaman." In *Spirit Possession in the Nepal Himalayas*, edited by John T. Hitchcock and Rex L. Jones, 343–361. Warminster: Aris and Phillips.

Badmaev, P. A. 2001. *Za kulisami tsarisma: Vospominaniia: Memuary* [Behind the Scenes of Tsarism: Memoirs]. Minsk: Kharvest.

Bahry, Donna. 2005. "The New Federalism and Paradoxes of Regional Sovereignty in Russia." *Comparative Politics* 37 (2): 127–146.

Bakic-Hayden, M. 1995. "Nesting Orientalisms: The Case of Former Yugoslavia." *Slavic Review* 54 (4): 917–931.

Baldano, M. N., and V. I. Diatlov. 2008. "Shenekhenskie buriaty: Iz diaspory v diasporu?" *Diaspory* 1:164–193.

Balzer, Marjorie Mandelstam. 1997. "Soviet Superpowers." *Natural History* 106 (2): 40–41.

———. 1999. *The Tenacity of Ethnicity: A Siberian Saga in Global Perspective.* Princeton: Princeton University Press.

Banzarov, Dorzhi. 1891. *Chernaia vera ili shamanstvo u mongolov i drugie stat'i* [Black Faith or Shamanism among the Mongols and Other Articles]. St. Petersburg: Imperial Academy of Sciences.

Baradiin, B. B. 1904. Dnevnik Badzara Baradiina, komandirovannogo Russkim Komitetom dlia izuchenia Srednei i Vostochnoi Azii v Zabaikal'e [Diary of Badzar Baradiin, Sent to the Transbaikal by the Russian Commitee for the Study of Central and Eastern Asia]. St. Petersburg Orientalist Archive, St. Petersburg, F. 87, D. 26.

———. 1908. "Puteshestvie v Lavran (Buddiiskii monastyr' na severovostochnoi okraine Tibeta) 1905–1907" [The Trip to Labrang (Buddhist Monastery on the Northeastern border of Tibet) 1905–1907]. *Izvestiia russkogo geograficheskogo obshchestva* [News of the Russian Geographic Society] 49 (4). Full text reprinted in Ermakova 1998, app. 5, 117–151.

———. 1926. "Buddiiskie monastyri: Kratkii ocherk" [Buddhist Monasteries: A Brief Sketch]. In *Ocherki istorii buriatskogo naroda* [Essays on the History of the Buryat People], edited by M. N. Bogdanov, 108–151. Verkhneudinsk: Buriat-mongol'skoe izdatel'stvo.

———. 2002. *Zhizn' v tangutskom monastyre Lavran: Dnevnik buddiiskogo palomnika (1906–1907)* [Life in the Tangut Monastery Labrang: A Diary of the Buddhist Pilgrim]. Ulan-Ude: Izdatel'stvo Buriatskogo nauchnogo tsentra.

Basaev, Sergei. 2008. "Dvorets dlia netlennogo tela" [Palace for the Incorruptible Body]. *Inform-Polis*, November 2. Accessed May 7, 2009. http://www .infpol.ru/newspaper/number.php?ELEMENT_ID=13237.

Basilov, V. N. 1984. *Izbranniki dukhov* [Chosen by the Spirits]. Moscow: Politizdat.

Bassin, Mark. 1999. *Imperial Visions: Nationalist Imagination and Geographical Expansion in the Russian Far East, 1840–1865.* Cambridge: Cambridge University Press.

Bataille, Georges. 1991. *The Accursed Share.* Vols. 2 and 3. Translated by Robert Hurly. New York: Zone Books.

Baudrillard, Jean. 1998. "Death in Bataille." In *Bataille: A Critical Reader*, edited by Fred Botting and Scott Wilson, 139–146. Oxford: Blackwell.

Bawden, Charles. 1961. *The Jebtsun Dampa Khutukhtus of Urga, Text Translation and Notes.* Wiesbaden: O. Harrassowitz.

———. 1985. *Shamans, Lamas, and Evangelicals: The English Missionaries in Siberia.* London: Routledge and Kegan Paul.

———, trans. 1997. *Tales of an Old Lama: From a Mongolian Text Recorded and Edited by Ts. Damdinsuren*. Tring: Institute of Buddhist Studies.

Belka, L. 2001. "K voprosy ob institute khubilganov v buriatskom buddizme" [About the Issue of Khubilgans in Buryat Buddhism]. In *Mir buddiiskoi kul'tury: Materialy mezhdunarodnogo simpoziuma 10–14 sentiabria 2001*, 120–126. Chita: ZabGPU.

Beloborodov, Stanislav. 2008. "Bitva po-monastyrski." *Rossiiskaia gazeta*, January 28. Accessed August 24, 2009. http://economy.buryatia.ru/index-n .htm?a=full&id=1226.

Benavides, Gustavo. 2005. "Economy." In *Critical Terms for the Study of Buddhism*, edited by Donald S. Lopez, 77–103. Chicago: University of Chicago Press.

Benjamin, Walter. 1969. *Illuminations: Essays and Reflections*. Translated by Harry Zohn. New York: Schocken.

———. 1998. *The Origin of the German Tragic Drama*. Translated by John Osborne. London: Verso.

Bernstein, Anya. 2002a. "Buddhist Revival in Buryatia: Recent Perspectives." *Mongolian Studies* 25:2–11.

———. 2002b. *Join Me in Shambhala*. Videorecording, 30 min. Watertown, MA: Documentary Educational Resources.

———. 2006. *In Pursuit of the Siberian Shaman*. Videorecording,72 min. Watertown, MA: Documentary Educational Resources.

———. 2008. "Remapping Sacred Landscapes: Shamanic Tourism and Cultural Production on the Olkhon Island." *Sibirica* 7 (2): 23–46.

———. 2009. "Pilgrims, Fieldworkers, and Secret Agents: Buryat Buddhologists and an Eurasian Imaginary." *Inner Asia* 11 (1): 23–45.

———. 2012. "More Alive Than All the Living: Sovereign Bodies and Cosmic Politics in Buddhist Siberia." *Cultural Anthropology* 27 (2): 261–285.

Bertagaev, T. A. 1970. "Ob etnonimakh 'buriat' i 'kurikan'" [On Ethnonyms "Buryat" and "Kurikan"]. In *Etnonimy* [Ethnonyms], edited by V. A. Nikonov. Moscow: Nauka.

Bishop, Peter. 1989. *The Myth of Shangri La: Tibet, Travel Writing, and the Western Creation of Sacred Landscape*. Berkeley: University of California Press.

Borenstein, Eliot. 1999. "Public Offerings: MMM and the Marketing of Melodrama." In *Consuming Russia: Popular Culture, Sex, and Society since Gorbachev*, edited by Adele M. Barker, 49–75. Durham: Duke University Press.

Borneman, John. 2004. *Death of the Father: An Anthropology of the End of Political Authority*. New York: Berghahn.

Boronoeva, Darima. 2003. "Rol' idei 'vozvrashcheniya na rodinu' v mirovozzrenii shenekhenskikh buriat" [The Role of the Idea of "Return to the Homeland" in the Worldview of the Shenekhen Buryats]. Paper read at the conference "Buddhism in the Historical, Ideological and Cultural Context of Central and Eastern Asia," Ulan-Ude.

Buck-Morss, Susan. 2000. *Dreamworld and Catastrophe: The Passing of Mass Utopia in East and West*. Cambridge, MA: MIT Press.

Budaeva, L. 2006. *Boginia Yanzhima: Fotoal'bom* [Goddess Ianzhima: A Photo Album]. Ulan-Ude: NovaPrint.

Bulag, Uradyn Erden. 1998. *Nationalism and Hybridity in Mongolia*. Oxford: Oxford University Press.

Buyandelger, Manduhai. 2013. *Tragic Spirits: Shamanism, Memory, and Gender in Contemporary Mongolia*. Chicago: University of Chicago Press.

Buyandelgerin, Manduhai. 2007. "Dealing with Uncertainty: Shamans, Marginal Capitalism, and the Remaking of History in Postsocialist Mongolia." *American Ethnologist* 34 (1): 127–147.

Cahn, Peter S. 2006. "Building Down and Dreaming Up: Finding Faith in a Mexican Multilevel Marketer." *American Ethnologist* 33 (1): 126–142.

Cattelino, Jessica R. 2008. *High Stakes: Florida Seminole Gaming and Sovereignty*. Durham: Duke University Press.

Chandra Das, Sarat. 1902. *Narrative of a Journey to Lhasa and Central Tibet*. New York: Dutton.

Cheah, Pheng, and Bruce Robbins. 1998. *Cosmopolitics: Thinking and Feeling beyond the Nation*. Edited by W. W. Rockhill. Minneapolis: University of Minnesota Press.

Chimitdorzhin, D. G. 2008. "Ivolginskii datsan" [Ivolginsk Monastery]. In *Zemlia Vadzhrapani: Buddizm v Zabaikal'e* [The Land of Vajrapāṇi: Buddhism in the Transbaikal], edited by Ts. P. Vanchikova, 423–435. Moscow: Dizain, Informatsiia, Kartografiia.

Clifford, James. 1988. *The Predicament of Culture: Twentieth-Century Ethnography, Literature, and Art*. Cambridge, MA: Harvard University Press.

Coffey, Wallace, and Rebecca Tsosie. 2001. "Rethinking the Tribal Sovereignty Doctrine: Cultural Sovereignty and the Collective Future of Indian Nations." *Stanford Law and Policy Review* 12 (2): 191–221.

Collins, Steven. 1997. "The Body in Theravada Buddhist Monasticism." In *Religion and the Body*, edited by Sarah Coakley, 185–205. Cambridge: Cambridge University Press.

Comaroff, Jean, and John L. Comaroff. 2000. "Millennial Capitalism: First Thoughts on a Second Coming." *Public Culture* 12 (2): 291–343.

Corwin, Julie A. 1999. "Controversy Doesn't End with Sacred Text's Return." *Radio Free Europe/Radio Liberty Newsline* 3, no. 191, pt. 1:30. Accessed July 31, 2009. http://www.hri.org/news/balkans/rferl/1999/99–09-30.rferl .html.

Cuevas, Bryan J., and Jacqueline Ilyse Stone. 2007. *The Buddhist Dead: Practices, Discourses, Representations*. Honolulu: Kuroda Institute with University of Hawai'i Press.

da Col, Giovanni. 2012a. "Five Armchair Reflections on Tibetan Personhood." *Cultural Anthropology* Hot Spots Forum: Self-Immolation as Protest in

Tibet, April. Accessed September 15, 2012. http://www.culanth
.org/?q=node/535.

———. 2012b. "The Elementary Economies of Dechenwa Life: Fortune, Vital-
ity, and the Mountain in Sino-Tibetan Borderlands." *Social Analysis* 56 (1):
74–99.

Dalai Lama the Fourteenth. 1997 [1962]. *My Land and My People: The Original
Autobiography of His Holiness the Dalai Lama of Tibet.* New York: Warner
Books.

———. 1999. *Kalachakra Tantra: The Rite of Initiation.* Somerville, MA: Wisdom
Publications.

David-Neel, Alexandra. 1965 [1932]. *Magic and Mystery in Tibet.* New York:
University Books.

Davidson, Ronald M. 2005. *Tibetan Renaissance: Tantric Buddhism in the Rebirth
of Tibetan Culture.* New York: Columbia University Press.

Derrida, Jacques. 1992. *Given Time: I. Counterfeit Money.* Translated by Peggy
Kamuf. Chicago: University Of Chicago Press.

Devonshire-Ellis, Chris. 2011. "Mongolia Enthrones Its Dalai Lama." *Investment
News and Commentary from Emerging Markets in Asia—China, India and
ASEAN,* December 5, op-ed commentary. Accessed March 2, 2012. http://
www.2point6billion.com/news/2011/12/05/mongolia-enthrones-its-dalai
-lama-10484.html.

Dierkes, Julian, with contributions from T. Shakya and Byambajav D. 2011.
"Dalai Lama on Surprise Visit to Mongolia." *Mongolia Today. Information
and Analysis of Contemporary Mongolia,* November 8. Accessed March 2,
2013. http://blogs.ubc.ca/mongolia/2011/dalai-lama-surprise-visit/.

Dinello, Natalia. 1998. "Russian Religious Rejections of Money and Homo Eco-
nomicus: The Self-Identifications of the 'Pioneers of a Money Economy' in
Post-Soviet Russia." *Sociology of Religion* 59 (1): 45–64.

Dirks, Nicholas. 2001. *Castes of Mind: Colonialism and the Making of Modern
India.* Princeton: Princeton University Press.

Dondokov, Boris. 2002a. "Menia oni ne uspeiut vziat'" [They Will Not Manage
to Capture Me]. *Inform-Polis,* September 18. Accessed December 5, 2009.
http://www.infpol.ru/newspaper/number.php?ELEMENT_ID=2519.

———. 2002b. "Telo lamy ostalos' netlennym" [The Lama's Body Remained
Incorruptible]. *Inform-Polis,* September 18. Accessed December 5, 2009.
http://www.infpol.ru/newspaper/number.php?ELEMENT_ID=2518.

Dorzhiev, Agvan. 1994 [1921]. *"Predanie o krugosvetnom puteshestvii" ili povest-
vovanie o zhizni Agvana Dorzhieva* ["Tale about the Trip around the World";
or, Life Story of Agvan Dorzhiev]. Ulan-Ude: Olzon.

Douglas, Mary. 2005 [1966]. *Purity and Danger.* London: Routledge.

Dragadze, Tamara. 1993. "The Domestication of Religion under Soviet Communism." In *Socialism: Ideals, Ideologies and Local Practice,* edited by Chris
Hann, 148–157. London: Routledge.

Dreyfus, George B. J. 2003. *The Sound of Two Hands Clapping: The Education of a Tibetan Buddhist Monk*. Berkeley: University of California Press.

Dyrkheeva, G. A. 2003. "Factors in National Language Development: The Buryat Example." Paper presented at the Conference "Language Development, Language Revitalization and Multilingual Education in Minority Communities in Asia," Bangkok. Accessed April 23, 2010. http://www.google.com/search?hl=en&client=firefox-a&rls=org.mozilla%3Aen-US%3Aofficial&q=buryat+%22russian-speaking%22&aq=f&aqi=&aql=&oq=&gs_rfai=.

Eck, Diana. 1998. *Darsan: Seeing the Divine Image in India*. New York: Columbia University Press.

Edensor, Tim. 2005. *Industrial Ruins: Space, Aesthetics, and Materiality*. New York: Berg.

Edou, Jérôme. 1996. *Machig Labdrön and the Foundations of Chöd*. Ithaca, NY: Snow Lion.

Elaeva, I. E. 2005. "Religioznost' v kontekste etnichnosti" [Religiosity in the Context of Ethnicity]. In *Buriatskaia etnichnost' v kontekste sotsiokul'turnoi modernizatsii: Postsovetskii period* [Buryat Ethnicity in the Context of Socio-cultural Modernization: Post-Soviet Period], edited by D. D. Amogolonova, I. E. Elaeva and T. D. Skrynnikova. Irkutsk: Radian. Accessed October 13, 2009. http://mion.isu.ru/filearchive/mion_publcations/buryat3/2_6.html.

Eliade, Mircea. 1964 [1951]. *Shamanism: Archaic Techniques of Ecstasy*. Princeton: Princeton University Press.

Elverskog, Johan. 2006. "Two Buddhisms in Contemporary Mongolia." *Contemporary Buddhism* 7 (1): 29–46.

———. 2007. "Tibetocentrism, Religious Conversion and the Study of Mongolian Buddhism." In *The Mongolia-Tibet Interface: Opening New Research Terrains in Inner Asia*, edited by Uradyn E. Bulag and Hildegard G. M. Diemberger, 59–81. Leiden: Brill.

Empson, Rebecca. 2007. "Enlivened Memories: Recalling Absence and Loss in Mongolia." In *Ghosts of Memory: Essays on Remembrance and Relatedness*, edited by Janet Carsten, 58–83. Oxford: Blackwell.

———. 2011. *Harnessing Fortune: Personhood, Memory, and Place in Mongolia*. Oxford: Oxford University Press.

Ensa Chöd, Russian translation from Tibetan. *Chöd linii preemstvennosti Ensa: Podnoshenie illiuzornogo tela dlia nakopleniia zaslug i obreteniia bystrogo rezul'tata v praktike metoda i mudrosti: "Daruemoe sokrovishche linii Ganden"* [Chöd of the Ensa Lineage: The Offering of the Illusionary Body for Merit Accumulation and Obtaining a Quick Result in the Practice of Method and Wisdom: "Gifted Treasure of the Ganden Lineage"]. Chöd ritual text.

Erbanov, N. I. 1959. *V chem vred religioznykh prazdnikov i obriadov lamaizma* [What the Harm Is of Lamaist Religious Holidays and Rituals]. Moscow:

Obshchestvo po rasprostraneniu politicheskikh i nauchnykh znanii RSFSR.

Ermakova, T. V. 1998. *Buddiiskii mir glazami rossiiskikh issledovatelei XIX–pervoi treti XX veka* [The Buddhist World through the Eyes of Russian Scholars, 19th–first third of the 20th centuries]. St. Petersburg: Nauka.

Evans-Wentz, W. Y. 2000. *Tibetan Yoga and Secret Doctrines.* Oxford: Oxford University Press.

Faure, Bernard. 1998. *The Red Thread: Buddhist Approaches to Sexuality.* Princeton: Princeton University Press.

———. 2003. *The Power of Denial: Buddhism, Purity, and Gender.* Princeton: Princeton University Press.

Feldman, Allen. 1991. *Formations of Violence: The Narrative of the Body and Political Terror in Northern Ireland.* Chicago: University of Chicago Press.

Filatov, Sergei. 2007. "Buriatiia: Evraziistvo v buddiiskom kontekste" [Buryatia: Eurasianism in the Buddhist Context]. *Russian Review of the Keston Institute* (in Russian), May 2007. Accessed May 10, 2009. http://www.keston.org.uk/russia/articles/rr20/02Buddhism.html.

Foucault, Michel. 1979 [1975]. *Discipline and Punish: The Birth of the Prison.* New York: Vintage Books.

———. 1980. *History of Sexuality.* Vol. 1. New York: Vintage Books.

———. 2003. *"Society Must Be Defended": Lectures at the Collège de France, 1975–1976.* New York: Picador.

Gal, Susan. 1991. "Bartók's Funeral: Representations of Europe in Hungarian Political Rhetoric." *American Ethnologist* 18 (3): 440–458.

Galdanova, G. P. 1987. *Dolamaistskie verovaniia buriat* [Pre-Lamaist Beliefs of the Buryats]. Novosibirsk: Nauka.

Galdanova, G. P., K. M. Gerasimova, and D. B. Dashiev. 1983. *Lamaizm v Buriatii XVIII–nachala XX v* [Lamaism in Buryatia from the 18th to the Beginning of the 20th Century]. Novosibirsk: Nauka.

Gardner, Alexander. 2006. "The Sa Chog: Violence and Veneration in a Tibetan Soil Ritual." *Études Mongoles et Sibériennes, Centrasiatiques et Tibétaines* 36–37:283–323.

Geary, Patrick. 1986. "Sacred Commodities: The Circulation of Medieval Relics." In *The Social Life of Things: Commodities in Cultural Perspective,* edited by Arjun Appadurai, 169–195. Cambridge: Cambridge University Press.

Gell, Alfred. 1998. *Art and Agency.* Oxford: Oxford University Press.

Gerasimova, K. M. 1957. *Lamaizm i natsional'no-kolonial'naia politika tsarizma v Zabaikal'e v XIX–nachale XX vekov* [Lamaism and National-Colonial Politics of Tsarism in the Transbaikal in the 19th–Beginning of the 20th Centuries]. Ulan-Ude: Buriat-mongol'skii nauchno-issledovatel'skii institut kul'tury.

———. 1964. *Obnovlencheskoe dvizhenie buriatskogo lamaistkogo dukhovenstva (1917–1930)* [Reformist Movement of the Buryat Clergy (1917–1930)]. Ulan-Ude: Buriatskoe knizhnoe izdatel'stvo.

———. 1998. "Shamanizm v Buriatii: Materialy polevykh issledovanii XIX–XX vekov" [Shamanism in Buryatia: Materials from Field Studies in the 19th–20th Centuries]. In *Kul'tura Tsentral'noi Azii: Pis'mennye istochniki* [Central Asian Culture: Written Sources], vol. 2. Ulan-Ude: SO RAN.

Germano, David. 1998. "Re-membering the Dismembered Body of Tibet: Contemporary Tibetan Visionary Movements in the People's Republic of China." In *Buddhism in Contemporary Tibet: Religious Revival and Cultural Identity*, edited by Melvyn C. Goldstein and Matthew T. Kapstein, 53–95. Berkeley: University of California Press.

Germano, David, and Kevin Trainor. 2004. *Embodying the Dharma: Buddhist Relic Veneration in Asia*. Albany: State University of New York Press.

Ginsburg, Faye D. 1989. *Contested Lives: The Abortion Debate in an American Community*. Los Angeles: University of California Press.

Goble, Paul. 2009. "National Republics Resist Moscow on Dropping References to Sovereignty." *Window on Eurasia*, June 20. Accessed February 5, 2010. http://windowoneurasia.blogspot.com/2009/06/window-on-eurasia -national-republics.html.

Goldstein, Melvyn C. 1973. "The Circulation of Estates in Tibet: Reincarnation, Land and Politics." *Journal of Asian Studies* 32 (3): 445–455.

———. 1998. "The Revival of Monastic Life in Drepung Monastery." In *Buddhism in Contemporary Tibet: Religious Revival and Cultural Identity*, edited by Melvyn C. Goldstein and Matthew T. Kapstein, 15–53. Berkeley: University of California Press.

Goldstein, Melvyn, and Paljor Tsarong. 1985. "Tibetan Buddhism Monasticism: Social, Psychological, and Cultural Implications." *Tibet Journal* 10 (1): 14–31.

Gombrich, Richard, and Gananath Obeyesekere. 1988. *Buddhism Transformed: Religious Change in Sri Lanka*. Princeton: Princeton University Press.

Grant, Bruce. 1999. "The Return of the Repressed: Conversations with Three Russian Entrepreneurs." In *Paranoia within Reason: A Casebook on Conspiracy as Explanation*, edited by George E. Marcus, 241–268. Chicago: University of Chicago Press.

———. 2009. *The Captive and the Gift: Cultural Histories of Sovereignty in Russia and the Caucasus*. Ithaca: Cornell University Press.

———. 2011. "Shrines and Sovereigns: Life, Death, and Religion in Rural Azerbaijan." *Comparative Studies in Society and History* 53 (3): 654–681.

Grant, Bruce, and Lale Yalçin-Heckmann. 2007. *Caucasus Paradigms: Anthropologies, Histories, and the Making of the World Area*. Berlin: LIT Verlag.

Grünwedel, Albert. 1900. *Mythologie du bouddhisme au Tibet et en Mongolie basée sur la collection lamaïque du Prince Oukhtomsky*. Leipzig: Brockhaus.

Gupta, Akhil. 2002. "Reliving Childhood? The Temporality of Childhood and Narratives of Reincarnation." *Ethnos* 67 (1): 33–56.

Gutschow, Kim. 2004. *Being a Buddhist Nun: The Struggle for Enlightenment in the Himalayas*. Cambridge, MA: Harvard University Press.

Gyatso, Janet. 1985. "The Development of the Gcod Tradition." In *Soundings in Tibetan Civilization*, edited by B. N. Aziz and M. Kapstein, 320–341. New Delhi: Manohar.

———. 1987. "Down with the Demoness: Reflections on the Feminine Ground in Tibet." *Tibet Journal* 12:38–53.

———. 1993. "The Logic of Legitimation in the Tibetan Treasure Tradition." *History of Religions* 33 (2): 97–133.

———. 1996. "Drawn from the Tibetan Treasury: The gTer ma Literature." In *Tibetan Literature: Studies in Genre*, edited by José Ignacio Cabezón and Roger R. Jackson, 147–170. Ithaca, NY: Snow Lion.

———. 2005. "Sex." In *Critical Terms for the Study of Buddhism*, edited by Donald S. Lopez, 271–291. Chicago: University of Chicago Press.

———. 2012. "Discipline and Resistance on the Tibetan Plateau." *Cultural Anthropology* Hot Spots Forum: Self-Immolation as Protest in Tibet, April. Accessed September 15, 2012. http://www.culanth.org/?q=node/528.

Hamayon, Roberte N. 1990. *La chasse à l'âme: Esquisse d'une théorie du chamanisme sibérien*. Nanterre: Société d'ethnologie.

———. 2002. "Emblem of Minority, Substitute for Sovereignty: The Case of Buryatia." *Diogenes* 49 (2): 16–21.

Hansen, Thomas Blom, and Finn Stepputat. 2004. "Sovereignty Revisited." *Annual Review of Anthropology* 35:295–315.

———. 2005. "Introduction." In *Sovereign Bodies: Citizens, Migrants, and States in the Postcolonial Period*, edited by Thomas Blom Hansen and Finn Stepputat, 1–36. Princeton: Princeton University Press.

Harvey, Peter. 2000. *An Introduction to Buddhist Ethics*. Cambridge: Cambridge University Press.

Havnevik, Hanna, Ragchaa Byambaa, and Agata Bareja-Starzynska. 2007. "Some Practices of the Buddhist Red Tradition in Contemporary Mongolia." In *The Mongolia-Tibet Interface: Opening New Research Terrains in Inner Asia*, edited by Uradyn E. Bulag and Hildegard G. M. Diemberger, 223–239. Leiden: Brill.

Heelas, Paul. 1996. *The New Age Movement: The Celebration of the Self and the Sacralization of Modernity*. Oxford: Blackwell.

Herzfeld, Michael. 1997. *Cultural Intimacy: Social Poetics of the Nation-State*. New York: Routledge.

Højer, Lars. 2009. "Absent Powers: Magic and Loss in Post-socialist Mongolia." *Journal of the Royal Anthropological Institute* 15 (3): 575–591.

Horkhang, Jampa Tendar. 2005. "The Geshe Chödrak That I Knew and His Dictionary." *Latse Library Newsletter* 3 (1): 19–25.

Horner, I. B., trans. 1982. *Vinaya-Pitaka (The Book of the Discipline)*. Vol. 1, *Suttavibhanga*. London: Routledge and Kegan Paul.

Huber, Toni. 1999. *The Cult of Pure Crystal Mountain: Popular Pilgrimage and Visionary Landscape in Southeast Tibet*. Oxford: Oxford University Press.

Humphrey, Caroline. 1999 [1983]. *Marx Went Away—but Karl Stayed Behind.* Ann Arbor: University of Michigan Press.

———. 1992. "The Moral Authority of the Past in Post-socialist Mongolia." *Religion, State and Society* 20 (3–4): 375–389.

———. 1994a. "Casual Chat and Ethnic Identity: Women's Second Language Use among Buryats in the USSR." In *Bilingual Women: Anthropological Approaches to Second Language Use,* edited by Pauline Burton, Ketaki Kushari Dyson, and Shirley Ardener, 65–80. Oxford: Berg.

———. 1994b. "Remembering an 'Enemy.' The Bogd Khaan in Twentieth-Century Mongolia." In *Memory, History, and Opposition under State Socialism,* edited by Rubie S. Watson, 21–44. Santa Fe: School of American Research Press.

———. 2002a. "'Eurasia,' Ideology and the Political Imagination in Provincial Russia." In *Postsocialism: Ideals, Ideologies and Practices in Eurasia,* edited by C. M. Hann, 258–277. London: Routledge.

———. 2002b. *The Unmaking of Soviet Life: Everyday Economies after Socialism.* Ithaca: Cornell University Press.

———. 2008. "Reassembling Individual Subjects: Events and Decisions in Troubled Times." *Anthropological Theory* 8:357–380.

Humphrey, Caroline, and David Sneath. 1999. *The End of Nomadism? Society, State, and the Environment in Inner Asia.* Durham: Duke University Press.

Hyer, Paul, and Sechin Jagchid. 1983. *A Mongolian Living Buddha: Biography of the Kanjurwa Khutughtu.* Albany: State University of New York.

Jeffrey, Lyn. 2001. "Placing Practices: Transnational Network Marketing in Mainland China." In *China Urban: Ethnographies of Contemporary Culture,* edited by N. Chen, C. Clark, S. Gottschang, and L. Jeffrey, 23–42. Durham: Duke University Press.

Kantorowicz, Ernst. 1957. *The King's Two Bodies: A Study in Mediaeval Political Theology.* Princeton: Princeton University Press.

Kaufman, Leslie. 2008. "Making Their Own Limits in a Spiritual Partnership." *New York Times,* May 15. Accessed July 22, 2009. http://www.nytimes.com/2008/05/15/garden/15buddhists.html?pagewanted=1&_r=1.

Kaufman, Sharon R., and Lynn M. Morgan. 2005. "The Anthropology of the Beginnings and Endings of Life." *Annual Review of Anthropology* 34:317–341.

Kawaguchi, Ekai. 1909. *Three Years in Tibet.* Madras: Theosophical Publishing Society.

Khangalov, M. N. 1958–1959. *Sobranie sochinenii v trekh tomakh* [Collected Works, 3 Volumes]. Edited by G. N. Rumiantsev. Ulan-Ude: SO RAN.

Kieschnick, John. 2008. "Celibacy in East Asian Buddhism." In *Celibacy and Religious Traditions,* edited by Carl Olson, 225–241. Oxford: Oxford University Press.

King, Richard. 1999. *Orientalism and Religion: Postcolonial Theory, India, and "The Mystic East."* London: Routledge.

Klima, Alan. 2002. *The Funeral Casino: Meditation, Massacre, and Exchange with the Dead in Thailand.* Princeton: Princeton University Press.

Klin, Boris. 2006. "Zhivee vsekh zhivykh ne Lenin, a lama Itigelov" [Itigelov, Not Lenin, Is More Alive Than All the Living]. *Izvestiia,* November 8. Accessed October 8, 2009. http://www.izvestia.ru/special/article3095502/.

Koreniako, V. A. 2001. "Prisoedinenie Buriatii k Rossii" [Joining of Buryatia to Russia]. In *Istoriko-kul'turnyi atlas Buriatii* [Historical and Cultural Atlas of Buryatia], edited by N. L. Zhukovskaia, 172–181. Moscow: Dizain, Informatsiia, Kartografiia.

Kotkin, Stephen. 2007. "Mongol Commonwealth? Exchange and Governance across the Post-Mongol Space." *Kritika: Explorations in Russia and Eurasian History* 8 (3): 487–531.

Kozhevnikova, Margarita. 1997. "Interview with Lama Ridgzin from the Religious Organization Lamrim, Ulan-Ude." *Buddizm v Rossii* 28:33–36. Accessed August 24, 2009. http://www.buddhismofrussia.ru/sangha/63/.

———. 2008. "Deiatel'nost' Bakuly Rinpoche v Rossii." In *Zemlia Vadzhrapani: Buddizm v Zabaikal'e* [The Land of Vajrapāṇi: Buddhism in the Transbaikal], edited by Ts. P. Vanchikova, 576–580. Moscow: Dizain, Informatsiia, Kartografiia.

Krist, Stefan. 2004. "When Going Back is a Step Forward: The Re-traditionalising of Sport Games in Post-Soviet Buryatiia." *Sibirica* 4 (1): 104–115.

Kyabje Zong Rinpoche. 2006. *Chöd in the Ganden Tradition: The Oral Instructions of Kyabje Zong Rinpoche.* Edited by David Molk. Ithaca, NY: Snow Lion.

Laidlaw, James. 2000. "A Free Gift Makes No Friends." *Journal of the Royal Anthropological Institute* 6:617–634.

Lamotte, Étienne. 1988. *History of Indian Buddhism from the Origins to the Saka Era.* Louvain: Catholic University of Louvain.

Lavine, Amy. 1998. "Tibetan Buddhism in America: The Development of American Vajrayana." In *The Faces of Buddhism in America,* edited by Charles S. Prebish and Kenneth K. Tanaka, 99–117. Berkeley: University of California Press.

Ledeneva, Alena. 1998. *Russia's Economy of Favors: Blat, Networking, and Informal Exchange.* Cambridge: Cambridge University Press.

Lemon, Alaina. 1998. "'Your Eyes are Green like Dollars': Counterfeit Cash, National Currency, and Currency Apartheid in 1990s Russia." *Cultural Anthropology* 13 (1): 22–55.

Lempert, Michael. 2012. *Discipline and Debate: The Language of Violence in a Tibetan Buddhist Monastery.* Berkeley: University of California Press.

Lindquist, Galina. 2000. "In Search of the Magic Flow: Magic and Market In Contemporary Russia." *Urban Anthropology* 29 (14): 315–357.

Livers, Keith A. 2004. *Constructing the Stalinist Body: Fictional Representations of Corporeality in the Stalinist 1930s.* Lanham, MD: Lexington Books.

Lock, Margaret, and Judith Farquhar. 2007. *Beyond the Body Proper: Reading the Anthropology of Material Life.* Durham: Duke University Press.

Lopez, Donald S. 1995a. *Curators of the Buddha: The Study of Buddhism under Colonialism.* Chicago: University of Chicago Press.

———. 1995b. "Foreigner at the Lama's Feet." In *Curators of the Buddha: The Study of Buddhism under Colonialism,* edited by Donald S. Lopez, 251–297. Chicago: University of Chicago Press.

———. 1995c. "Introduction." In *Curators of the Buddha: The Study of Buddhism under Colonialism,* edited by Donald S. Lopez, 1–31. Chicago: University of Chicago Press.

———. 1997. "Introduction." In *Religions of Tibet in Practice,* edited by Donald S. Lopez, 3–39. Princeton: Princeton University Press.

———. 1998. *Prisoners of Shangri-La: Tibetan Buddhism and the West.* Chicago: University of Chicago Press.

———. 2002a. "Introduction." In *Modern Buddhism: Readings for the Unenlightened,* edited by Donald S. Lopez, ix–xliii. London: Penguin.

———. 2002b. *The Story of Buddhism: A Concise Guide to Its History and Teachings.* New York: HarperOne.

Luehrmann, Sonja. 2011. *Secularism Soviet Style: Teaching Atheism and Religion in a Volga Republic.* Bloomington: Indiana University Press.

Machik Labdrön. 2003. *Machik's Complete Explanation: Clarifying the Meaning of Chöd: A Complete Explanation of Casting Out the Body as Food.* Translated by Sarah Harding. Ithaca, NY: Snow Lion.

Makhachkeev, Aleksandr. 2004a. "Buddiiskie sokrovishcha v Khorinske" [Buddhist Treasures in Khorinsk]. *Inform-Polis,* March 3. Accessed May 7, 2009. http://www.infpol.ru/newspaper/number.php?ELEMENT_ID =2864.

———. 2004b. "MVD i lamy: Konflikt ischerpan" [MVD and Lamas: Conflict Is Over]. *Inform-Polis,* December 29. Accessed May 7, 2009. http://www .infpol.ru/newspaper/number.php?ELEMENT_ID=3415.

———. 2004c. "Prezident i Khambo Lama poshli na sblizhenie" [President and Khambo Lama Started the Rapprochement]. *Inform-Polis,* December 22, 6.

———. 2005. "Naidena unikal'naia kniga Itigelova" [A Unique Book by Itigelov Has Been Found]. *Inform-Polis,* April 6, 5.

———. 2008a. "Buddy i sablia" [The Buddhas and a Sword]. *MK v Buriatii,* December 3. Accessed May 9, 2009. http://mk.burnet.ru/index.php? option=com_content&task=view&id=2348&Itemid=12—comment-847.

———. 2008b. "Voprosy k ierarchu" [Questions to the Hierarch]. *MK v Buriatii,* March 26. Accessed May 7, 2009. http://mk.burnet.ru/index .php?option=com_content&task=view&id=1663&Itemid=12.

———. 2009a. "Filosofiia kumysa" [The Philosophy of Kumys]. *Inform-Polis,* July 11. Accessed August 27, 2009. http://www.infpol.ru/newspaper/ number.php?ELEMENT_ID=21428.

———. 2009b. "Nevyezdnoi Itigelov" [Itigelov's Travel Banned]. *Inform-Polis,* June 3. Accessed June 4, 2009. http://www.infpol.ru/news/number .php?dd=1243999800&ELEMENT_ID=20100&PAGEN_2=2.

Makley, Charlene E. 2005. "The Body of a Nun." In *Women in Tibet*, edited by Janet Gyatso and Hanna Havnevik, 259–285. New York: Columbia University Press.

———. 2007. *The Violence of Liberation: Gender and Tibetan Buddhist Revival in Post-Mao China*. Berkeley: University of California Press.

———. 2012. "The Political Lives of Dead Bodies." *Cultural Anthropology* Hot Spots Forum: Self-Immolation as Protest in Tibet, April. Accessed September 15, 2012. http://www.culanth.org/?q=node/538.

Malinowski, Bronislaw. 1961 [1922]. *Argonauts of the Western Pacific*. New York: E. P. Dutton and Co.

———.1926. *Crime and Custom in Savage Society*. London: Kegan Paul.

Mandel, Ruth, and Caroline Humprey. 2002. *Markets and Moralities: Ethnographies of Postsocialism*. Oxford: Berg.

Mauss, Marcel. 2000 [1925]. *The Gift: The Form and Reason for Exchange in Archaic Societies*. New York: W. W. Norton.

Mbembe, Achille. 2003. "Necropolitics." *Public Culture* 15 (1): 11–40.

McLagan, Meg. 2002. "Spectacles of Difference: Cultural Activism and Mass Mediation of Tibet." In *Media Worlds: Anthropology on a New Terrain*, edited by Faye D. Ginsburg, Lila Abu-Lughod, and Brian Larkin, 90–115. Berkeley: University of California Press.

Metzo, Katherine R. 2009. "The Formation of Tunka National Park: Revitalization and Autonomy in Late Socialism." *Slavic Review* 68 (1): 50–70.

Mikhailov, T. M. 1998. "Buriaty" [Buryats]. In *Narody i religii mira: Entsyklopediia* [Peoples and Religions of the World], edited by V. A. Tishkov. Moscow: Bol'shaia Rossiiskaia entsyklopediia.

Mills, Martin A. 2000. "Vajra Brother, Vajra Sister: Renunciation, Individualism and the Household in Tibetan Buddhist Monasticism." *Journal of the Royal Anthropological Institute* 6 (1): 17–34.

Minear, Richard H. 1998. "Orientalism and the Study of Japan." In *History of Contemporary Japan, 1945–1998*, edited by E. R. Beauchamp, 1–13. New York: Garland.

Moran, Peter. 2004. *Buddhism Observed: Travelers, Exiles and Tibetan Dharma in Kathmandu*. London: RoutledgeCurzon.

Morgan, David. 1999. *Visual Piety: A History and Theory of Popular Religious Images*. Berkeley: University of California Press.

Mrozik, Susanne. 2007. *Virtuous Bodies: The Physical Dimensions of Morality in Buddhist Ethics*. Oxford: Oxford University Press.

———. 2009. "A Robed Revolution: The Contemporary Buddhist Nun's (Bhikshuni) Movement." *Religion Compass* 3 (3): 360–378.

Mueggler, Erik. 2001. *The Age of Wild Ghosts: Memory, Violence, and Place in Southwest China*. Berkeley: University of California Press.

Mukhanov, Igor'. 2005. *Dozhd' iz tsvetov: Buriatskie buddiiskie pritchi* [Rain of Flowers: Buryat Buddhist Parables]. Moscow: Agarti.

Mumford, Stan Royal. 1989. *Himalayan Dialogue: Tibetan Lamas and Gurung Shamans in Nepal*. Madison: University of Wisconsin Press.

Namsaraeva, Sayana. 2010. "The Metaphorical Use of Avuncular Terminology in Buriad Diaspora Relationships with Homeland and Host Society." *Inner Asia* 2 (210): 201–230.

Natsov, G. D. 1998. *Materialy po lamaizmu v Buriatii* [Materials on Lamaism in Buryatia]. Ulan-Ude: BNTs.

Nattier, Jan. 1991. *Once upon a Future Time: Studies in a Buddhist Prophecy of Decline*. Berkeley: Asian Humanities Press.

Nimaev, D. D., and L. L. Abaeva. 2004. "Vvedenie." In *Buriaty*, edited by L. L. Abaeva and N. L. Zhukovskaia. Moscow: Nauka.

Norbaev, Danzan. 1927. "Pis'mo v redaktsiiu" [Letter to the Editor]. *Buriat-Mongol'skaia pravda*, 11 September. St. Petersburg Orientalist Archive, St. Petersburg, Razr. 2, Op. 1, #374.

Norbu, Thupten Jigme. 1986 [1960]. *Tibet Is My Country: Autobiography of Thubten Jigme Norbu, Brother of the Dalai Lama, as Told to Heinrich Harrer*. London: Wisdom Publications.

Novik, E. S. 2004 [1984]. *Obriad i fol'klor v sibirskom shamanizme* [Ritual and Folklore in Siberian Shamanism]. Moscow: Vostochnaia literatura.

Nyima, Agvan. 1996. *Pereprava cherez reku sansary: Avtobiografiia* [Crossing the River of Samsara: An Autobiography]. Translated from Tibetan by Bair Ochirov. Ulan-Ude: Tsentral'noe dukhovnoe upravlenie buddistov Rossiiskoi Federatsii.

Obeyesekere, Gananath. 2002. *Imagining Karma: Ethical Transformation in Amerindian, Buddhist, and Greek Rebirth*. Berkeley: University of California Press.

Ochirov, Bair. 2008. "Traditsiia Chod v Buriatii" [Tradition of Chöd in Buryatia]. In *Zemlia Vadzhrapani: Buddizm v Zabaikal'e* [The Land of Vajrapāṇi: Buddhism in the Transbaikal], edited by Ts. P. Vanchikova, 158–172. Moscow: Dizain, Informatsiia, Kartografiia.

Ohnuma, Reiko. 2007. *Head, Eyes, Flesh, and Blood: Giving Away the Body in Indian Buddhist Literature*. New York: Columbia University Press.

"O kontseptsii natsional'noi bezopasnosti Rossiiskoi Federatsii, 10 January 2000" [President's Edict on National Security Policy]. 2000. Ukaz Prezidenta RF. Accessed March 7, 2009. http://www.ln.mid.ru/dip_vest.nsf/99b 2ddc4f717c733c32567370042ee43/83162ad8bc89e61ec32568cc00253b6c? OpenDocument.

Olson, Carl. 2008. "Celibacy and the Human Body: An Introduction." In *Celibacy and Religious Traditions*, edited by Carl Olson, 3–21. Oxford: Oxford University Press.

Oushakine, Serguei Alex. 2009. *Patriotism of Despair: Nation, War, and Loss in Russia*. Ithaca: Cornell University Press.

Parry, Jonathan. 1986. "The Gift, the Indian Gift, and the 'Indian Gift.'" *Man* 21 (3): 453–473.

———. 1989. "On the Moral Perils of Exchange." In *Money and the Morality of Exchange*, edited by Jonathan Parry and Maurice Bloch, 64–93. Cambridge: Cambridge University Press.

Parry, Jonathan, and Maurice Bloch. 1989. "Introduction." In *Money and the Morality of Exchange*, edited by Jonathan Parry and Maurice Bloch, 1–33. Cambridge: Cambridge University Press.

Patico, Jennifer. 2009. "Spinning the Market: The Moral Alchemy of Everyday Talk in Postsocialist Russia." *Critique of Anthropology* 29 (2): 205–224.

Patrul, Rinpoche. 1998. *The Words of My Perfect Teacher.* Boston: Shambhala.

Pedersen, Morten Axel. 2002. "In the Hollow of the Taiga." Doctoral dissertation, King's College, University of Cambridge.

———. 2011. *Not Quite Shamans: Spirit Worlds and Political Lives in Northern Mongolia.* Ithaca: Cornell University Press.

Pesmen, Dale. 2000. *Russia and Soul: An Exploration.* Ithaca: Cornell University Press.

Petri, B. E. 1928. *Staraia vera buriatskogo naroda: Nauchno-populiarnyi sbornik* [Old Faith of the Buryat Peoples: Popular Scientific Anthology]. Irkutsk: Vlast' truda.

Plate, Brent, ed. 2002. *Religion, Art, and Visual Culture: A Cross-Cultural Reader.* New York: Palgrave Macmillan.

Pollock, Sheldon. 1993. "Deep Orientalism? Notes on Sanskrit and Power Beyond the Raj." In *Orientalism and the Post-colonial Predicament*, edited by Carol A. Breckenridge and Peter Van der Veer. Philadelphia: University of Pennsylvania Press.

Poppe, N. N., trans. 1940. *Letopisi khorinskikh buriat: Khroniki Tuguldur Toboeva i Vandana Iumsunova* [Chronicles of Khori Buryats: Chronicles of Tuguldur Toboev and Vandan Iumsunov]. Moscow: Izdatel'stvo akademii nauk.

———. 1983. *Reminiscences.* Bellingham: Western Washington University.

Potanin, G. N. 1883. *Ocherki Severo-Zapadnoi Mongolii* [Sketches on North-West Mongolia]. St. Petersburg: Russian Geographic Society.

Powers, John. 2009. *A Bull of a Man: Images of Masculinity, Sex, and the Body in Indian Buddhism.* Cambridge, MA: Harvard University Press.

Pozdneev, A. M. 1887a. "K istorii razvitiia buddizma v Zabaikal'skom krae" [On the History of the Development of Buddhism in the Transbaikal]. In *Zapiski Vostochnogo otdeleniia Imperatorskogo archeologicheskogo obshchestva* [Proceedings of the Eastern Division of the Imperial Archaeological Society], 169–188. St. Petersburg.

———. 1887b. *Ocherki byta buddiiskikh monastyrei i buddiiskogo dukhovenstva v Mongolii v sviazi s otnosheniami sego poslednego k narodu* [Essays on the Mongolian Monasteries and Clergy, Related to Its Relationship with the People]. St. Petersburg: Imperatorskaia akademiia nauk.

———. ca. 1888. "Buddhizm v Zabaikal'e" [Buddhism in the Transbaikal]. St. Petersburg Orientalist Archive, St. Petersburg, F. 44, Op. 1, D. 128.

———. 1897. *Skazanie o khozhdenii v tibetskuiu stranu maloderbetskogo Baaza-bakshi* [Tale of the Travel to the Tibetan Country by the Maloderbet Baaza-Bakshi]. Translated from Kalmyk by A. M. Pozdneev. St. Petersburg: Imperatorskaia akademiia nauk.

Quijada, Justine Buck. 2009. "Opening the Roads: History and Religion in Post-Soviet Buryatia." PhD dissertation, University of Chicago.

———. 2012. "Soviet Science and Post-Soviet Faith: Etigelov's Imperishable Body." *American Ethnologist* 39 (1): 138–155.

Raheja, Gloria Goodwin. 1988. *The Poison in the Gift: Ritual, Prestation, and the Dominant Caste in a North Indian Village*. Chicago: University of Chicago Press.

Ram, Harsha. 2001. "Imagining Eurasia: The Poetics and Ideology of Olzhas Suleimenov's AZ i IA." *Slavic Review* 60 (2): 289–311.

Rawski, Evelyn S. 1998. *The Last Emperors: A Social History of Qing Imperial Institutions*. Berkeley: University of California Press.

Roach, Michael. 2000. *The Diamond Cutter: The Buddha on Managing Your Business and Your Life*. New York: Doubleday.

———. 2008. *Almaznyi ogranshchik: Budda o tom kak upravliat' biznesom i lichnoi zhizn'u* [The Diamond Cutter: The Buddha on Managing Your Business and Your Life]. Translated by Vadim Kovalev. Moscow: Otkrytyi mir.

Rogers, Douglas. 2005a. "Introductory Essay: The Anthropology of Religion after Socialism." *Religion, State, and Society* 33 (1): 5–18.

———. 2005b. "Moonshine, Money, and the Politics of Liquidity in Rural Russia." *American Ethnologist* 32 (1): 63–81.

———. 2009. *The Old Faith and the Russian Land: A Historical Ethnography of Ethics in the Urals*. Ithaca: Cornell University Press.

Rupen, Robert A. 1956. "The Buryat Intelligentsia." *Far Eastern Quarterly* 15 (3): 282–398.

———. 1964. *Mongols of the Twentieth Century*. Bloomington: Indiana University Press.

Sahlins, Marshall. 1987. *Islands of History*. Chicago: University of Chicago Press.

Said, Edward. 1991. *Orientalism: Western Conceptions of the Orient*. London: Penguin.

Samuel, Geoffrey. 1993. *Civilized Shamans: Buddhism in Tibetan Societies*. Washington, DC: Smithsonian Institution Press.

Sanders, Fabian. 2001. "The Life and the Lineage of the Ninth Khalkha Jetsun Dampa Khutukhtu of Urga." *Central Asiatic Journal* 45 (2): 273–303.

Sanzheev, G. D. 1983. "Nekotorye voprosy etnonimiki i drevnei istorii mongol'skikh narodov" [Some Issues on the Ethnonyms and Ancient History of Mongol Peoples]. In *Etnicheskie i istoriko-kul'turnye sviazi mongol'skikh narodov* [Ethnic, Historical and Cultural Links of the Mongol Peoples], edited by T. M. Mikhailov, G. N. Zaiatuev, and D. D. Nimaev. Ulan-Ude: SO RAN.

Sanzhikhaeva, Zhanna. 2004. "Vechera na khutore bliz Alari" [Evenings on a Farm Near Alar']. *Inform-Polis*, August 11, 27.

Sas, Ivan. 2010. "Ne donor—ne sub"ekt" [Not a Donor—Not a Subject]. *Rossiiskaia gazeta*, January 22, 2010. Accessed February 5, 2010 http://www.rg.ru/2010/01/22/grizlov.html.

Sazykin, A. G. 1986. "Opisanie Tibeta, sostavlennoe v XVIII v. buriatskim palomnikom Damba-Dorzhi Zaiaevym" [The Description of Tibet Compiled in the 18th Century by the Buryat Pilgrim Damba-Dorzhi Zaiaev]. In *Strany i narody Vostoka*, 117–125. Moscow: Vostochnaia literatura.

Schimmelpenninck van der Oye, David. 2001. *Toward the Rising Sun: Russian Ideologies of Empire and the Path to War with Japan*. DeKalb: Northern Illinois University Press.

———. 2010. *Russian Orientalism: Asia in the Russian Mind from Peter the Great to the Emigration*. New Haven: Yale University Press.

Schönle, Andreas. 2006. "Ruins and History: Observation on Russian Approaches to Destruction and Decay." *Slavic Review* 65 (4): 649–669.

Schopen, Gregory. 1990. "The Buddha as an Owner of Property and Permanent Resident in Medieval Indian Monasteries." *Journal of Indian Philosophy* 18:181–217.

———. 2004a. *Buddhist Monks and Business Matters: Still More Papers on Monastic Buddhism in India*. Honolulu: University of Hawai'i Press.

———. 2004b. "Diamond Sutra." In *Encyclopedia of Buddhism*, edited by Robert E. Buswell, Jr., 227–228. New York: Macmillan.

Schulter, Susan. 2000. "The Making of *National Geographic*: Science, Culture, and Expansionism." *American Studies* 41:5–29.

Schwab, Raymond. 1984. *The Oriental Renaissance: Europe's Rediscovery of India and the East, 1680–1880*. New York: Columbia University Press.

Semennikov, V. P. 1925. *Za kulisami tsarizma: Arkhiv tibetskogo vracha Badmaeva* [Behind the Scenes of Tsarism: The Archive of the Tibetan Doctor Badmaev]. Leningrad: Gosudarstvennoe izdatel'stvo.

Shadaeva, A. T. 1998. *Nekotorye problemy etnokul'turnoi istorii buriat* [Some Problems of the Ethno-cultural History of Buryats]. Ulan-Ude: BGU.

Shakya, Tsering. 1999. *The Dragon in the Land of the Snows: A History of Modern Tibet since 1947*. New York: Columbia University Press.

Sharp, Leslie A. 2007. "Commodification of the Body and Its Parts." *Annual Review of Anthropology* 29:287–328.

Shaumian, T. 2000. *Tibet: The Great Game and Tsarist Russia*. New Delhi: Oxford University Press.

Shils, Edward. 1956. *The Torment of Secrecy: The Background and Consequences of American Security Policies*. Carbondale: Southern Illinois University Press.

Simmel, Georg. 2004 [1900]. *The Philosophy of Money*. London: Routledge.

Skrynnikova, T. D. 1997. "Traditsionnoe mirovozzrenie buriat i shamanizm" [Traditional Buryat Worldview and Shamanism]. In *Metodologicheskie i teo-

reticheskie aspekty izucheniia dukhovnoi kul'tury Vostoka [Metodological and Theoretical Aspects of the Study of Eastern Cultures], 2:3–19. Ulan-Ude: SO RAN.

Slezkine, Yuri. 1994. *Arctic Mirrors: Russia and the Small Peoples of the North.* Ithaca: Cornell University Press.

Snellgrove, David, and Hugh Richardson. 1995 [1968]. *A Cultural History of Tibet.* Boston: Shambhala.

Snelling, John. 1993. *Buddhism in Russia: The Story of Agvan Dorzhiev, Russian Emissary to the Tsar.* Shaftesbury: Element Books.

Starks, Tricia. 2008. *The Body Soviet: Propaganda, Hygiene, and the Revolutionary State.* Madison: University of Wisconsin Press.

Steinberg, Mark D., and Catherine Wanner. 2008. *Religion, Morality, and Community in Post-Soviet Societies.* Washington, DC: Woodrow Wilson Center Press; Bloomington: Indiana University Press.

Stewart, Charles. 2003. "Dreams of Treasure: Temporality, Historicization and the Unconscious." *Anthropological Theory* 3 (4): 481–500.

Stoler, Laura Ann. 2008. "Imperial Debris: Reflections on Ruins and Ruination." *Cultural Anthropology* 23 (2): 191–219.

Strathern, Marilyn. 1990. *The Gender of the Gift: Problems with Women and Problems with Society in Melanesia.* Berkeley: University of California Press.

Strong, John S. 2004. *Relics of the Buddha.* Princeton: Princeton University Press.

Tambiah, Stanley. 1984. *The Buddhist Saints of the Forest and the Cult of Amulets.* Cambridge: Cambridge University Press.

Taussig, Michael. 1998. "Transgression." In *Critical Terms for Religious Studies*, edited by Mark C. Taylor, 349–365. Chicago: University of Chicago Press.

Teiser, Stephen F. 1988. *The Ghost Festival in Medieval China.* Princeton: Princeton University Press.

Tenchoy. 2004. *Rasskazy o praktike chod* [Stories about the Practice of Chöd]. Moscow: Globus.

Terrone, Antonio. 2008. "Tibetan Buddhism beyond the Monastery: Revelation and Identity in Rnying Ma Communities of Present Day Kham." In *Images of Tibet in the 19th and 20th Centuries*, edited by Monica Esposito, 747–779. Paris: École française d'Extrême-Orient.

Todorova, Maria N. 2009. *Bones of Contention: The Living Archives of Vasil Levski and the Making of Bulgaria's National Hero.* Budapest: Central European University Press.

Tolz, Vera. 2011. *Russia's Own Orient: The Politics of Identity and Oriental Studies in the Late Imperial and Early Soviet Periods.* New York: Oxford University Press.

Trautmann, Thomas R. 1981. *Dravidian Kinship.* Cambridge: Cambridge University Press.

Trepavlov, V. V. 2007. *"Belyi tsar'": Obraz monarkha i predstavlenie o poddanstve u narodov Rossii XV–XVII veka* ["The White Tsar": The Image of the Monarch and Notion of Loyalty of Peoples of Russia in 15th–17th Centuries]. Moscow: Vostochnaia literatura.

Trungpa, Chögyam. 2000. *Born in Tibet*. Boston: Shambhala.

Trusler, John. 1788. *The habitable world described, or the present state of the people in all parts of the globe, from north to south; shewing the situation, extent, climate, . . . including all the new discoveries: . . . With a great variety of maps and copper-plates, . . .* London: Printed for the author, at the Literary-Press, no. 62, Wardour-Street, Soho; and sold by all booksellers, 1788–97.

Tsedroen, Jampa. 2006. "Bhikṣuṇī Ordination." In *Out of the Shadows: Socially Engaged Women*, edited by Karma Legshe Tsomo, 305–309. Delhi: Sri Satguru Publications.

———. 2008. "Generation to Generation: Transmitting the Bhikṣuṇī Lineage in the Tibetan Tradition." In *Buddhist Women in a Global Multicultural Community: 9th Sakyadhita International Conference*, edited by Karma Legshe Tsomo, 205–215. Kuala Lumpur: Sukhi Hotu Publications.

Tsybikov, G. Ts. 1981 [1919]. "Buddist-palominik u sviatyn' Tibeta" [A Buddhist Pilgrim at the Sacred Places of Tibet]. In *Izbrannye trudy v dvukh tomakh* [Selected Works in Two Volumes], 1:1–256. Novosibirsk: Nauka.

Tsydendambaev, Ts. B. 1972. *Buriatskie istoricheskie khroniki i rodoslovnye* [Buryat Historical Chronicles and Lineages]. Ulan-Ude: Buriatskoe knizhnoe izdatel'stvo.

Tsyrempilov, N. V. 2008a. "Poema L. S. Tsydenova 'Lechu po nebu'" [The Poem "I Am Flying in the Sky" by L. S. Tsydenov]. In *Zemlia Vadzhrapani: Buddizm v Zabaikal'e* [The Land of Vajrapāṇi: Buddhism in the Transbaikal], edited by Ts. P. Vanchikova, 292–295. Moscow: Dizain, Informatsiia, Kartografiia.

———. 2008b. "Tsyden Sodoev (1846–1916)." In *Zemlia Vadzhrapani: Buddizm v Zabaikal'e* [The Land of Vajrapāṇi: Buddhism in the Transbaikal], edited by Ts. P. Vanchikova, 282–286. Moscow: Dizain, Informatsiia, Kartografiia.

———. 2009. "Za sviatuiu dkharmu i belogo tsaria: Rossiiskaia imperiia glazami buriatskikh buddistov XVIII—nachala XX vekov" [For the Holy Dharma and the White Tsar: The Russian Empire through the Eyes of Buryat Buddhists in the 18th–Early 20th Centuries]. *Ab Imperio* 2: 105–130.

Tulokhonov, M. I. 1973. *Buriatksie istoricheskie pesni* [Buryat Historical Songs]. Ulan-Ude: Buriatskii nauchnyi tsentr.

Tumarkin, Nina. 1997. *Lenin Lives! The Lenin Cult in Soviet Russia*. Cambridge, MA: Harvard University Press.

Tuttle, Gray. 2005. *Tibetan Buddhists in the Making of Modern China*. New York: Columbia University Press.

Ukhtomskii, E. E. 1896–1900. *Travels in the East of His Imperial Majesty Czar Nicholas II of Russia, When Cesarewitch, 1890–1891*. Translated by R. Goodlet. Edited by Sir G. Birdwood. Westminster: Archibald Constable.

———. 1904. *Iz oblasti lamaizma: K pokhodu anglichan na Tibet* [About Lamaism: Regarding the British Invasion of Tibet]. St. Petersburg: Vostok.

Urban, Hugh B. 1998. "The Torment of Secrecy: Ethical and Epistemological Problems in the Study of Esoteric Religious Traditions." *History of Religions* 37 (3): 209–148.

Vanchikova, Ts. P. 2006. *Istoriia buriatskogo buddizma: Pis'mennye istochniki* [History of Buryat Buddhism: Written Sources]. Ulan-Ude: Institut mongolovedeniia, buddologii i tibetologii RAN.

Van Tuyl, Charles D. 1979. "Mi-ra ras-pa and the gCod ritual." *Tibet Journal* 4 (1): 34–40.

Vashkevich, V. V. 1885. *Lamaity Vostochnoi Sibiri* [Lamaists of Eastern Siberia]. St. Petersburg: Ministerstvo vnutrennikh del.

Vasil'ev, V. P. 1873. *Religii Vostoka: Konfutsianstvo, buddizm i daoizm* [Religions of the East: Confucianism, Buddhism, Taoism]. St. Petersburg: Imperatorskaia akademia nauk.

———. 1888. "Retsenziia na knigu A. M. Pozdneeva 'Ocherki byta buddiiskikh monastyrei i buddiiskogo dukhovenstva v Mongolii v sviazi s otnosheniiami sego poslednego k narodu'" [The Review of A. M. Pozdneev's Book *Essays on the Mongolian Monasteries and Clergy, Related to Its Relationship with the People*]. *Zhurnal Ministerstva narodnogo prosveshcheniia*, chast' 257, otdel 2: 417–438.

Verdery, Katherine. 1991. "Theorizing Socialism: A Prologue to the 'Transition.'" *American Ethnologist* 18 (3): 419–439.

———. 1996a. "Faith, Hope, and Caritas in the Land of the Pyramids, Romania, 1990–1994." In *What Was Socialism and What Comes Next?*, edited by Katherine Verdery, 168–204. Princeton: Princeton University Press.

———. 1996b. *What Was Socialism and What Comes Next?* Princeton: Princeton University Press.

———. 1999. *The Political Lives of Dead Bodies: Reburial and Postsocialist Change.* New York: Columbia University Press.

Vitebsky, Pier. 1995. *The Shaman.* Boston: Little, Brown, and Company.

Volkhonskii, Boris. 2007. "Prosvetlenie i skotovodstvo" [Enlightenment and Cattle-Herding]. *Kommersant Vlast'*, April 2. Accessed April 22, 2010. http://www.kommersant.ru/doc.aspx?DocsID=755024.

Von Hagen, Mark. 2004. "Empires, Borderlands, and Diasporas: Eurasia as Anti-paradigm for the Post-Soviet Era." *American Historical Review* 109 (2): 445–468.

Waddell, Laurence Austin. 1905. *Lhasa and Its Mysteries.* New York: Dutton.

Waller, Derek 1990. *The Pundits: British Exploration of Tibet and Central Asia.* Lexington: University Press of Kentucky.

Weber, Max. 1993 [1922]. *The Sociology of Religion.* Translated by Ephraim Fischoff. Boston: Beacon Press.

———. 1958 [1930]. *The Protestant Ethic and the Spirit of Capitalism.* Translated by Talcott Parsons. New York: Scribner's Sons.

————. 1958. *The Religion of India: The Sociology of Buddhism and Hinduism*. Translated by Hans H. Gerth and Don Martindale. Glencoe, IL: Free Press.

Wiles, Peter. 1965. "On Physical Immortality." *Survey* 56:125–143.

Willerslev, Rane. 2007. *Soul Hunters: Hunting, Animism, and Personhood among the Siberian Yukaghirs*. Berkeley: University of California Press.

————. 2009. "The Optimal Sacrifice: A Study of Voluntary Death among the Siberian Chukchi." *American Ethnologist* 36 (4): 693–704.

Williams, Paul. 1989. *Mahāyāna Buddhism: The Doctrinal Foundations*. London: Routledge.

————. 1997. "Some Mahayana Buddhist Perspectives on the Body." In *Religion and the Body*, edited by Sarah Coakley, 205–231. Cambridge: Cambridge University Press.

Wilson, Ara. 1999. "The Empire of Direct Sales and the Making of Thai Entrepreneurs." *Critique of Anthropology* 19 (4): 401–422.

Winegar, Jessica. 2006. "Cultural Sovereignty in a Global Art Economy: Egyptian Cultural Policy and the New Western Interest in Art from the Middle East." *Cultural Anthropology* 21 (1): 173–204.

Wylie, Turrell V. 1978. "Reincarnation: A Political Innovation in Tibetan Buddhism." In *Proceedings of the Csoma de Koros Memorial Symposium*, edited by Louis Ligetti, 579–586. Budapest: Akademiai Kiado.

Ya, Hanzhang. 1991. *The Biographies of the Dalai Lamas*. Translated by Wang Wenjiong. Beijing: Foreign Languages Press.

Yurchak, Alexei. 2006. *Everything Was Forever, Until It Was No More*. Princeton: Princeton University Press.

Zaiatuev, G. N. 1991. *Tsanid-khambo Agvan Dorzhiev, 1853–1938 gg*. Ulan-Ude: Ob"edinenie detskikh pisatelei Buriatii.

Zalkind, E. M. 1958. *Prisoedinenie Buriatii k Rossii* [The Joining of Buryatia to Russia]. Ulan-Ude: Buriatskoe knizhnoe izdatel'stvo.

Zhambalova, S. G. 2000. *Profannyi i sakral'nyi miry ol'khonskikh buriat* [Profane and Sacred Worlds of the Olkhon Buryats]. Novosibirsk: Nauka.

Zhamtsarano, Tsyben. 2001. *Putevye dnevniki 1903–1907* [Travel Diaries, 1903–1907]. Ulan-Ude: BNTs SO RAN.

Zhironkina, Iulia. 2006. *Predsedatel' TsDub: Buriatskii narod nedoumevaet* [The Leader of the Central Committee of Buddhists: Buryat People Are Bewildered]. http://www.savetibet.ru/1157315682.html, accessed April 20, 2009.

Zhukovskaia, N. L. 1968. "Vliianie mongolo-buriatskogo shamanizma i doshamanskikh verovanii na lamaizm [The Influence of Mongol-Buryat Shamanism and Pre-shamanic Beliefs on Lamaism]." In *Problemy etnografii i etnicheskoi istorii narodov Vostochnoi i Iugo-Vostochnoi Azii*, 162–175. Moscow: Nauka.

————. 1997. "Buddizm v Buriatii: Problemy i perspektivy" [Buddhism in Buryatia: Problems and Perspectives]. *Issledovaniia po prikladnoi i neotlozhnoi etnologii* 104:1–17.

————. 1999. "Buriatskii shamanizm segodnia: Vozrozhdenie i evoliutsiia" [Buryat Shamanism Today: Revival and Evolution]. In *Materialy mezhdun-arodnogo kongressa "Shamanizm i inye traditsionnye verovaniia i praktiki"* [Materials of the International Congress "Shamanism and Other Traditional Beliefs and Practices"], 162–175. Moscow: RAN.

————, ed. 2001. *Istoriko-kul'turnyi atlas Buriatii* [Historical and Cultural Atlas of Buryatia]. Moscow: Dizain, Informatsiia, Kartografiia.

Zolotarev, Viktor. 2009. "Buriatiia ne popala v chernyi spisok" [Buryatia Did Not Get Blacklisted]. *Nomer Odin*, April 9. Accessed December 12, 2009. http://pressa.irk.ru/number1/2009/17/002001.html.

Zoriktuev, B. P. 1996. "O proiskhozhdenii i semantike etnonima buriat" [On the Origin and Semantics of the Ethnonym Buryat]. In *Mongolo-buriatskie etnonimy* [Mongol-Buryat Ethnonyms], edited by A. Ochir and B. P. Zorik-tuev, 8–31. Ulan-Ude: SO RAN.

Index

Page numbers in italics refer to illustrations.